Manliness and Masculinities in Nineteenth-Century Britain

WOMEN AND MEN IN HISTORY

This series, published for students, scholars and interested general readers, will tackle themes in gender history from the early medieval period through to the present day. Gender issues are now an integral part of all history courses and yet many traditional texts do not reflect this change. Much exciting work is now being done to redress the gender imbalances of the past, and we hope that these books will make their own substantial contribution to that process. We hope that these will both synthesise and shape future developments in gender studies.

The General Editors of the series are *Patricia Skinner* (University of Southampton) for the medieval period; *Pamela Sharpe* (University of Bristol) for the early modern period; and *Penny Summerfield* (University of Lancaster) for the modern period. *Margaret Walsh* (University of Nottingham) was the Founding Editor of the series.

Published books:

Imperial Women in Byzantium, 1025–1204: Power, Patronage and Ideology *Barbara Hill*

Masculinity in Medieval Europe *D. M. Hadley (ed.)*

Gender and Society in Renaissance Italy *Judith C. Brown and Robert C. Davis (eds)*

Widowhood in Medieval and Early Modern Europe *Sandra Cavallo and Lyndan Warner (eds)*

Gender, Church and State in Early Modern Germany: Essays by Merry E. Wiesner *Merry E. Wiesner*

Manhood in Early Modern England: Honour, Sex and Marriage *Elizabeth W. Foyster*

English Masculinities, 1600–1800 *Tim Hitchcock and Michele Cohen (eds)*

Disorderly Women in Eighteenth-Century London: Prostitution in the Metropolis, 1730–1830 *Tony Henderson*

Gender, Power and the Unitarians in England, 1760–1860 *Ruth Watts*

Practical Visionaries: Women, Education and Social Progress, 1790–1930 *Mary Hilton and Pam Hirsch (eds)*

Women and Work in Russia, 1880–1930: A Study in Continuity through Change *Jane McDermid and Anna Hillyar*

More than Munitions: Women, Work and the Engineering Industries, 1900–1950 *Clare Wightman*

Women in British Public Life, 1914–1950: Gender, Power and Social Policy *Helen Jones*

The Family Story: Blood, Contract and Intimacy, 1830–1960 *Leonore Davidoff, Megan Doolittle, Janet Fink and Katherine Holden*

Women and the Second World War in France, 1939–1948: Choices and Constraints *Hanna Diamond*

Men and the Emergence of Polite Society, Britain 1660–1800 *Philip Carter*

Everyday Violence in Britain, 1850–1950: Gender and Class *Shani D'Cruze (ed.)*

Women and Ageing in British Society Since 1500 *Lynn Botelho and Pat Thane (eds)*

Medieval Memories: Men, Women and the Past, 700–1300 *Elisabeth van Houts (ed.)*

Family Matters: A History of Ideas about Family since 1945 *Michael Peplar*

Domestic Service and Gender, 1660–1750 *Tim Meldrum*

Blood, Bodies and Families in Early Modern England *Patricia Crawford*

A History of Women in Ireland, 1500–1800 *Mary O'Dowd*

Manliness and Masculinities in Nineteenth-Century Britain *John Tosh*

Manliness and Masculinities in Nineteenth-Century Britain

Essays on gender, family and empire

John Tosh

Harlow, England • London • New York • Boston • San Francisco • Toronto
Sydney • Tokyo • Singapore • Hong Kong • Seoul • Taipei • New Delhi
Cape Town • Madrid • Mexico City • Amsterdam • Munich • Paris • Milan

PEARSON EDUCATION LIMITED

Edinburgh Gate
Harlow CM20 2JE
United Kingdom
Tel: +44 (0)1279 623623
Fax: +44 (0)1279 431059
Website: www.pearsoned.co.uk

First edition published in Great Britain in 2005

© Pearson Education Limited 2005

The right of John Tosh to be identified as author
of this work has been asserted by him in accordance
with the Copyright, Designs and Patents Act 1988.

ISBN 0 582 40449 5

British Library Cataloguing in Publication Data
A CIP catalogue record for this book can be obtained from the British Library

Library of Congress Cataloging in Publication Data
A CIP catalog record for this book can be obtained from the Library of Congress

10 9 8 7 6 5 4 3 2
08 07 06 05 04

Set by 35 in 9/13.5pt Stone Serif
Printed in Malaysia

The Publisher's policy is to use paper manufactured from sustainable forests.

Contents

Acknowledgements

Over the ten years in which the essays in this volume were written, a great many people have given invaluable help and advice. I am particularly grateful to Michèle Cohen, Leonore Davidoff, Megan Doolittle, Catherine Hall, Jim Hammerton, Tim Hitchcock, Angela John, Ludmilla Jordanova, Keith McClelland, Michael Roper and Bob Shoemaker: to all I have accumulated debts over several years. Both the University of North London and the University of Surrey Roehampton have generously supplied research leave. The final two chapters bear the imprint of a term visiting the History Department of the University of Natal at Durban, and for that I warmly thank Jeff Guy.

For permission to reprint copyrighted material I am grateful to Oxford University Press (for Chapter 2), the Royal Historical Society (for Chapter 4), Basil Blackwell (for Chapter 6) and the Ecclesiastical History Society (for Chapter 7).

Caroline White has provided support and respite in more ways than she probably realizes.

John Tosh
London, April 2004

Introduction

This book brings together a body of exploratory work which I have written over the past ten years. In 1994, when the earliest piece was published, it was far from clear what the history of masculinity comprised, and to the majority of historians the very idea was eccentric and provocative. Certainly a book of this kind was inconceivable. A decade later masculinity is a recognized area of enquiry. There is a steady flow of monographs, and if the field does not have its own journal, it has a ready entry into many others, which is a rather more telling indication of its maturity. The essays collected here serve to document the rapid emergence of a new and increasingly important field, partly by proposing new frameworks of interpretation, and partly by exploring the broader implications of work done by other scholars. All of the essays, including the more narrowly focused ones, were intended to take forward the definition of this new field.

It would, however, be misleading to regard this book as a comprehensive guide. It could only be that if the history of masculinities were a thematically and theoretically coherent field. In fact, like so many other new areas of research, masculinity is studied in a variety of ways. The current constitution of the field accurately reflects the tension between social and cultural approaches which characterizes so much of academic history at the present time.[1] In the case of nineteenth-century Britain the divergence can be conveyed by contrasting two influential works on the middle class: Leonore Davidoff and Catherine Hall's *Family Fortunes* and Claudia Nelson's *Boys Will Be Girls*.[2] The first offers an analysis of the relationship between gender and class, rooted in the material realities of household and occupation; the second investigates the changing interaction of sex and gender in the portrayal of boys in juvenile literature. This book is aligned more closely with the first model than the second. My perspective is that of a social historian, concerned (with the single exception of Chapter 4) with questions of experience and agency. For projects of this kind the cultural historian's subject-matter of discourse and representation is indispensable, but as a means to a more nuanced account of social experience, rather than as an end in itself. Thus in looking at the place of gender in British imperial expansion (Chapters 8 and 9), I place more weight on the pattern of motive and aspiration among emigrants and adventurers than on the handful of iconic literary texts through which their experience has been represented to posterity.[3]

At first glance, the history of masculinity might appear to be another example of 'identity' history, in which the distinctive or exclusive experience of a specific social grouping stakes its claim for attention. Early work in the field sought to identify aspects of male experience which could be classified as 'gendered', by concentrating on activities which were self-evidently for men only: for example, single-sex schools and youth organizations.[4] But it soon became clear that to treat the history of masculinity in this way was a category error. The history of masculinity does not deal with a neglected group, nor can it be placed under the banner of 'history from the margins'.[5] Rather, it is a new perspective which potentially modifies our view of every field of history in which men are the principal subject-matter – which is to say the overwhelming majority of written history. The implications of treating men as gendered persons are so all-embracing that it makes little sense to concentrate on exclusively male contexts. That level of permeation is still a long way from being realized, but this book is intended to indicate what we might expect, by reviewing both the general questions raised by the historicization of masculinity and the specific contributions it can make in two areas – the history of the family and the history of the British Empire.

The title of the book brings together two words which make rather uneasy bedfellows. *Manliness* was the most clearly articulated indicator of men's gender in the nineteenth century. Always used in the singular, it implied that there was a single standard of manhood, which was expressed in certain physical attributes and moral dispositions. It was defined in different variants, according to class and religion, but each version claimed an exclusive authority. *Masculinities* is of much more recent coinage, and in common parlance dates no further back than the 1970s. The use of the plural accurately conveys the prevalent view in present-day Western society that masculinity is anything but a monolith: it should not be subject to prescription, and it should ideally express individual choice. Whereas manliness was treated essentially as a social attainment in the gift of one's peers, masculinity is an expression of personal authenticity, in which being true to oneself counts for much more than conforming to the expectations of others. The subject of this book is the gendered lives of men in nineteenth-century Britain: 'manliness' was the only term through which considerations of gender could then be aired. In a contradiction which is familiar from other branches of history, the explanations offered in this book depend on a set of concepts which was quite foreign to the period itself.

The contrasting meanings of manliness and masculinity say something about gender in England today. 'Manliness' denoted those attributes which men were happy to own, which they had often acquired by great effort, and which they frequently boasted about – as in 'manly character' or 'manly figure'. 'Masculinity', on the other hand, is more neutral and matter-of-fact: it can be used in a prescriptive way, for instance by labelling someone as 'unmasculine', but its essential thrust is descriptive and inclusive. Masculinity is deployed in a far greater variety of contexts than manliness was, even in its heyday. Its meaning is mediated not only through class, but through ethnicity and – most important of all – through sexuality. It relates not just to bodily distinctions or to formal precept. At one moment masculinity appears to be an almost entirely visual metaphor, achieved through negotiation with fashion and style. In the next moment it invites an intrusion into the fantasies and insecurities of the individual psyche. Masculinity is the appropriate label for a culture which is obsessed by gender, but as an individual possession rather than a group characteristic. And masculinity carries nothing like the same positive freight as 'manliness' did, partly because it is too fractured to do so, and partly because men do not any longer lay exclusive claim to the active virtues. Instead we value gender choice and the lack of moral pretension which seems to go with it. For that reason, perhaps, manliness belongs to another era. 'Masculinities' fits with the post-modernist vision of the world, with its proliferation of identities and its contradictory discourses.

To recognize that 'manliness' is redundant is only another way of saying that its common usage was rooted in historically specific conditions. That is one reason why manliness featured prominently in the earliest work on the nineteenth-century history of masculinities. Here was a clearly delineated discourse which set out what was expected of men, and which was particularly directed to young men and their instructors. The centrality of manliness to a range of nineteenth-century cultural contexts has been fully documented by more recent work, but initially the ideological moorings of manliness were presented in a much narrower frame. It was most clearly articulated in church, chapel and school, by middle-class exponents for middle-class consumption. Its impact was measured with reference to all-male institutions, such as sports and youth organizations. This was the dominant perspective in the path-breaking collection, *Manliness and Morality*, which appeared in 1987. The results were illuminating, but they had the effect of making masculinity seem less like an integral dimension of all social relations than a marginal ideological add-on.[6]

In order to overcome this limitation, there needed to be a conscious engagement with gender theory. The late 1980s and early 1990s were a period of intense theoretical work, particularly among feminists and within the gay movement.[7] Through a growing familiarity with the pioneer conceptual work of other disciplines, historians began to register the full implications of the relational character of masculinity. This meant resisting the tendency to study masculinity in isolation. It also meant recognizing the centrality of social power – of men over women, and of heterosexual men over homosexual men. The implications of a radical sexual politics for historical work on masculinity were addressed in *Manful Assertions* (1991), edited by Michael Roper and myself: the volume came out of a two-year discussion group which had explored ways of formulating an agenda along these lines.[8] Three years later, in 'What should historians do with masculinity?' (Chapter 2 below), I set out to apply the theoretical perspectives we had explored in *Manful Assertions* to the field of British social history in the nineteenth century. The article sets the categories of masculinity in the context of the British class structure, and by drawing on R.W. Connell's theory of hegemonic masculinity it puts forward a framework for establishing the extent to which gender operated in tandem with, or independently from, class.[9]

The most insistent question posed in these early contributions was whether masculinity was wholly subsumed in patriarchy. This was partly because 'patriarchy' summed up most of what women's history had to say about men at that point, and it seemed important to develop a position from a men's perspective. It was also because a historical analysis informed by patriarchy promised an extended historical reach, from the structure of the household to the hidden gender dynamics of political power. Two essays reprinted here exemplify this approach. In Chapter 3 the 'old Adam' of the title is a reference to deep-seated patriarchal features, notably the sexual licence of young bachelors and the enforcement of domestic authority, which persisted unchanged through the tumultuous economic and political changes of the period 1750–1850. Chapter 5 analyzes middle-class masculinity as a contribution to understanding men's responses to the women's suffrage movement of the late Victorian and Edwardian periods. Given that context, it is not surprising that the limelight falls on the patriarchal aspect of men's relations with women in the family and in the public sphere.

The limitations of the emphasis on patriarchy can be signalled by observing that neither of these essays has much to say about manliness. This is an inevitable consequence of treating patriarchy as the central issue in the history of masculinity. Although all codes of manliness laid down the lineaments of proper conduct towards women, that was never their prime concern. Manliness was fundamentally a set of values by which men judged other men, and it is a mistake to suppose that those values were exclusively – or even mainly – to do with maintaining control over women. As Chapter 4 explains, assertiveness, courage, independence and straight-forwardness were the common currency of manliness, on which a highly varied superstructure was built by different classes and denominations. Those qualities provided the basis of a pecking order among men, and as the Victorian period proceeded they also furnished the basis of a political persona suited to the requirements of an expanded Parliamentary representation. But they had little to do with the upholding of patriarchy. The prevalence of manly discourse is an effective reminder that masculinity is as much about homosociality as about patriarchy.

Nowhere has the impact of the history of masculinity been more marked than in the study of the family. The history of men in families simply did not exist until quite recently. The successes achieved in this field have not only made it possible to understand the family as an interactive group, instead of as a zone cordoned off for women and children; they have also begun to break down the gulf which historians traditionally observed between men's public lives and their emotional and domestic selves. Until the 1980s family history was largely the preserve of demographic historians who were little interested in the quality of relationships within the family. That scale of priorities was turned upside down by feminist scholars who brought the power relations of the family to the fore, in the belief that the family was the foundation of patriarchy (as the etymology of the word implies).[10]

The patriarchal certainties of that generation of scholars did not last long. In Britain, as in America, the outcome of close research in personal materials has been a recognition that historically families were constituted by a range of social and cultural factors, only some of which could be described in terms of sexual inequality. Davidoff and Hall's *Family Fortunes* was the pioneering work in this regard (as in so many others). Separate spheres existed in the sense that occupational discrimination left husbands with most of the wealth, but their account foregrounds marital partnerships and 'nursing fathers'; patriarchal villains are in short supply. An even more positive picture is painted in M. Jeanne Peterson's account of Victorian professional families.[11] My article on Victorian fatherhood (Chapter 6) is an attempt to carry this perspective forward. It juxtaposes the requirements of paternal authority with the impulse to nurture and play: the growing moral prestige of motherhood made paternal authority less secure, while the direct engagement of fathers with their offspring was validated by the compelling Romantic image of the child (and the child within the adult). I document a range of paternal types, but the overall effect of the piece is to foreground the intimate father at the expense of the absent or tyrannical father.[12]

The least theorized piece is the article on domesticity among middle-class Methodists (Chapter 7). My choice of three individuals (Joshua Pritchard, Isaac Holden and Cornelius Stovin) cannot be described as an exercise in sampling. It is determined by the vagaries of documentary survival – intimate family materials written by or to husbands and fathers being frustratingly scarce. What sets the framework of analysis is the religious and social contexts which are so vividly captured in the sources – the tightly knit community of class and chapel, and (except in Pritchard's case) the close proximity of work and home. Here too the effect of following through personal experience is to undermine any notion of patriarchal consistency. The article also shows how the Methodist world-view furnished resources to both husbands and wives in achieving their aspirations within marriage. What was true of these Methodists applied across a wide swathe of Evangelicals, since the Methodists were typical of many denominations in elevating the home as a site of religious life.

Unlike the family, the empire has been a staple of historical enquiry for generations. Only very gradually has a gender perspective begun to make inroads into the conventional definition of the field.[13] When R.W. Connell remarked in 1993 that 'imperialism was a massively important event in gender history',[14] he had in mind the modification or obliteration of gender regimes in *colonized* societies. The small amount of work he was able to draw on then has been significantly expanded during the past ten years by scholars chiefly concerned to include women in the ranks of the 'subaltern'.[15] But imperialism raises another set of questions with regard to the *colonizing* society: what did the acquisition of empire imply about the gender order of the imperialists? Answers to this question certainly require attention to the role of women in supporting or opposing imperialism within Britain. But the main focus needs to be on men, because empire was above all a massive assertion of masculine energies. That imperial history is today one of the last bastions of gender-blind history reflects the near-monopoly which men had on the colonial enterprise itself. We need to ask in what senses the empire was 'a man's world' and to what extent it proffered specifically masculine attractions.

In 'All the masculine virtues' (Chapter 8) my focus is one of the most tangible – but most neglected – expressions of British imperialism on the ground: the emigration of British people to those countries which came to be called 'the colonies of white settlement'. Given the numerical preponderance of men among British emigrants and their institutionalized power to make decisions on behalf of the women, what was the masculine appeal of the colonies? In what sense were the colonies seen as the answer to a masculine predicament; or, to put it another way, how did men think that the colonies would enhance their manhood? Popular notions of manliness are central to answering these questions, in terms of both the personal courage which emigrating required, and the 'independence' which life in the colonies was expected to deliver.

In the final chapter I propose a re-evaluation of the New Imperialism of the late nineteenth century. The basis of the social support for empire within Britain has been the least studied aspect of the New Imperialism, and the gendered dimensions of this support have been virtually ignored. The imperial project was presented to the public in unequivocally masculine terms, partly with the intention of encouraging young men to pursue their careers overseas as soldiers, administrators or emigrants at a time when the empire was believed to be under stress. The extent to which this propaganda succeeded was conditioned by how far popular images of the empire resonated with masculine aspirations. This was a critical factor in the 1890s when the phenomenon of the New Woman released a great deal of status anxiety on the part of men, particularly in the lower middle and middle classes. Imperial enthusiasm often ran in parallel with hostility to women's rights, and in many instances appears to have been embraced by men as a means of suppressing gender insecurity.

In addressing the concerns of a traditional branch of scholarship – imperial history – the last two chapters highlight a key issue in the current historiography. For reasons which are set out in Chapter 1 the earliest exponents of the history of masculinity aimed to write a new history of men which would bring their gender centre-stage and thus end their unmarked status: like class and nation, masculinity would have its own history.[16] The outcome was to be a new overarching narrative framework, analogous in some ways to those which have been propounded in women's history. But most historians of masculinity today do not see their work as contributing to a 'men's history' of this kind. They are more concerned with how their distinctive perspective can enrich 'mainstream' history. Sooner or later most branches of history which began on the margins seek some such accommodation, usually when enough work has been done to ensure that integration does not mean elimination; but in this case the issue is posed less starkly, since the subjects of the history of masculinity are intrinsically no different from the subjects of political or social history.[17] What this process of integration implies in practice is that historians of masculinity are now much more interested in exploring the social and cultural meanings of masculinity in specific historical conjunctures, where other identities and other structuring principles are also in play.[18] This means re-examining fields which are not obvious candidates for the practice of gender history. Imperialism is only one of these. Fruitful work is now also being carried out on the most traditional topics of political history.[19] Contextualization and interconnectedness are cardinal features of these endeavours. What the history of masculinity has lost in ideological clarity it has certainly gained in academic rigour. Ten years ago I anticipated that the work of historians of masculinity would be 'central to how we as historians think about our subject'.[20] There is some way to go before that point is reached. But in the meantime masculinity has become integral to the way in which some of the key themes of the subject are viewed. The discipline of history can only be the richer for that.

Notes and references

1 The current state of the debate is well captured in the special issue on the state of social history, *Journal of Social History* 37, i (Fall, 2003).

2 Leonore Davidoff and Catherine Hall, *Family Fortunes: Men and Women of the English Middle Class, 1780–1850* (London, 1987); Claudia Nelson, *Boys Will Be Girls: the Feminine Ethic and British Children's Fiction* (New Brunswick, 1991).

3 These texts would include the endlessly reinterrogated *Heart of Darkness* by Conrad and Rider Haggard's *She*.

4 J.A. Mangan and J. Walvin (eds), *Manliness and Morality: Middle-Class Masculinity in Britain and America, 1800–1940* (Manchester, 1987).

5 Cf. Leonore Davidoff, *Worlds Between: Historical Perspectives on Gender and Class* (Cambridge, 1995), p. 1.

6 Mangan and Walvin, *Manliness and Morality*.

7 Particularly influential were R.W. Connell, *Gender and Power* (Cambridge, 1987); Lynne Segal, *Slow Motion: Changing Masculinities, Changing Men* (London, 1990); Eve K. Sedgwick, *Between Men: English Literature and Male Homosexual Desire* (New York, 1985); Jeffrey Weeks, *Sexuality and Its Discontents* (London, 1985).

8 See especially Michael Roper and John Tosh, 'Historians and the politics of masculinity', in M. Roper and J. Tosh (eds), *Manful Assertions: Masculinities in Britain since 1800* (London, 1991), pp. 1–24.

9 For a full assessment of Connell's theory, see John Tosh, 'Hegemonic masculinity and the history of gender', in S. Dudink, K. Hagemann and J. Tosh (eds), *Masculinities in Politics and War: Gendering Modern History* (Manchester, 2004), pp. 41–58.

10 For a highly nuanced theorization of the field, see Leonore Davidoff *et al.*, *The Family Story: Blood, Contract and Intimacy, 1830–1960* (London, 1999), pp. 16–97.

11 M. Jeanne Peterson, *Family, Love and Work in the Lives of Victorian Gentlewomen* (Bloomington, 1989).

12 This perspective was further developed in my book, *A Man's Place: Masculinity and the Middle-Class Home in Victorian England* (London, 1999), chs 4 and 5.

13 The status quo is conveyed in Andrew Porter (ed.), *Oxford History of the British Empire*, vol. III (Oxford, 1999); out of thirty chapters, only four make more than passing mention of gender issues.

14 R.W. Connell, 'The big picture: masculinities in recent world history', *Theory & Society* 22 (1993), p. 606.

15 See for example Antoinette Burton, *Burdens of History: British Feminists, Indian Women, and Imperial Culture, 1865–1915* (Chapel Hill, 1994); Clare Midgley (ed.), *Gender and Imperialism* (Manchester, 1998). See also the special issue on gendered colonialism in *Gender & History* 8 (1996).

16 Peter N. Stearns, *Be a Man! Males in Modern Society* (New York, 1979).

17 For an interesting attempt to combine contextualization with an extended sense of period, see the special issue on masculinities in British history, guest edited by Alexanda Shepard and Karen Harvey, *Journal of British Studies*, forthcoming.

18 Mrinalini Sinha, 'Giving masculinity a history: some contributions from the historiography of colonial India', *Gender & History* 11 (1999), p. 446.

19 Dudink, Hagemann and Tosh, *Masculinities in Politics and War*.

20 'What should historians do with masculinity?', Chapter 2 below.

PART ONE

Agendas

CHAPTER 1

The making of manhood and the uses of history

My title refers to the two areas of work in which I have been engaged in recent years. 'The making of manhood' perhaps suggests something new and challenging, and I hope to show that the history of masculinities is just that. But the second phrase – 'the uses of history' – sounds a lot less challenging until one recalls that most historians are not particularly concerned about the broader application of their subject: if pressed they are likely to take refuge in some notion of cultural capital – while quickly denying that this has anything to do with 'heritage'. I have been exercised by the question of relevance ever since, as a research student in African history, I wondered what contribution my study of the Lango people of Uganda might make to the process of nation-building.[1]

I shall return at the end of this lecture to the responsibility which historians have to the wider community. But the history of masculinity is a particularly good vantage point from which to make a general argument for the relevance of history. The first steps within the field of British history (less than thirty years ago) were influenced as much by activists as academics, and those ideological traces are still present today. Yet ultimately, I want to argue, the claims of this history on a wider public depend not on its overtones of political correctness, but on its participation in a shared scholarly discourse.

I

Fifty years ago, mention of 'manhood' was most likely to signal a pep-talk about courage and duty addressed to teenage boys. It was associated with public-school values, and with the mass movement which did so much to disseminate those values – the Boy Scouts. Today that use of the word has disappeared entirely: adult men don't any longer claim the authority

Inaugural lecture delivered at the University of Surrey Roehampton, 17 March 2003.

to instil gender ideals in the young. Instead, 'manhood' has become a concept in a critical discourse of gender. It signals not an affirmation of masculinity, but a dissection of its social privileges – as, for example, in Anthony Rotundo's history, *American Manhood* (1993), or the recent work by Elizabeth Foyster, *Manhood in Early Modern England* (1999).

What does it mean to speak of 'the making of manhood'? From the perspective of the individual male, manhood is 'made' in the sense of being a personal accomplishment. In many small-scale societies in the world this is marked by a formalized initiation rite, usually in seclusion from women, in which boys graduate to manhood by instruction and by submitting to painful physical tests.[2] In British society of the recent past both public-school education and apprenticeship to working-class trades included elements of this kind. But even when there is no institutional support, manhood was still essentially an achieved status. It was not a birthright, but lay within the power of one's peers to confirm or deny. Manhood was 'made' in the course of proving oneself 'one of the lads', by demonstrations of physical strength, sporting ability, sexual prowess, and so on. Moreover, manhood was made in a fixed mould. The injunction 'Be a man!' implied that there were only certain ways in which one *could* be a man, and that they demanded a high degree of effort and a suppression of self. Proving one's manhood was an experience with profoundly oppressive implications.

You will notice I have put this scenario into the past tense. Although recent research in secondary schools shows that the traditional masculine value system is alive and well,[3] we live now in a culture which is much more open to gender diversity. Masculinity has fractured into a spectrum of identities. Though there were always distinctions of class, there was little room for manoeuvre within one's class. But now masculine identity is also defined in relation to sexuality, ethnicity, even consumer choice: we are no longer surprised when individuals redefine their masculinity, and the visual metaphors of gender which they deploy are themselves constantly shifting in meaning. The making of manhood now has a much more voluntaristic character, suggesting not so much a single path as a range of alternatives. Significantly, 'manliness', the traditional word for prescriptive masculinity, has vanished from the lexicon. The masculine monolith is a thing of the past.

And – here we come to the second part of my title – history has been a vital resource in charting that course. For what historians have done is to demonstrate that manhood is not only made in the individual sense, but made in the historical sense of being a changing construct over time. That we now talk so readily of *masculinities* is itself testimony to the fruitful enquiries of historians. Aspects of manhood which were once central have disappeared – notably the martial honour which, as my colleague Robin Headlam Wells has shown, permeates Shakespeare's plays.[4] Conversely, critical aspects of today's masculinity are of recent origin. Take for example the male work ethic. Protestantism spiritualized work, and made of it the pre-eminent demand on a man's time and energy, the proof of his self-denial and perseverance. The notion of work as a creative act, the expression of one's very self, barely existed before the Industrial Revolution. Earlier generations had regarded labour as the wages of original sin, and certainly not as a means of gratification. It was the nineteenth-century bourgeoisie that saddled men with the full rigours of a self-punishing commitment to work.[5]

If masculinity was variable in the past, then logically it has the potential for change in the present and future. Awareness of something like the full range of historical masculinities challenges the aura of inevitability which attaches to mainstream notions of manhood, and it provides solid evidence of the alternatives. The way is then open to a critical appraisal of the codes by which men live in the present. This objective was uppermost in my mind when I convened an informal study group on men's history in 1988 (around ten people meeting in my living room in north London). As someone formed by a military background and a particularly hidebound public school, I felt acutely the need for this kind of perspective. I'm glad to say that we stayed the course and collaborated fruitfully on the book I co-edited with Michael Roper in 1991, *Manful Assertions*. The subjects included the Victorian skilled artisan, the company executive of recent decades, and the culture of all-male middle-class institutions as seen through the medium of critical autobiography.[6] It was the work we did on that book which convinced me that the history of masculinities had a serious future.

II

Where did this new approach to the past come from? It began roughly twenty-five years ago as part of a radical sexual politics. It may seem paradoxical that it was closely associated with women's history. After all, the early exponents of women's history believed that one of the principal uses of history hitherto had been to reinforce patriarchy by focusing exclusively on men's achievements in the past. But the relationship between masculinity and history soon became part of a wider feminist project. A number of feminist historians realized that it was not enough to restore women to a place in history; they must also critique the assumptions which had led to men monopolizing the record. Furthermore, if feminists were serious about understanding the historical dynamic of women's oppression, they must investigate the nature of men's stake in that oppression: gender was a power structure which must be analyzed as a system embracing both sexes.[7] That approach had a growing following among feminist historians during the 1980s, and it was carried over into the journal *Gender & History*, founded by Leonore Davidoff in 1989.[8]

Where were the men in all this? Most male historians were hostile or at best indifferent, and they continued to work without regard to the gender of their subjects. But on the fringes of academia there was a small group associated with the 'men's movement'. During the last ten years that phrase has come to denote a backlash against feminism and women's rights, based on the recovery of an exclusive and supposedly 'authentic' masculinity. (Robert Bly is the best-known guru.) But back in the 1980s that backlash had not yet taken shape. The men's movement was a loose association of men's groups who *supported* feminism both materially and in print – in magazines like *Achilles Heel*.[9] One facet of that support was a merciless autocritique of conventional masculinity, echoing the grounds of feminist attack in what to some seemed a self-indulgent guilt trip. But the appraisal of masculinity also reflected a more inward-looking preoccupation with the sources of oppression among men. The priority given to bread-winning and to public life was blamed for suppressing men's nurturing side. Upholding patriarchy was attacked as a burden which disfigured men's natures, even as it ground women down.[10] A comparable perspective was applied to institutionalized homophobia. Long before Queer Theory directed a deconstructionist gaze at heterosexuality, gay historians showed how the rigid division between straight and gay not only oppressed gay men but censored intimacy between straight men. Gay and pro-feminist male historians worked closely together, and were sometimes – like Jeffrey Weeks for example – the same people, committed to an inclusive emancipatory project.[11]

Since women's history was by this time a highly effective arm of the women's movement, it is not surprising that this pro-feminist stance among men carried with it a historical agenda. The ideological imperative was sometimes quite clear. I recall attending a workshop in the mid-1980s organized by *Marxism Today*, where one of the participants spoke eloquently about the need for a new kind of male hero – one who would provide a role model for the anti-sexist man (or 'new man', as he was beginning to be called). One promising candidate was John Stuart Mill.

Mill was not only the most eminent liberal philosopher of his age. From his twenties onwards he never wavered in his belief in the equal rights of women. He introduced the first motion in favour of a gender-blind franchise in the House of Commons in 1866, and when he married Helen Taylor in 1851 he insisted on signing a legal instrument renouncing the powers that marriage conferred on him as husband.[12] On the other hand, Mill had much less to say about masculinity. For the early advocates of an inspirational men's history, Mill yielded place to Edward Carpenter, seer, social critic and grass-roots socialist. Carpenter was not only a committed supporter of feminism. In books like *Love's Coming of Age* (1896) he attacked the dead weight of sexual hypocrisy in late Victorian society, and deplored the emotional illiteracy of men, especially middle-class man – 'man the ungrown' as he called him.[13] Above all, for thirty years Carpenter led the life of an openly gay man with his partner George Merrill, risking prosecution under the law which had brought down Oscar Wilde. He was among the first sexual radicals to identify an 'intermediate sex', more adaptable and more creative because freed from the constraining stereotypes of masculine and feminine.

Another of the early aspirations of a new men's history was for a 'good' past, a golden age when patriarchs were benevolent, when sexuality was non-prescriptive, and when men and women enjoyed a relationship of mutual respect. One early survey characterized pre-industrial society in terms of 'a sharing of personal and productive life by men, women and children', with the implication that something like these conditions might be restored when capitalist patriarchy had been dismantled.[14] Robert Bly located men's ills in the failure of fathers to pass on to their sons the wisdom of the elders; so his golden age existed before the Industrial Revolution, which in his view sundered the bond between father and son.[15] The aspiration for a good past has survived longest in the historical treatment of homosexuality in eighteenth-century London. The late Alan Bray was the first to offer a scholarly treatment of the 'molly-houses', those places of homosexual resort where same-sex practices, cross-dressing and camp behaviour flourished.[16] This culture was lavishly celebrated to popular acclaim in Mark Ravenhill's play *Mother Clap's Molly House* at the National Theatre in 2001; the text drew heavily on the book of the same title by the historian Rictor Norton.[17]

A good past and inspiring heroes have always featured prominently in the political appropriation of the past. They are certainly not confined to movements of personal liberation. Mainstream politics regularly resorts to such rhetoric. But neither a golden age nor the quest for heroes makes for a very accurate picture of the past. Too much wishful thinking is involved. John Stuart Mill was in some ways the prototypical 'new man', but he took for granted the female labour that made his home comforts possible; his sole domestic duty was to make tea when he arrived home from the office at 6 p.m.[18] Gay liberationists today tend to gloss over Edward Carpenter's sexual puritanism: he deplored masturbation and promiscuity, and he looked forward to a progressive future in which the carnal expression of intimate relationships would increasingly be sublimated. Neither of these exemplars had children, by the way. Equally, believers in a pre-industrial or pre-Enlightenment golden age also tend to be selective; for instance, they cast a veil over the double standard which condoned men's sexual escapades while cracking down on any deviance on the part of women. Both the search for heroes and the longing for a golden age represent crude and fundamentally flawed ways of adapting the findings of historical enquiry to a new agenda.

Today liberationist politics are much less evident in writing on the history of masculinity. The subject has become academically respectable. Of course it still has the ability to provoke. Suggest to a traditional political historian that the masculinity of, say, Gladstone or Churchill should be examined and you will certainly raise hackles. But the history of masculinities is now firmly lodged within academia. The aim has been to further the gendering of history – to show how many historical situations cannot be fully understood without articulating the masculinity of the participants. Thus when Leonore Davidoff and Catherine Hall contextualized their path-breaking book *Family Fortunes* in 1987, they acknowledged the influence of the women's liberation movement, yet the chief impact of their work has been on the academic study of class formation during the period of the Industrial Revolution.[19] As masculinity has become more accepted as a historical problematic, the historians who study it have become immersed in debates which are largely internal to the discipline. Indeed the rest of my lecture could easily have been devoted to the debate between materialist and cultural approaches to social history which has been hotly pursued in this field, as in so many others. But where does that leave the lay audience whose demands were so vociferous twenty years ago? What does the historical study of masculinity have to say to the broader community of those with a critical interest in contemporary issues of gender?

III

I have suggested one answer already: history has already proved a vital resource in breaking down essentialist or monolithic notions of masculinity. The rich variety of the past has proved a welcome solvent of some of the rigidities in the way gender is thought and lived. I now want to take the analysis further by applying some historical perspective to the dominant outlook on masculinity today. This could be summed up as a sense of alarm, little short of a collective panic: what it means to be a man has become a deeply troubling question, as the traditional benchmarks of masculinity have been swept away. It has become a commonplace to speak of a 'crisis of masculinity'. Back in the 1970s crisis in traditional masculinity was a matter for celebration among writers of a liberationist hue.[20] But by the 1990s it had become a rhetoric of complaint, signalling a much more negative reaction to the loss of identity and power by men on all fronts. This was the message of several bestsellers – like Anthony Clare's *On Men: Masculinity in Crisis* (2000) and Susan Faludi's American blockbuster *Stiffed: the Betrayal of the Modern Man* (1999).

This media hype is founded on a number of anxieties. First and most important is the fear that men are losing the battle of the sexes. Women are said to have won advancement at the expense of men in the workplace and in public life, and much anxiety is now focused on the extent to which boys' performance in school is slipping behind that of girls. The balance of power has also shifted in the family: divorce proceedings are more often than not initiated by wives, and child custody is awarded to the mother. Secondly, there are the changing labour needs of the economy – much stressed by Faludi. There is less and less demand for the unskilled physical strength of young school-leavers, while in the professions men can no longer expect their working life to be shaped by the unilinear career in which so much of middle-class masculine identity has been invested. 'If work used to define masculinity,' writes Anthony Clare, 'it does not do so any more.'[21] Thirdly, masculinity has been redefined by profound changes in sexuality. Gay liberation was the catalyst for opening up a strictly heterosexual male culture to a kaleidoscopic diversity of styles and practices: heady liberation for some, but profoundly disorienting for those whose chief aim is to 'fit in'. Then there is the AIDS epidemic, at its height a threat to all who are sexually active, but a threat in particular to the time-honoured equation of masculine prestige with sexual 'scoring'. This tale of woe might be summed up by saying that men are not only losing power and influence, but have forfeited their legitimacy as the dominant sex. We have become familiar with the veil of ironic parody through which masculinity is represented in film, television and novels.[22] More serious – though less noticed – is the rise in suicide among men, especially young men.[23]

Of course, not all of these manifestations of crisis are in play at the same time. Sometimes the pressure point is perceived to be the dysfunctional family, sometimes unemployment and sometimes the scourge of sexually transmitted disease. But they are all regarded as manifestations of 'crisis'. Now 'crises' are the stock-in-trade of the historian. As we never tire of telling our students, to gauge the severity of a crisis requires a close look at what came before. The very idea of crisis assumes a pre-existing stability, when change was minimal and behaviour predictable. Much of the media comment on men in travail makes just this assumption. It invokes a vanished world of dogged bread-winning, self-deprecating chivalry and understated heroism. Susan Faludi shows a fine regard for the idiosyncrasies of men's lives, but at bottom her analysis in *Stiffed* is an elegy for a world of vanished certainties: dignified labour, honourable wars and the call of the untamed frontier.

Academic comment, on the other hand, tends to take the opposite tack, by stressing the inherent and continuing *insecurity* of masculinity. If, as I suggested at the beginning, attaining manhood is a matter of jumping over a succession of hurdles, the fear must always be that the odds will be loaded against one by adverse circumstances. A rise in unemployment, for example, will place the bread-winner role out of many men's reach, with crucial consequences for their masculine standing: this was the case during both the 1930s and 1980s.[24] Michael Kimmel, a leading pro-feminist writer on men's issues in the United States, asserts 'that the current malaise among men has a long history, and that the way men are responding these days bears a startling resemblance to men's responses over the course of American history'; men are 'chronically anxious' because 'manhood is a relentless test'.[25]

Lynne Segal places the issue squarely within the power dynamic of gender relations. Men's sense of their masculinity, she maintains, is complicated by the fact that manhood carries immense symbolic weight. It is equated with power, especially power over women, to an extent which can never be fully realized. Hence men are always open to the charge – or the self-reproach – that they have failed to 'measure up'. As a result quite trivial shifts in gender relations, instead of being evaluated on their merits, are immediately perceived to be a threat. Even a slightly higher profile for women in the media or in the workplace is then experienced as a curtailment of masculinity. Segal argues that the advances of feminism have had a quite disproportionate impact on the poise and confidence of men; conversely there can be a crisis of masculinity even when women continue to face systemic sex discrimination. Her point is that masculine insecurity does not depend on extraneous social circumstances; it is part of the logic of gender hierarchy. 'Masculinity is always in crisis', she says.[26]

I am almost persuaded by this argument, but not quite. Uncertainty about their gender identity is a very common experience among men. And much of it (though not all) hinges on their position *vis-à-vis* the opposite sex. Indeed it might be regarded as an occupational hazard of masculinity, in the sense that men typically experience periods of considerable gender anxiety during their lives (most of it unacknowledged, of course). But a crisis of masculinity is surely more than the sum of individual anxieties. Nor does it make sense to reduce it to a steady state, since crisis is by definition a departure from the common run. The term should be reserved for those times when men's gender expectations are being frustrated across the board, and when the structure of relations between men and women has altered in some fundamental way. Changes on this scale are likely to give rise to a discourse of 'crisis', whereas the inherent anxieties around power and autonomy which Segal pinpoints generally do not.[27] So, rather than go along with the 'continuous crisis' thesis, I prefer to pose the question: is crisis in the more structural sense particularly characteristic of our time? Is it as unprecedented as popular comment suggests?

To a remarkable extent the gender troubles of the 1990s were presaged by those of the 1890s. Indeed this was the premise of Elaine Showalter's popular text on the *fin de siècle*, *Sexual Anarchy* (1990). The masculinity of the middle and upper classes was brought into question on two fronts. First, by what the media of the day called the New Woman, or in a rather more precise catch-phrase – 'the revolt of the daughters': educated young women of the middle class who renounced the protection of home in order to lead independent working lives as journalists or teachers. They lived alone or with a woman friend; they mixed freely without a chaperone – a social trend perfectly symbolized by the woman cyclist; and they claimed intellectual equality with men.[28] In the lower middle class an increasing proportion of clerical work was being performed by women, and this was a significant inroad on the traditional male monopoly of office work.

Second, although the New Woman label was applied only to unmarried women, changes in the status of wives were equally far-reaching. The married woman of the 1890s was the beneficiary of a series of legal reforms over the previous twenty years which had enhanced her rights of property, her rights of child custody, and her right to seek redress against marital assault. Many observers believed that apart from their legal significance, these changes gave wives a new dignity and confidence, prompting them to seek a separation in some cases.[29] As one legal commentator put it, there had been not merely an alteration in the law, but a revolution.[30] At just the time when young men were having to negotiate with women on more equal terms, the rights of husbands over their wives were becoming conditional. It was a widely held view that patriarchy would never be the same again.

How did men react? Leaving aside a small group of progressive pro-feminists like Edward Carpenter, the dominant reaction was to reaffirm sexual difference – to define masculinity in terms which made the least possible concession to the feminine.[31] Manliness was given a sharper, more aggressive edge. Physical courage and stoic endurance became the exemplary masculine virtues, ruthlessly imposed on the young, especially in schools. They were seen to best advantage in the lives of military men like Gordon or Kitchener who not only never married but kept women at arm's length. But this was more than a pulling up of the drawbridge in the sex war. Fear of women in the social arena was closely associated with fear of the feminine within. The door was shut on emotional disclosure for men by the new cult of the 'stiff upper lip'. Above all, the man who engaged in same-sex practices was pathologized as 'the homosexual', degenerate and effeminate – indeed degenerate *because* he was effeminate. That image became firmly lodged in popular consciousness as a result of the trials of Oscar Wilde in 1895. And because homosexuality was pathologized in this way, it was obsessively detected – on the streets of the metropolis, in the public schools and in high places. The same moral canker which Edward Gibbon had blamed for the decline of the Roman Empire would, it was feared, bring down its successor. Sanity in same-sex relations was a casualty of a hegemonic masculinity fighting to keep the feminine at bay.[32]

IV

One conclusion, then, is that men today are not battling with unprecedented setbacks. Just as manhood has been made in many historical constructions, so too it can be 'unmade'. It has always depended on certain preconditions which are historically contingent. When those conditions have ceased to apply, men have undoubtedly lost out. The parallels between the 1890s and the recent *fin de siècle* are particularly striking, as Elaine Showalter emphasized: the general assertion of women's rights, the rise in female employment, the shifting balance within marriage, and the cultural disorientation arising from ambiguous sexualities. Even AIDS was foreshadowed by the highly publicized scourge of syphilis.

Recognizing that we are not in entirely uncharted territory opens up a second line of enquiry, and that is to distinguish the genuinely new from the recurrent. The historical parallels between the 1890s and the present should not be overstated. The extent and nature of the male response is very different. Commentators today speak glibly of a male backlash, but the current campaigns to restore the custody rights of fathers or to reverse the scholastic lead of girls over boys seem small beer compared with the growth in separatist masculinity at the end of the nineteenth century or the stigmatizing of deviants as 'degenerate'. The implication that permissiveness was common to both eras is also hard to sustain. 'Sexual anarchy' makes a striking label for the 1890s, but it is fundamentally misleading. High culture reflected a preoccupation with ambiguous sexualities, but the numbers of men who were in a position to benefit from a less conventional sexuality were minuscule; and those who engaged in physical relations of any kind with other men were open to the serious charge of 'gross indecency' – the catch-all label under which most sexual offenders were prosecuted after 1885. There is simply no comparison with the visible and accessible gay culture we have known since the 1970s, or with the real sense of choice which men now have in defining their sexual orientation. A similar caution must be applied to the New Woman. Today's feminist is right to recognize kinship with her, particularly in the ideological sense of treating entitlement to gender equality as a given. But the scale of women's advances now dwarfs anything achieved in the 1890s: in employment, especially the employment of married women, in educational attainment, and in equality within marriage and parenting.

The contrast is so pronounced that the resemblances between then and now are best viewed not as repetition, but as evidence of a cumulative process of change over time; and that process is the mounting demand of the capitalist economy for female labour. Today's assumption that a majority of both middle- and working-class women will be in employment is the latest stage in a story which takes us back to the opening up of clerical work to young women in the late nineteenth century. In fact it goes back a hundred years before that, to the recruitment of a predominantly female workforce in the Lancashire cotton mills which powered the Industrial Revolution.[33] What drove this process forward at every stage was the determination of employers to increase the pool of workers and to increase the proportion of workers who, in a convenient evasion, required not a 'family wage' but an individual wage.[34] Identifying process is rather more useful than noticing repetition, because it suggests that we ourselves are in mid-trajectory, situated in a process not yet completed. Given the history of the labour market over the past two hundred years, it seems most unlikely that the proportion of women in the workforce will decline or remain static in the future. The logic of capitalism will continue to work itself out in higher levels of female employment. At every stage, men have protested against the slur on their masculinity represented by women working outside the home. In a famous passage Engels graphically described the unmanning of Manchester workers forced to act as house-husbands while their wives were at the mill; such a predicament, he wrote, 'unsexes the man and takes from the woman all womanliness'.[35] But given the direction of historical change, shifts in the gendered access to the labour market are better seen as an occupational hazard. Men need to brace themselves for further instalments, to adapt rather than resist.

In some ways, however, making that kind of adjustment is more difficult than it used to be. That may sound rather surprising. Surely we have the advantage over our forebears of sophisticated analytical tools which enable us to understand what is happening and to formulate constructive responses? The reason why I question that upbeat approach is that the notion of a 'crisis of masculinity' itself is not conducive to purposeful action. The point of the phrase is its generalizing, abstract quality. It suggests a universal malaise, a disempowerment striking at the very heart of manhood. It points to a dysfunction so fundamental and so pervasive that it can scarcely be delineated, much less subjected to effective social action. The reason why we feel overwhelmed lies in the word 'masculinity' itself. It denotes all the attributes – physical, emotional and social – which define a masculine identity, and in highlighting 'identity' it prioritizes the interiority of being, or feeling, a man. But this is a comparatively recent concept. Only at the close of the nineteenth century did 'masculinity' begin to be used in this way, and only after the Second World War did it enter general currency.[36] Until then 'masculinity' had a much more restricted meaning, denoting the legal prerogatives of the male sex (such as primogeniture).[37] The abstract nouns which conveyed the condition of being a man were 'manhood' and 'manliness'. These terms referred primarily to a man's appearance – as in 'manly posture' – and his actions – as in 'proving one's manhood'. They did not refer to the interior core of inner identity which, in 'masculinity', is what holds the disparate elements together and binds them into an authentic whole. If the word 'masculinity' were not in common currency, we would be analyzing a crisis of employment, a crisis of the family and a crisis of sexuality. We would not be subsuming these separate phenomena into an overarching crisis of masculinity, with its implied assault on men's sense of self. In many contexts use of the word 'masculinity' has enabled

scholars to deconstruct conventional gender stereotyping. But here, paradoxically, it has an essentializing effect. The sense of embattled masculinity which
so many men evidently feel is caused by the belief that its constituents are
fixed, and that what is disappearing is not merely certain contingent
definitions but masculinity itself. The truth is that those definitions have
never been stable, and are no more likely to persist today than they were
a hundred years ago. 'Masculinity' is a term that we cannot do without,
but the history I have been examining suggests that we should be on our
guard against its essentialist implications. Talk of a crisis of masculinity is
not so much a realistic analysis as a surrender to impotent despair.

V

My premise during this lecture has been that our current preoccupations
about masculinity can be illuminated by applying a historical perspective.
Obviously I am not making a case which is exclusive to gender. I am applying some general propositions about the value of historical knowledge to a
specific instance. These propositions are generic: that history provides an
inventory of human experience on which we can draw to expand the choices
available to us now; that history can illuminate the contingent circumstances
in which particular features of our world came into being; and that history
reveals some of the trajectories which are being played out in our lives.
Without the contribution of historians, we would be more inclined to regard
our social arrangements as 'timeless', and less equipped to distinguish what
is genuinely new from what has endured over time.

   Put like that, the assertion that history is 'relevant' may not sound very
adventurous. In fact it is highly contentious – not least within the historical profession itself. Most historians are extremely cautious about claim-
ing that their scholarship might have practical application. This is partly
because, in the nineteenth century, the academic discipline of history was
established in the teeth of distorted and present-minded interpretations of
the past which were then current; and partly because during the twentieth
century 'relevant' history so often meant propaganda written by state
apparatchiks or their radical opponents.[38] The professional integrity of historians came to be identified with 'history for its own sake', conducted in an
ivory tower hopefully untouched by the world in which historians actually
lived. It may not be easy to draw a line between politically motivated
history and scholarly history from which lessons can be learned, but the
energies of historians would be better spent exploring that distinction than

in rejecting all notion of topicality out of hand. That is why I distinguished between the naive one-track expectations which were invested in the history of masculinity back in the 1980s and the insights which have flowed from the scholarly study of the subject since then.

But even more depressing are the expectations laid on history and the rest of the humanities by our political paymasters. Here the demand is for relevance, but relevance of an almost wilfully blinkered kind. Every pronouncement to come out of the Department for Education and Skills testifies to a diminishing commitment to intellectual and scholarly values. Historians certainly train their students in 'skills': years of essay-writing and seminar participation teach them to organize and voice their thoughts, and we can also take credit for the more distinctive experience which our students get in problem-solving and the weighing up of evidence. But none of this reflects what is most valuable and distinctive about a historical education. Ultimately this is not about skills, but about modes of thought that give us a stronger purchase on the world around us. We might call it 'applied history'. I prefer to flag up its social benefits, and to call it 'education for citizenship'. This country still subscribes to a model of the active, informed citizen – in the voting booth, the local council, the voluntary body and the letter pages of the dailies. That kind of participation gains immeasurably from a shared ability to deploy the insights of past experience. The prime reason why history continues to be taught in this university is not that it teaches our students to communicate and analyze, or that it starts some of them on the road to research, but that it equips them to be informed and critical citizens.

Notes and references

1 John Tosh, *Clan Leaders and Colonial Chiefs in Lango: the Political History of an East African Stateless Society, 1800–1939* (Oxford, 1978).

2 David D. Gilmore, *Manhood in the Making* (New Haven, 1990).

3 Stephen Frosh, Ann Phoenix and Rob Pattman, *Young Masculinities* (Basingstoke, 2002); Mike O'Donnell and Sue Sharpe, *Uncertain Masculinities: Youth, Ethnicity and Class in Contemporary Britain* (London, 2000).

4 Robin Headlam Wells, *Shakespeare on Masculinity* (Cambridge, 2000).

5 Walter E. Houghton, *The Victorian Frame of Mind, 1833–1870* (New Haven, 1957), pp. 242–62; Daniel T. Rodgers, *The Work Ethic in Industrial America, 1850–1920* (Chicago, 1974).

6 Contributions by Keith McClelland, Michael Roper and Peter M. Lewis to
   M. Roper and J. Tosh (eds), *Manful Assertions: Masculinities in Britain since 1800*
   (London, 1991).

7 Natalie Zemon Davis, '"Women's history" in transition: the European case',
   Feminist Studies 3 (1975–6), pp. 83–103.

8 See esp. the forum 'Formations of masculinity', *Gender & History* 1, ii (1989),
   pp. 159–212.

9 *Achilles Heel* began publication in 1979. See Victor J. Seidler, *The Achilles Heel
   Reader* (London, 1991).

10 Victor J. Seidler, *Re-Discovering Masculinity* (London, 1989).

11 Sheila Rowbotham and Jeffrey Weeks, *Socialism and the New Life: the Personal
   and Sexual Politics of Edward Carpenter and Havelock Ellis* (London, 1977);
   Weeks, *Sex, Politics and Society: the Regulation of Sexuality since 1800* (Harlow,
   1981).

12 M. St-J. Packe, *John Stuart Mill* (London, 1954).

13 Edward Carpenter, *Love's Coming of Age* (London, 1916, first pub. 1896),
   pp. 25–34.

14 Donald Bell, 'Up from patriarchy: men's role in historical perspective', in
   Robert A. Lewis (ed.), *Men in Difficult Times* (Englewood Cliffs, 1981), p. 313.

15 Robert Bly, *Iron John: a Book About Men* (Rockport MA, 1990).

16 Alan Bray, *Homosexuality in Renaissance England* (London, 1982), ch. 4.

17 Rictor Norton, *Mother Clap's Molly House: Gay Subculture in England, 1700–1830*
   (London, 1992).

18 Packe, *John Stuart Mill*, p. 355.

19 Leonore Davidoff and Catherine Hall, *Family Fortunes: Men and Women of the
   English Middle Class, 1780–1850* (London, 1987), p. 11.

20 See for example Andrew Tolson, *The Limits of Masculinity* (London, 1977).

21 Anthony Clare, *On Men: Masculinity in Crisis* (London, 2001), p. 69.

22 Rosalind Coward, *Sacred Cows: Is Feminism Relevant to the New Millennium?*
   (London, 1999), pp. 92–4.

23 Clare, *On Men*, pp. 82–5.

24 For a revealing comparison, see David J. Morgan, *Discovering Men* (London,
   1992), pp. 99–119.

25 Michael Kimmel, *Manhood in America: a Cultural History* (New York, 1996),
   pp. viii–x.

26 Lynne Segal, 'Back to the boys? Temptations of the good gender theorist',
   inaugural lecture, Birkbeck College, January 2001, p. 9. See also her
   Why Feminism?, (Cambridge, 1999), pp. 160–9.

27 Bruce Traister, 'Academic viagra: the rise of American masculinity studies', *American Quarterly* 52 (2000), pp. 287–93.

28 David Rubinstein, *Before the Suffragettes: Women's Emancipation in the 1890s* (Brighton, 1986).

29 A. James Hammerton, *Cruelty and Companionship: Conflict in Nineteenth-Century Married Life* (London, 1992), pp. 143–9.

30 Montague Lush, 'Changes in the law affecting the rights, status and liabilities of married women', in *A Century of Law Reform* (London, 1901), p. 342.

31 John Tosh, *A Man's Place: Masculinity and the Middle-Class Home in Victorian England* (London, 1999), pp. 172–94.

32 From a voluminous literature on Wilde, this aspect is best dealt with in Ed Cohen, *Talk on the Wilde Side* (New York, 1993).

33 Deborah Valenze, *The First Industrial Woman* (New York, 1997); Maxine Berg, 'What difference did women's work make to the Industrial Revolution?', *History Workshop Journal* 35 (1993), pp. 22–44.

34 Wally Seccombe, *Weathering the Storm: Working-Class Families from the Industrial Revolution to the Fertility Decline* (London, 1993).

35 Friedrich Engels, *Condition of the Working Class in England* (Harmondsworth, 1990, first pub. 1844), p. 168.

36 Gail Bederman, *Manliness and Civilization* (Chicago, 1995), pp. 17–19.

37 *OED*, 'masculinity'.

38 Marc Ferro, *The Use and Abuse of History* (London, 1987).

CHAPTER 2

What should historians do with masculinity? Reflections on nineteenth-century Britain

A ny call for historians to take masculinity seriously is exposed to objection on three fronts. It can be seen as an unwelcome take-over bid, as unacceptably subversive or as a modish irrelevance. Though none of these objections has produced an articulate critique, they are no less powerful for that; together I suspect they account for most of the reluctance of the historical profession to explore the potential of this new perspective.

The first position is taken by those who see the history of masculinity as a not-so-subtle attempt to infiltrate women's history and blunt its polemical edge. The appropriate response was given as long ago as 1975 by Natalie Zemon Davis. Addressing a feminist audience, she remarked:

It seems to me that we should be interested in the history of both women and men, that we should not be working only on the subjected sex any more than an historian of class can focus entirely on peasants. Our goal is to understand the significance of the sexes, of gender groups in the historical past.[1]

This analogy is not to do with symmetry or balance, but about the need to understand a system of social relations *as a whole* – class in the first instance, gender in the second. Davis was arguing that unless the field of power in which women have lived is studied, the reality of their historical situation

Reprinted with minor revisions from *History Workshop Journal* 38 (Oxford University Press, 1994), pp. 179–202.

will always be obscured. On those grounds alone, the gendered study of men must be indispensable to any serious feminist historical project. There are still no doubt students who object to the inclusion of masculinity in women's studies courses, but within academia Davis's point has been repeatedly made by feminist historians in recent years.[2]

One reason why feminists have come to feel happier with the study of masculinity is that its full subversive potential is becoming visible. It is this realization which shapes the second line of attack. One of the problems of women's history has been that so much of its output has concerned areas like family, philanthropy and feminist politics which can be shrugged off by mainstream historians as a minority pursuit with no bearing on their work (they are of course mistaken). But the history of masculinity cannot be cordoned off in this way. It must either be rejected, or incorporated into the traditional heartland. In an edited collection, *Manful Assertions*, which appeared in 1991, Michael Roper and I brought together essays on labour, business, religion, education and national identity in Britain over the past two hundred years, and were we assembling the volume now we would be able to include material on institutional politics too.[3] In other words, historians of masculinity are in a strong position to demonstrate (not merely assert) that gender is inherent in all aspects of social life, whether women are present or not.

Perhaps the commonest response among historians is an all-too-familiar weary scepticism. Masculinity according to this view is merely the latest in a series of ideological red herrings which will add nothing to what we already know about identity, social consciousness and social agency in the past – and indeed will probably obscure what we *do* know. It is easy to write off this attitude as a symptom of intellectual fatigue. But in fact it relates to a crucial feature of masculinity in most societies that we know about, and certainly modern Western ones, namely its relative invisibility. Men were the norm against which women and children should be measured. Women were 'carriers' of gender, because their reproductive role was held to define their place in society and their character. Masculinity remained largely out of sight since men as a sex were not confined in this or any other way: as Rousseau bluntly put it, 'The male is only a male at times; the female is a female all her life and can never forget her sex'.[4] This view proved remarkably enduring. Even in the late Victorian heyday of scientific belief in sexual difference, little was made of men's distinctive biology and the character traits that might flow from it, compared with the volume of comment on women.[5] Men's nature was vested in their reason, not their bodies. A profound dualism in Western thought has served to keep the spotlight away from men. In the historical record it is as though mascu-linity is everywhere but nowhere.

I

Given this frustrating situation, it is hardly surprising that historians inter-ested in moving towards a gendered history of men have seized upon any-thing that looks like an explicit ideology of masculinity. Hence the renewed interest in codes of chivalry and honour.[6] For the nineteenth-century historian the situation is at first sight particularly encouraging because of the hundreds of volumes written on the subject of 'manliness' – a high-profile ideology of masculinity, if ever there was one. It was elaborated, reiter-ated, contested and adapted – by preachers, schoolmasters and novelists. It was treated as the essence of civic virtue and the root of heroic achieve-ment, while at the same time being scaled down to everyday proportions as a guide for the little man. As one of the key concepts in the moral uni-verse of the Victorians, manliness has been well suited to the skills of the intellectual and cultural historian. Walter Houghton allows only a brief discussion in his classic *The Victorian Frame of Mind* (1957), but were he writ-ing today manliness would surely enjoy a higher profile. David Newsome began the work of reclamation with his fine pioneer studies of public-school culture. J.A. Mangan has charted the relationship between manliness and athleticism. Norman Vance and Claudia Nelson have considered the place of manliness in Victorian fiction, and Stefan Collini has weighed its significance for some of the heavy-weight liberal thinkers of the day.[7]

The outcome of all this work is not only to document a number of important strands within manliness, but to identify a broad shift over the Victorian era from the earnest, expressive manliness of the Evangelicals to the hearty, stiff-upper-lip variant in the era of Kitchener and Baden-Powell. Manliness expresses perfectly the important truth that boys become men not just by growing up, but by acquiring a variety of manly qualities and manly competencies as part of a conscious process which has no close par-allel in the traditional experience of young women (try adapting 'Be a man!' for use by the other sex). If men are the sex at large in society, they must live by a code which affirms their masculinity. As such a code, Victorian manliness was not only taken very seriously by pundits and preachers; it was also manifest in the lives of countless young men, who saw it as an expression of their manhood in keeping with their religious convictions, or their social aspirations, or both together. So for anyone concerned to historicize masculinity, manliness is an obvious starting-point – and it is where I began too.[8]

The results of this emphasis have been distinctly mixed. The problem is not that manliness was a cultural representation of masculinity rather than a description of actual life. Modern theorists of gender are correct in attributing great power to such representations, and their argument is only partly contingent on the high profile of the mass media today.[9] Case studies on the nineteenth and early twentieth centuries have shown how lived masculine identities drew on a repertoire of cultural forms – I am thinking here of Graham Dawson's work on the psychic meaning of military heroes, Joseph Bristow on adventure fiction and Kelly Boyd on boys' story papers.[10] The problem is rather that Victorian manliness was an *elite* cultural form, of an often crudely didactic kind. This is one reason, of course, why it is such a relief to move from the sermonizing of *Tom Brown's Schooldays* or *John Halifax Gentleman* to the more relaxed adventure fiction of Rider Haggard and G.A. Henty. But these late-Victorian bestseller authors were permeated by the values of the coming code of imperial manliness, and their role in propagating these values to a mass audience is clear. It would be a great mistake to suppose that the cultural representation of Victorian masculinity was an entirely elite affair, but the mistake is easily made because scholarly work has been so tilted in this direction. We need to know much more about the gender models conveyed by music-hall song – like Peter Bailey's suggestive account of 'Champagne Charlie', the popular stage swell of the late 1860s, with his narcissism, his convivial consumerism and his assertive sexuality.[11] And until we do, we should be cautious about assuming much permeation by the dominant manly values beyond the ranks of the lower middle class.

Another problem with manliness is its cerebral and bloodless quality – closely related, of course, to its elite provenance. While manliness can in theory be defined as a mingling of the ethical and the physiological,[12] a great deal of the literature of the day left the overwhelming impression that masculine identification resided in the life of the mind (heavily overlaid by conscience) rather than the body. This was certainly no longer the case at the end of the nineteenth century, when there was a growing tension between the moral and physical criteria of manliness.[13] But for most of the Victorian era the high ground was held by the moralists, who either believed that the body would take care of itself, or else favoured 'manly exercises' for their salutary moral effect. Even Thomas Hughes, creator of the highspirited Tom Brown and advocate of boxing for the working man, maintained that manliness was about moral excellence, and as likely to be found in a weak body as a strong.[14] The aristocracy, in keeping with its traditional claim to be a military as well as a ruling caste, took sporting prowess and physical hardiness much more seriously, but their code of manliness was of declining influence from the 1830s onwards. Only at times of popular alarm about the nation's military readiness, like the late 1850s and 1860s[15] and the first decade of the twentieth century,[16] did vestiges of aristocratic manliness reappear in the mainstream. For the most part, the Victorian code of manliness made scant acknowledgement of the body.[17]

Nowhere was this distortion more pronounced, of course, than with regard to sexuality. Public teaching on manliness was almost unanimous in enjoining purity on young men, and in casting a veil over sex within marriage. The eighteenth-century tension between manliness as enjoyment and manliness as abstinence was emphatically resolved.[18] The nearest that any variant of manliness came to acknowledging the reality of the sexual impulse was Charles Kingsley's spirited defence of the 'divineness of the whole manhood',[19] but his influence in this regard was slight. Yet alongside this massive silence has to be placed the incontrovertible evidence of large-scale prostitution. Where this conflicts most directly with the pieties of manly discourse is not so much the sanctity of the marriage vow as the purity of young men. These probably accounted for the vast majority of the prostitutes' clients: bachelors postponing marriage until their prospects had improved, middle-class youths who heeded their doctors' warnings about the danger of complete continence, soldiers and sailors, young migrant or transient workers, and so on.[20] The implication is that, except for those men who came from devout or otherwise highly respectable families, commercial sex was a masculine rite of passage, and in many cases a routine erotic outlet. Yet it is still extraordinarily difficult to incorporate this fact into our picture of the Victorians. The 'gay life' was very widespread, but it remained firmly out of sight.

So far as marriage is concerned, Peter Gay's attempt to rehabilitate bourgeois Victorians would suggest that their masculinity was more at ease with the erotic life than had been supposed.[21] Although too few of Gay's case studies are drawn from England for the case to be regarded as proven, I cannot resist mentioning two of the middle-class men whom I have studied in detail – Edward Benson and Isaac Holden of Bradford. Both possessed a strong and guilt-free desire for erotic satisfaction in marriage despite profound religious convictions in each case.[22] It is also interesting that public figures who were widely believed to practise abstinence in marriage, like John Stuart Mill or John Ruskin, suffered a definite loss of masculine reputation. But the point I wish to emphasize is that our ignorance in this area is compounded by the tendency in some quarters to equate manliness with masculinity. Certainly, if we take nineteenth-century discourses of manliness at face value there is no scope for exploring the meanings given to sexual identity and sexual desire which are fundamental to masculinity.

But the key problem is that 'manliness' was only secondarily about men's relations with women. Of course it embraced notions of chivalry – that is, the protection due to sisters, then wives, and by extension any respectable woman.[23] Anna Clark is surely right to see the foregrounding of this ideal in place of libertinism as central to early Victorian manliness.[24] But this was not the main thrust of public discourse. Writers on manliness were essentially concerned with the inner character of man, and with the kind of behaviour which displayed this character in the world at large. The dominant code of Victorian manliness, with its emphasis on self-control, hard work and independence, was that of the professional and business classes, and manly behaviour was what (among other things) established a man's class credentials *vis-à-vis* his peers and his subordinates. Of course, as Leonore Davidoff and Catherine Hall have stressed, the labour and support of female family members was essential to this public face,[25] but the tenets of manliness made absolutely no acknowledgement of this fact. Nor were explicit contrasts between the sexes much emphasized by the pundits. The distinction which exercised them (following the influential Dr Arnold of Rugby) was that between men and boys; worries about immaturity counted for much more than the fear of effeminacy, at least until the 1880s.[26] That perhaps is why so many recent historical writings on manliness have been quite innocent of gender. They are certainly helpful in giving some historical particularity to notions of masculinity. But they also convey the decidedly unfortunate impression that men can be satisfactorily studied in isolation from women, thus obscuring the crucial *relational* quality of all masculinities. Manliness presents a convenient target for gender historians, but a fundamentally misleading one. It is certainly not the master concept which will unlock the puzzle of Victorian masculinity.

II

To a greater or lesser degree, the same limitations apply to most ideologies of masculinity, and the explanation is simple. For underlying them all was the incontrovertible fact of men's social power. As a general rule, those aspects of masculinity which bear most directly on the upholding of that power are least likely to be made explicit. More specifically, men have seldom advertised the ways in which authority over women has sustained their sense of themselves as men. Even in areas of obvious contention between the sexes like the suffrage, men's opposition to measures of reform was much more likely to cite women's mission or women's inferiority than to dwell on men's stake in sexual power.[27] But the fact that such things were not much spoken of is no reason to doubt their importance – in fact rather the reverse. One explanation for John Stuart Mill's intense unpopularity in conservative circles is that he voiced unpalatable truths in precisely this area – like his assertion in *The Subjection of Women* that 'the generality of the male sex cannot yet tolerate the idea of living with an equal'.[28] The rage with which very modest reforms in the law on the custody of children were greeted is some measure of the extent to which men felt their identity to be vested in the exercise of domestic authority.[29]

What then is the historical connection between patriarchy[30] and masculinity? As I have shown, the answer offered by recent work on manliness is: not much. To move beyond that rather bland disclaimer, we have to turn from masculinity as a set of cultural attributes to consider masculinity as a social status, demonstrated in specific social contexts. I say 'demonstrated' because public affirmation was, and still is, absolutely central to masculine status. Here it is worth taking note of some of the earlier findings of feminist anthropology. Michelle Rosaldo pointed to a critical distinction between the upbringing of boys and girls in almost all societies. Whereas girls are expected to graduate to womanhood in a largely domestic setting under a mother's tutelage, boys have to be prepared for a more competitive and demanding arena. Their qualification for a man's life among men – in short for a role in the public sphere – depends on their masculinity being tested against the recognition of their peers during puberty, young adulthood and beyond. As Rosaldo put it,

A woman becomes a woman by following in her mother's footsteps, whereas there must be a break in a man's experience. For a boy to become an adult, he must prove himself – his masculinity – among his peers. And although all boys may succeed in reaching manhood, cultures treat this development as something that each individual has achieved.[31]

What precisely has to be achieved varies a lot between cultures, but in modern Western societies the public demonstration of masculinity occurs in three linked arenas: home, work and all-male associations. I would like to dwell on the gendered meaning of each of these contexts in nineteenth-century Britain, because I think that together they account for much of the reason why masculinity should matter to social historians.

In most societies that we know of, setting up a new household is the essential qualification for manhood. The man who speaks for familial dependants and who can transmit his name and his assets to future generations is fully masculine. The break is all the clearer when it is recognized that marriage requires setting up a new household, not forming a sub-unit within the parental home. In the nineteenth century this was a governing condition of the transition to adult life. Bachelorhood was always an ambivalent status, though its cultural appeal was greater at some times than others – particularly at the end of the century. Once established, a household had to be sustained by the man's productive activities. In the eighteenth century this condition was met in many areas by household production, with the man directing the labour of family members and other dependants.[32] As this pattern declined during the following century, increasing emphasis was placed on the man's unaided labours. Notwithstanding the prevalence of women's employment in the working class, the cultural weight attached to the *male* bread-winner was overwhelming. It was reflected positively in the demand for a 'family wage', and negatively in the humiliation of the unemployed man obliged to depend on his wife's earnings, and in the anger of the skilled artisan displaced by female labour. 'What is the feeling of a man in this position?' asked a Kidderminster carpet weaver in 1894. 'Has it not a tendency to reduce him and create a *littleness* when he is no longer the bread-winner of the family?' (emphasis added).[33]

The location of authority within the household was the other key determinant of masculine status here. The power of the *paterfamilias* is most assured when he controls the labour of household members, which is why household production is usually taken to imply a patriarchal family. By the mid-nineteenth century economic organization had moved sharply away from this pattern, but patriarchal values still held sway. The belief in the household as a microcosm of the political order, vigorously restated by Evangelicals, underlined the importance of the man being master in his own home.[34] The law remained pretty unyielding. The husband was legally responsible for all members of the household, including servants, and only in cases of extreme cruelty (mental or physical) was his authority over wife or children at risk. In cultural terms, up-to-date notions of domesticity and companionate marriage may have carved out a more autonomous sphere for the wife, especially in middle-class families, but the ultimate location of authority was seldom in doubt. Indeed, as Jim Hammerton has recently pointed out, companionate marriage often led the husband to be *more* assertive and heavy-handed, not less.[35] Home might be the 'woman's sphere', but the husband who abdicated from his rights in the cause of a quiet life was in common opinion less than a man, and he was a frequent butt of music-hall humour.[36]

Maintenance of a household at a level of comfort appropriate to one's social status presupposed an income from work – the second leg of masculine reputation. But not just *any* work. It wasn't enough that the work be dependable or even lucrative – it had to be dignified, and the wide currency of this notion is one of the most distinctive features of the nineteenth-century gender regime. For middle-class work to be dignified, it had to be absolutely free from any suggestion of servility or dependence on patronage. 'Look not for success to favour, to partiality, to friendship, or to what is called interest,' declared William Cobbett; 'write it on your heart that you will depend solely on your own merit and your own exertions.'[37] Neither the practice of a profession nor the running of a business was represented as a mere burden. It might become so in particular instances – if one found oneself in the wrong occupation, or wrecked one's constitution through over-work – but fundamentally a man's occupation in life was his 'calling', often seen as subject to the workings of Providence. The idea that what a man did in his working life was an authentic expression of his individuality was one of the most characteristic – and enduring – features of middle-class masculinity.[38]

Inevitably the scope for these values in the working class was limited. But the idea that the working man's property lay in his skill, acquired by apprenticeship or training under his father's eye, carried a comparable load of moral worth, and it was the basis on which craft unions demanded the continuation of traditional labour relations based on respect for the masculine skills of the men.[39] Among the manual working class, it seems highly likely that the aggressive celebration of physical strength as an exclusive badge of masculinity, described by Paul Willis in the 1970s,[40] prevailed in Victorian times too. The hapless office clerk fell between two stools: in middle-class terms his occupation was servile, while the labourer despised his soft hands and poor physique.[41] In each case masculine self-respect demanded the exclusion of women. The gender coding of the world of work could accept the reality of women's labour in the domestic setting as servants or home-workers. But the entry of women into formal paid work out of the home – whether it was mill-girls at the beginning of the century or female office-clerks at the end – always occasioned strain, not only because there might be less work (or less well-paid work) for men, but because their masculine identity as the working sex was at stake.[42]

The third leg of men's social identity is less familiar, and certainly much less developed in the theoretical literature. But all-male associations are integral to any notion of patriarchy beyond the household. They embody men's privileged access to the public sphere, while simultaneously reinforcing women's confinement to household and neighbourhood. This perception has made little impact on historical work on modern Western societies. 'Male bonding' would be a handy label, if it did not suggest something primal and trans-historical.[43] For we are dealing here with quite a wide variety of social forms. Some, like craft guilds or chambers of commerce or professional bodies, existed to promote the pursuit of business, and might therefore be subsumed under my second heading of work. But there were far too many men's associations which had little or nothing to do with work. I am thinking of the voluntary associations and pressure groups whose voices together made up 'public opinion', and the clubs, taverns and bars which oiled the wheels of friendship, politics and leisure (as well as business).

The salience of these groups is partly determined by the life cycle. The appeal of all-male conviviality is probably greatest among young unmarried men who are temporarily denied the full privileges of masculinity: the journeymen's association, the street gang, the sports club. Schooling often intensifies it. In the second half of the nineteenth century the public schools were patriarchal institutions not only because they excluded women, but because they instilled an enduring preference for all-male sociability. But the appeal of associational life goes well beyond youth. In the nineteenth century this was most evident in the United States, where the hold of fraternal lodges over the leisure time and the purses of urban men of all classes in the generation after the Civil War was truly remarkable.[44] Britain boasted an array of institutions for men of all ages, ranging from the pub, the friendly society and the working men's club through to the middle-class voluntary association and the West End club.[45]

All of these arenas were at one time or another correctly perceived by women as contributing to the edifice of male exclusionary power. They sustained the powerful myth that masculinity is about the exclusive company of men, and of course most work settings reinforced this. What the literary critic Eve Sedgwick has dubbed the 'homosocial alliance' is fundamental to masculine privilege. At the same time, as she points out, it operates within clear limits, for in the interests of protecting the key patriarchal institution of marriage, desire between males is inadmissible; camaraderie must remain just that. So while male bonding is prescribed, homosexuality is proscribed.[46] It was no coincidence that the first modern homosexual panic occurred in the 1880s, when the clubability of the propertied classes was particularly pronounced and their age of marriage (around thirty for men) unprecedentedly late. Any hint of erotic charge or emotional excess

between men, such as had been commonplace in polite society a generation earlier, now aroused suspicion. W.T. Stead's remark to Edward
Carpenter in 1895 that 'a few more cases like Oscar Wilde's and we should
find the freedom of comradeship now possible to men seriously impaired'[47]
proved all too accurate. All-male associations sustained gender privilege, while
at the same time imposing a discipline on individuals in the interests of
patriarchal stability.

III

In dwelling on the importance of home, work and association as minimal
components of masculine identity, I have doubtless laboured the obvious.
My reason for doing so is that I have wanted to prepare the ground for the
more interesting claim that the precise character of masculine formation
at any time is largely determined by the balance struck *between* these three
components. It is now widely recognized that constant emphasis on the
'separation of spheres' is misleading, partly because men's privileged ability
to pass freely between the public and the private was integral to the
social order. And some notion of complementarity is always implied by that
key nineteenth-century indicator of masculinity achieved, 'independence',
combining as it did dignified work, sole maintenance of the family, and
free association on terms of equality with other men. But it is much rarer
to see these elements considered as a linked system – characterized, as any
such system must be, by contradiction and instability. Yet this, it seems
to me, is one of the most promising ways of pinning down the social
dynamics of masculinity.

Consider, first of all, the Victorian middle class. Any notion of a solid
bourgeois masculinity is not tenable. The balance between my three components was inherently unstable and often gave visible signs of strain.
Essentially this was because the ideology of domesticity raised the profile
of home life far beyond its traditional place in men's lives, and hence posed
in an acute form the conflict between the private and public constituents
of masculinity. Already in Cobbett's writings one can see the tensions between
family life and 'the gabble and balderdash of a club or pot-house company'.[48]
By mid-century, when middle-class mores placed the tavern off-limits, this
conflict was less stark. The decorous entertainment of lectures and concerts,
not to mention collective action in the public interest, appeared to be in
less conflict with domestic values, though real devotees of domestic comfort had to be reminded that duty in the public sphere might require some

personal sacrifice.[49] More fundamental was the clash between work and home. In which sphere was a man really himself? The implications of the work ethic, in its unyielding Victorian form, were clear, and in spelling them out Carlyle had immense and enduring influence. But there was a strong current running the other way. The adage 'an Englishman's home is his castle', which enjoyed wide currency by the 1850s,[50] conveyed a double meaning of pos-session against all comers, and of refuge or retreat from the world beyond. This second meaning spoke with special force to those middle-class men who experienced the world of work as alienating or morally undermining. From Froude through Dickens to William Hale White, Victorian fiction pro-pounds the notion that only at home can a man be truly himself; as Froude put it in *The Nemesis of Faith* (1849), 'we lay aside our mask and drop our tools, and are no longer lawyers, sailors, soldiers, statesmen, clergymen, but only men'.[51] And, lest you should suppose that historians were above this alienation, Coventry Patmore (writing in the same vein) specifically included the scholar 'wearying his wits over arid parchments'.[52]

By the 1880s the balance had shifted. For the professional classes at least, domesticity was increasingly associated with ennui, routine and feminine constraint.[53] The result was a higher rate of male celibacy, rising club mem-bership and a vogue for 'adventure' – both in the real-life hazards of moun-taineering and the rougher sports, and in what Sir Arthur Conan Doyle admiringly called 'the modern masculine novel' of Robert Louis Stevenson and Rider Haggard.[54] For middle-class men at the turn of the century the respective pulls of home and the homosocial world were much more evenly matched than they had been for their grandfathers. Perhaps no clearer evidence could be found than the enormous appeal of Scouting to boys and scoutmasters alike: the camp fire was all that the domestic hearth was not.[55]

In the working class, men's commitment to home was more problem-atic still. In most cases there was of course far less to hold the working man there. If his home served also as a workshop it was unlikely to boast the modicum of amenities which might draw him to his own fireside. If he was an employee on average earnings or less, his wife's work at home combined with domestic overcrowding were likely to increase the attractions of the pub. There were plenty of people within the working class who deplored this state of affairs. Anna Clark has drawn attention to that strand within Chartism which advocated a domesticated manhood, like the London Working Men's Association which denied 'the attributes and characters of *men*' to those who were forgetful of their duties as fathers and husbands.[56] By the 1870s the claim to a dignified home life was part of the stock-in-trade of trade union leaders.[57]

It seems clear that in the late Victorian period there was a growing minority of comparatively well-paid skilled workers who entirely supported the household and spent much of their leisure time there. Yet the reality could be very different outside this privileged group. Both Ellen Ross and Carl Chinn describe an urban working-class world from which private patriarchy had almost disappeared. The husband was often made to feel like a bull in a china shop, excluded from the emotional currents of the family. More likely than not, as a boy he would have developed domestic and nurturing skills, but an important part of his growing up to manhood was to 'forget' these skills. The wife, on the other hand, was the one who maintained vital neighbourhood support, who negotiated with landlords and welfare workers, and who supervised the children's schooling. Even moving house was often her decision. London magistrates sometimes spoke of the wife's 'headship of the home'. This was in the context of domestic assault – surely a symptom of the acute masculine ambivalence experienced by men married to women who so effectively controlled the domestic sphere.[58] One can argue whether working men's attachment to convivial drinking was cause or effect of their discomfort in the home, but cutting a figure in the pub was clearly a far less equivocal sign of masculine status than presiding over the home. Charting the ebb and flow of men's commitment to domestic life, whether in the working class or the bourgeoisie, has much to reveal about the dynamics of masculinity – then and now.

IV

Although this is far from being a comprehensive account, it should be clear that in the nineteenth century masculinity had multiple social meanings. Citing this kind of historical material has become a standard procedure for students of gender who wish to emphasize masculinity as multiform.[59] It is obviously important to dispose once and for all of the argument that masculinity is 'natural' and thus beyond history. But well-documented diversity raises the opposite problem that masculinity may be merely a second-order feature, contingent on other social identities: teasing out the play of masculinity in Chartism or the bourgeois work ethic may add colour to our understanding, but it does not introduce a new dynamic.

There is some truth in this. For example, it is a fair inference from Davidoff and Hall's *Family Fortunes* that domesticated manliness was essentially the character-set of a more devout and materially confident middle class expressed in gender terms. Particular classes are sometimes associated with a distinctive masculinity. In the nineteenth century upwardly mobile men had to adapt themselves to different masculine expectations, like the artisan rising into 'respectability',[60] or the young Thomas Carlyle railing against the enfeebled masculinity of the London men of letters whose ranks he sought to join.[61] There is a sense, too, in which ruling classes may propagate their distinctive masculine codes to the society at large, just as they disseminate their political values. It has often been pointed out, for example, that Baden-Powell's intention in setting up the Boy Scouts was to introduce boys from the lower middle and working classes to public-school manliness, as the best basis for physical fitness, an ethic of service and patriotism. (It should be noted that the exercise was selective: while the public schools aimed to train boys in obedience and then command, the second stage was played down in the Scouts.[62])

But gender status cannot be reduced to class status. Even when the two are running in parallel, so to speak, interpretation of experience and action is likely to be significantly modified by taking masculinity into account. It makes a difference to recognize that unemployment not only impoverished workers but gravely compromised their masculine self-respect (including their ability to demand respect from women). In late nineteenth-century London the industrialization of traditional workshop trades not only made earnings more precarious; it also destroyed the father's ability to endow his son with a craft or a job, and was resented for this reason.[63] Again, if domestic violence is placed in the context of a volatile power relationship between the sexes at home, we can move beyond trite commonplaces about the power of cheap liquor. In short, consideration of masculinity (like femininity) enlarges the range of factors relevant to the historian of social identity or social change. It is precisely because Davidoff and Hall structure *Family Fortunes* around masculinity and femininity that we now have a different view of the middle class in the early nineteenth century; their achievement is not to fill out the gender attributes of a class we already know about, but to place gender at the centre of class formation itself.

But there is a further reason why masculinity is resistant to incorporation within other social categories. It has its own pecking order which is ultimately to do with upholding patriarchal power rather than a particular class order. Ruling groups do not only valorize particular features of their own masculine code; they often marginalize or stigmatize other masculine traits in a way which cuts across more familiar social hierarchies. This will be clear if we look at the two categories most often repressed, young bachelors and homosexuals. In most societies the energy of young men who are physically mature but not yet in a position to assume the full duties or privileges of an adult is combustible, to say the least. Much of the offence that they give is because they precociously affect fully adult modes of masculine behaviour in exaggerated or distorted forms. Since the heyday of the disorderly apprentice, young men have been a by-word for brawling, drunkenness, sexual experiment and misogyny (the last two being entirely compatible of course). Lyndal Roper's recent work vividly evokes this aspect of sixteenth-century Augsburg.[64] In the modern period, societies have varied greatly in how they have approached this issue, sometimes allowing the breathing space of a Bohemian lifestyle as in France, sometimes employing a combination of control and diversion as in middle-class Britain.[65]

The targeting of social control at homosexuals was of course historically much more specific. Only in the late nineteenth century did the now familiar polarization between 'normal' heterosexual and 'deviant' homosexual finally take shape. Just when homosexuality (as distinct from homosexual behaviour) 'emerged' has become a contentious area of scholarship in recent years. There can be little doubt that a vigorous gay sub-culture existed in early eighteenth-century London, or that 'molly-houses' periodically attracted draconian repression.[66] But the stigmatization of homosexuals as an aberrant category of men set apart from the 'normal' seems only to have fully developed at a highly specific conjuncture in the late nineteenth century: when medical theory identified a congenitally defective 'third sex', when a strident Social Purity movement seized on homosexuality as a metaphor for national decline, and when homosexuals themselves developed an emancipatory 'Uranian' identity. From then on the figure of the homosexual was established as a patriarchal scapegoat – someone who struck at the roots of the family, flouted the work ethic and subverted the camaraderie of all-men association.[67]

One can say, therefore, that the dominant masculinity is constructed in opposition to a number of subordinate masculinities whose crime is that they undermine patriarchy from within or discredit it in the eyes of women. Sometimes an entire persona is demonized, as in the case of the homosexual; sometimes specific forms of male behaviour are singled out. A good example of this second category is wife-beating. In the course of the nineteenth century domestic violence became increasingly unacceptable to 'respectable' opinion. As is well known, the campaign which culminated in the Matrimonial Causes Act of 1878 was headed by Frances Power Cobbe. But the fight in Parliament was led by Henry Labouchère, who saw in wife-beating a damnable slur on the honour of the male sex.[68]

Both the disciplining of subordinate masculinities and the modification of gender norms imposed on the majority of men illustrate the workings of what is sometimes called 'hegemonic masculinity'. This concept has been developed by the sociologist R.W. Connell in order to explain the gender structure of contemporary societies. Connell maintains that one neglected explanation for patriarchy's successful survival and adaptation is the solidarity of men in upholding it – in not 'rocking the boat'. 'Hegemonic masculinity' denotes those expressions of masculinity – like exclusive heterosexuality or the double standard or the assumption that paid work is a male birthright – which serve most effectively to sustain men's power over women in society as a whole. From this perspective, the dominant forms of masculinity are those which marshall men with very different interests behind the defence of patriarchy.[69] The historical application of Connell's theory is limited by the central role he accords to the powerful images of mainstream masculinity put out by the modern mass media, but it becomes increasingly relevant from the 1880s, when the role of the stage and the printed word in shaping gender identification was already in evidence.[70] 'Hegemonic masculinity' is a convenient phrase because it reminds us that masculinity carries a heavy ideological freight, and that it makes socially crippling distinctions not only between men and women, but between different categories of men – distinctions which have to be maintained by force, as well as validated through cultural means.

V

Once we are clear about the ways in which masculine identities diverge from – and in some contexts overlay – class identities, it is easier to understand why masculine insecurity has had such wide social ramifications in the past, as today. Masculinity is insecure in two senses: its social recognition depends on material accomplishments which may not be attainable; and its hegemonic form is exposed to resistance from both women and subordinated masculinities. (There is a third sense in which masculinity tends to insecurity, arising out of its psychic constitution, to which I turn in the next section.)

In discussing the three foundations of work, home and association, I showed how the social definition of masculinity was determined by the balance between them – and how that balance was inherently variable. However, my argument needs to be taken one stage further. Each of these bases of masculine identification was itself uncertain. This was particularly true of the first two. A proper job and a viable household were highly vulnerable to the vicissitudes of the economic cycle. Individual men might experience acute loss of masculine self-respect through a lack of housing, a shortage of apprenticeships, being thrown out of work, and so on. It is to the credit of recent historians like Sonya Rose and Keith McClelland that we can now grasp the gender implications of these familiar vicissitudes of working-class life.[71] The argument here is not that masculinity was *always* experienced as something contingent and vulnerable. It is not difficult to think of categories of men who never had any reason to doubt their social qualifications for manhood once they had attained adulthood. Nor should one forget those men who were able to make a virtue of their gender non-conformity – the Bohemian, the club *habitué*, the member of a homo-sexual coterie.[72] My point is rather that, for the majority of men who wielded comparatively little social and economic power, loss of masculine self-respect was as much an occupational hazard as loss of income.

As for hegemonic masculinity, any system of hegemony is by definition liable to insecurity. Holding the line on forms of masculinity intended to uphold patriarchy is always open to the danger of contestation and sub-version. This, after all, was the thrust of much action by women in the public sphere – notably successive campaigns for marriage-law reform, and the crusade for Social Purity.[73] The New Woman was, of course, widely construed as a threat to the patriarchal order. Of greater substance perhaps were the female plaintiffs in the post-1857 Divorce Court, whose courage in exposing their painful circumstances to the glare of publicity brought (as Hammerton has shown) the long-term benefit of raising socially acceptable standards of men's marital conduct.[74] At various times during the nineteenth century the subordinated masculinities whom I mentioned earlier were also seen as a threat. In his various manifestations as the lout, the loafer and the hooligan, the unmarried youth was consistently condemned – either as a threat to patriarchal order in the present, or (by the turn of the century) as a degenerate who threatened the manly vigour of future generations.[75] During the nineteenth century the ability of homosexual men to achieve changes in the organization of patriarchy was much less than has been the case in the last thirty years, but it was in the 1880s that the typecasting of gays as everything that the front-line troops of patriarchy are not began to assume its modern shape.

This is the context in which to consider the idea of a 'crisis in masculinity'. As used by present-day theorists, the term denotes a situation in which the traditionally dominant forms of masculinity have become so blurred that men no longer know what is required to be a 'real man' – either because of structural changes or because of challenging critique, or both.[76] There is the drawback that, if we speak of 'crisis', we imply stability the rest of the time. But there is a difference between the individual's insecurity and the undermining of masculinity across a swathe of society, especially when this is articulated and acted upon.

Elaine Showalter has popularized the notion of a 'masculine crisis' in *fin-de-siècle* Britain, mostly on the strength of the cultural challenge posed by the New Woman and the visible homosexual.[77] I would like to offer a brief example which pays more attention to shifts in the social underpinnings of masculinity in the same period – namely, popular support for imperialism. This is a promising context, because the empire's masculine associations were so strong, and so much of its significance to the British represented a displacement of domestic concerns. An important strand of jingo sentiment was the male clerical workers of the lower middle class, noted for their uninhibited participation in Mafeking night, their enlistment in volunteer army units – and also their taste for imperial adventure fiction.[78] They are of course a classic example of a marginal class, balanced precariously between the workers and the bourgeoisie, and hence likely to make a very public avowal of what they perceived to be respectable or patriotic values. But we must also take note of their masculine job anxieties. From the 1880s onwards, more and more clerical work was being given to women – up to a quarter in some cities – and male clerks protested at this slur on their manhood.[79] A hearty, and above all a *physical* identification with the quintessentially masculine ethos of empire was one very effective way in which that slur could be countered. On this reading, male clerks were a class fraction undergoing acute gender insecurity at this time, and they grasped the most easily improvised way of reaffirming their masculinity. As a form of political identification (and also, it might be said, as a career choice[80]) the empire served to underpin beleaguered masculinities at home. The components of masculine status have, I would argue, been too long taken for granted as a fixture largely outside the narratives of social change. As this neglect is rectified, other features of the historical landscape, no less familiar than imperialism, are likely to change their configuration too.

VI

So far, in treating masculinity as a social identity – as an aspect of the structure of social relations – I have reflected the dominant trend in this country in historical writing about gender. But of course this is not the only approach, nor the most challenging one. Masculinity is more than social construction. It demands to be considered also as a *subjective* identity, usually the most deeply experienced that men have. And this brings into play the early formation of the gendered personality in the intimate relations of family life. What men subsequently seek to validate through recognition of their peers has been shaped in infancy and childhood in relations of nurture, desire and authority. It is therefore a mistake to treat masculinity merely as an outer garment or 'style', adjustable according to social circumstances.[81] Nor does it make much sense to baldly equate masculinity with the reflexes which serve to maintain gender inequality. Subjectivity is the other, indispensable part of the picture. This is where the problems of conceptualization and analysis are most acute. For all the gaps and speculations in my discussion of masculinity and patriarchy, the issues I raised were at least issues of social and intellectual history, to be addressed by well-tried research methods. Masculinity as subjective identity, on the other hand, has received far less attention and raises much greater scepticism in the profession. The quicksand of psychoanalytic theory, combined with serious technical problems of sources and sampling, has undoubtedly been a deterrent to historians in Britain, where these matters have tended to be left to cultural studies.

This is not the place to enter a discussion of the subtleties of competing interpretations within the psychoanalytic tradition – for which I am anyway not qualified – but I do want to stress the key psychodynamics of masculinity which feature in most variants of the tradition. All gender identities are unstable and conflictual because the growing infant has to negotiate a path through a dual identification – with both parents (or their surrogates) – and because so much of his/her adult identity is formed in this way (rather than through biological endowment or cultural influences). The outcome of this process of growth is that men have feminine bits of themselves (just as women have masculine bits). Peer-group pressure among men in the public arena requires them to disown their feminine side, in the process setting very rigid boundaries for the self. And the unacknowledged feminine within is disposed of by being projected onto other categories of men, often with socially repressive results, as in the case of homosexuals. Men's conflict with the feminine within is sometimes treated as a psychic universal, with the kind of baleful consequences that make it hard to have any optimism about a more equitable gender order in the future. To the extent that all boys have to go through a separation from infant identification with the mother which can never be fully accomplished, there is a universal pattern here. But what this perspective loses sight of is that cultures vary immensely in how much significance they accord to mothering, how far they permit men to express feminine qualities, and how far they insist that masculinity should, so to speak, be all of a piece. These questions are the realm of the historian *par excellence*.[82]

We are a long way from approaching these questions in a systematic fashion. But I would like to discuss two contrasted contexts where the benefits of a psychically informed approach are beginning to come into view. The first takes me back to the subject of manliness with which I began. Here we have a code of masculinity which demands to be treated as a *public* code – a guide to masculine performance in the public sphere. The mistake is to regard such codes as pertaining to the public sphere alone. We need to ask the question, who taught young men about manliness? – and to go further than the more obvious answers. There has been much emphasis on the public schools.[83] But what is often forgotten is that the public schoolboy was not a *tabula rasa* at thirteen; he was someone whose formative years had been spent in an upper- or middle-class home, and who continued to spend considerable stretches of each year there. His first and most enduring instructors in manliness were his parents.

A good deal turns on which parent took the lead. And here the vital context is the relatively recent elevation of the mother's role. Whereas in the eighteenth century mothers had been thought of as too indulgent to be trusted with their sons for long, by the 1830s moral motherhood was well into its stride, at least in middle-class circles. Wives were increasingly seen as morally superior to their husbands and as the conscience of the home.[84] Their role as guide and teacher of the young, especially boys, was accordingly extended. Fathers might continue to engage in 'serious talk' with their sons on the quandaries of adult life, but mothers, particularly those married to remote aristocratic husbands or to overworked middle-class ones, now had control over a large area of moral education, and it is clear that this included 'manliness'. Mary Benson was married to a bishop who regarded himself as an expert on the subject (having been a public-school headmaster for thirteen years); but it was she who urged on their twelve-year-old son in 1879 with these words: 'I want you to be manly and all that we have ever talked of tends to this. . . . Stir yourself up then, my boy, and be a man'.[85]

Middle-class males in late Victorian Britain thus tended to face a difficult transition to an adult masculine identity. Not only did they have to deal with an infant separation trauma enhanced by a pronounced emphasis on maternal nurture; they also had the unsettling awareness that what they knew of manliness had, to some degree at least, been filtered through a feminine sensibility. Their own code of manliness was accordingly more brittle and less tolerant of the 'feminine' within.[86] Thus, whereas young men earlier in the century were often able to express intense feelings in public – in tears, hugs and so forth – this became increasingly rare in their sons and grandsons. The dominant code of manliness in the 1890s, so hostile to emotional expression and so intolerant of both androgyny and homosexuality, can be interpreted as a by-product of a raised imperial consciousness – especially with regard to the imperial frontier and the manly qualities required there.[87] But this is to see manliness as rooted only in the public sphere. I am suggesting that its late nineteenth-century version was also the outward symptom of a need to repress the feminine within – a psychic universal maybe, but one which had been greatly exacerbated by the distinctive domestic regime of the middle and upper classes over the previous generation or so. Psychic and social were inextricably intertwined in this, as in so many other aspects of gender.

My second example takes us beyond the world of home and school and considers some of the wide-ranging implications of projection. I say 'wide-ranging' because it is this aspect which best explains why gender identities rooted in intimate experience spill over into social consciousness and sometimes political action. Any identity, and especially an insecure one, is partly constructed in juxtaposition to a demonized 'other' – an imagined identity composed of all the relevant negatives, and pinned onto its nearest approximation in the real world. This aspect of masculine identity is now best recognized in historical studies of culture conflict and colonialism, and the explanation is straightforward enough. Confronted by forms of racism which strike us in retrospect as bizarre in the extreme, we are more likely to take seriously a framework of explanation which moves beyond instrumental rationality. For it is clear that the deep investment of British society in empire arose not just from profit and career but from compelling fantasies of mastery. And these appealed not only to colonial whites who had face-to-face contact with other races, but to men in Britain who had never travelled beyond Europe. Thomas de Quincey's violent racial fantasies (as analyzed by John Barrell) are a telling instance of this, and on a broader canvas Catherine Hall's recent work (though less psychoanalytic) is intended to show how English national identities were constructed through powerful notions of sexual and racial difference.[88] The production of images of Africa, India or the Caribbean shifted the meanings attached to being white and male (and female too).

The psychic structure of colonial discourse was certainly not uniform. On one level, it was about idealized masculinities like those of the so-called 'martial races' – embodying desirable qualities which had been 'lost' or marginalized by the British and might now be repossessed through imperial control – a theme which runs through Baden-Powell's *Scouting for Boys* (1908) and was to account for much of T.E. Lawrence's popular appeal.[89] Alternatively colonial subjects were viewed as children – a popular fantasy with paternalistic officials and missionaries, despite the long-term implications of equality and displacement. But most powerful of all was the projection of femininity, because this combined disparagement and desire in a heady mixture. What white men thought they recognized in the other reflected both the compulsion to disown their own feminine and their attraction to those same feminine qualities. Sometimes the feminine was ascribed to whole regions, as in the allure of the Dark Continent awaiting penetration and mastery. More often it was attached to colonized men specifically. Colonial discourse was full of the effeminate and devious Bengali, or the docile and affectionate slave in the West Indies. Sexual expression was more relaxed overseas, the work ethic often non-existent. Local lifestyles which for the Englishman in the tropics were the road to a ruined career could appeal as unrestrained fantasy back home, one moment speaking to hidden desires, and the next moment informing violently punitive impulses.[90]

This is the point at which to reintroduce masculinity as cultural representation. For the power of these images of the 'other' to shape masculine identities in Britain itself (as distinct from the colonies) depended on their presence in visual and literary culture. By 'culture' here I do not of course mean the explicit and self-conscious culture of manliness, but rather the contingent and contradictory meanings inscribed in the culture at large, where gendered distinctions abounded in popular forms, ranging from missionary magazines through travel writing and adventure fiction to popular ballad and music hall. Here one certainly finds the portrayal of imperial paragons and heroes, like Henty's boy adventurers or the figure of Allan Quatermain. But I suspect that the strongest hold was exercised by the evocation of 'the other', especially the negative racial stereotypes I have just mentioned. The artisan, the clerk and the shop-worker were invited to participate in imperial fantasies of mastery and thereby find new ways of expressing (and perhaps containing) the tensions in their own gender identity.[91] The popular assumption of superiority over other races in the empire operated at a much deeper level than a complacent comparison of material circumstances. It follows that the questions we have to ask about the quickening of imperial consciousness in late Victorian Britain include not only how it was affected by changes in the social underpinnings of masculinity at home, but what changes occurred in the imagined relationship between masculinities in Britain and the empire overseas.

VII

Masculinity as I have analyzed it in this paper is both a psychic and a social identity: psychic, because it is integral to the subjectivity of every male as this takes shape in infancy and childhood; social, because masculinity is inseparable from peer recognition, which in turn depends on performance in the social sphere. It is the uneasy and complex relation between these two elements which explains masculinity's power to shape experience and action, often in ways beyond the conscious grasp of the participants. At one and the same time, men pursue practical goals of gender aggrandizement and are guided by unacknowledged fantasies designed to defend the psyche.[92] That is what patriarchy means. Most patriarchal forms in history have arisen from psychic needs combined with a perception of the material advantage to be derived from power over women. Tracing the interconnections and weighing their social impact is clearly a major task for historians. The challenge was thrown down by Sally Alexander and Barbara Taylor as long ago as 1981,[93] and it must be said that only very slow progress has so far been made.

The other task which I would highlight relates to my discussion of masculine hierarchies. It is certainly vital to establish that these hierarchies had a life of their own, not reducible to distinctions of class, ethnicity or religion. This is why, when we bring gender into social history, we are not simply contextualizing people's reactions more richly – we are shifting the weight of explanation. But that makes the question of determination all the more pressing. What was the dynamic behind the fluctuating balance between work, home and association which I have identified as the key arenas of masculine recognition? What shaped the dominant or hegemonic practices of masculinity in any given society? And how should we conceive of the relation between the discursive and the social when dealing with structures of power that often remained hidden? All the resources of the cultural and social historian will surely be needed in these endeavours. The answers, I suggest, will not be the province of yet another sub-specialism, but will be central to how we as historians think about our subject.

Notes and references

1 Natalie Zemon Davis, '"Women's History" in transition: the European case', *Feminist Studies* 3 (1975), p. 90.

2 See for example Jane Lewis, *Labour and Love: Women's Experience of Home and Family, 1850–1940* (Oxford, 1986), editor's introduction, p. 4; Gisela Bock,

'Women's history and gender history: aspects of an international debate', *Gender & History* 1 (1989), p. 18.

3 Michael Roper and John Tosh (eds), *Manful Assertions: Masculinities in Britain since 1800* (London, 1991). For masculinity and institutional politics, see Jon Lawrence, 'Class and gender in the making of urban Toryism, 1880–1914', *English Historical Review* 108 (1993), pp. 629–52.

4 William Boyd (ed. and trans.), *Emile for Today: the Emile of Jean Jacques Rousseau* (London, 1956), p. 132.

5 Cynthia Eagle Russett, *Sexual Science: the Victorian Construction of Womanhood* (Cambridge, 1989).

6 Robert A. Nye, *Masculinity and Male Codes of Honor in Modern France* (New York, 1993).

7 David Newsome, *Godliness and Good Learning* (London, 1961); J.A. Mangan, *Athleticism in the Victorian and Edwardian Public School* (Cambridge, 1981); Norman Vance, *The Sinews of the Spirit: the Ideal of Christian Manliness in Victorian Literature and Religious Thought* (Cambridge, 1985); Stefan Collini, *Public Moralists* (Oxford, 1991); Claudia Nelson, *Boys Will Be Girls: the Feminine Ethic and British Children's Fiction 1857–1917* (New Brunswick, 1991). For a representative collection of work, see J.A. Mangan and James Walvin (eds), *Manliness and Morality: Middle-Class Masculinity in Britain and America, 1800–1940* (Manchester, 1987).

8 John Tosh, 'Domesticity and manliness in the Victorian middle class: the family of Edward White Benson', in Roper and Tosh, *Manful Assertions*, pp. 44–73.

9 Antony Easthope, *What a Man's Gotta Do: the Masculine Myth in Popular Culture* (London, 1986); Peter Middleton, *The Inward Gaze: Masculinity and Subjectivity in Modern Culture* (London, 1992).

10 Graham Dawson, *Soldier Heroes: British Adventure, Empire and the Imagining of Masculinities* (London, 1994); Joseph Bristow, *Empire Boys: Adventures in a Man's World* (London, 1991); Kelly Boyd, 'Exemplars and ingrates: imperialism and masculinity in the boys' story paper, 1880–1930', *Historical Research* 67 (1994), pp. 143–55.

11 Peter Bailey, 'Champagne Charlie: performance and ideology in the music-hall swell song', in J.S. Bratton (ed.), *Music Hall: Performance and Style* (Milton Keynes, 1986), pp. 49–69.

12 Collini, *Public Moralists*, p. 113.

13 See esp. the essays in Mangan and Walvin, *Manliness and Morality*.

14 Thomas Hughes, *The Manliness of Christ* (London, 1880), p. 25.

15 Bruce Haley, *The Healthy Body and Victorian Culture* (Cambridge, 1978), ch. 6.

16 John Springhall, *Youth, Empire and Society: British Youth Movements 1883–1940* (London, 1977); Tim Jeal, *Baden-Powell* (London, 1989).

17 The counter-argument to this generalization is most effectively made in Haley, *Healthy Body*.

18 John Barrell, *The Birth of Pandora and the Division of Knowledge* (London, 1992), ch. 4.

19 *Charles Kingsley: His Letters and Memories of His Life*, ed. F. Kingsley (London, 1877), vol. II, p. 186.

20 J.A. Banks, *Prosperity and Parenthood* (London, 1954); J.A. Banks and Olive Banks, *Feminism and Family Planning in Victorian England* (Liverpool, 1964); J.A. Banks, *Victorian Values, Secularism and the Size of Families* (London, 1981); Judith R. Walkowitz, *Prostitution and Victorian Society* (Cambridge, 1980).

21 Peter Gay, *The Bourgeois Experience: Victoria to Freud*, vol. II (New York, 1986), esp. pp. 14–21, 30–4, 297–311, 419–22.

22 On Benson, see Tosh, 'Domesticity and manliness'. On Holden, see John Tosh, 'From Keighley to St-Denis: separation and intimacy in Victorian bourgeois marriage', *History Workshop Journal* 40 (1995), pp. 193–206.

23 See Mark Girouard, *The Return to Camelot: Chivalry and the English Gentleman* (New Haven, 1981).

24 Anna Clark, *Women's Silence, Men's Violence: Sexual Assault in England 1770–1845* (London, 1987), pp. 23, 110–13.

25 Leonore Davidoff and Catherine Hall, *Family Fortunes: Men and Women of the English Middle Class, 1780–1850* (London, 1987), esp. chs 6 and 8.

26 Newsome, *Godliness and Good Learning*, esp. pp. 195–8, 207–11, and Nelson, *Boys Will Be Girls*.

27 Brian Harrison, *Separate Spheres: The Opposition to Women's Suffrage in Britain* (London, 1978), ch. 4.

28 John Stuart Mill, *The Subjection of Women* (London, 1983, first pub. 1869), p. 91. For an equally forthright view on men's power over children, see Mill's *On Liberty* (1974, first pub. 1859), p. 175.

29 John Killham, *Tennyson and The Princess* (London, 1958), pp. 150–66; Mary L. Shanley, *Feminism, Marriage and the Law in Victorian England, 1850–1895* (Princeton, 1989), ch. 5.

30 I use the term 'patriarchy' aware of the misgivings which its use has recently aroused. I make no assumptions about the biological or trans-historical character of men's power over women; nor am I concerned to identify a specifically patriarchal mode of production at a given time. I use the term descriptively to indicate those areas of life where men's power over women and children constitutes a significant form of stratification. The broader debate can still be usefully followed in the exchange between Sheila Rowbotham, Sally Alexander and Barbara Taylor, in Raphael Samuel (ed.), *People's History and Socialist Theory* (London, 1981). See also Michael Roper and John Tosh,

'Historians and the politics of masculinity', in Roper and Tosh, *Manful Assertions*, pp. 8–11.

31 Michelle Z. Rosaldo, 'Woman, culture and society: a theoretical overview', in M.Z. Rosaldo and L. Lamphere (eds), *Woman, Culture and Society* (Stanford, 1974), p. 28. For a plethora of ethnographic examples, see David D. Gilmore, *Manhood in the Making: Cultural Concepts of Masculinity* (New Haven, 1990).

32 Maxine Berg, *The Age of Manufactures, 1700–1820* (London, 1985), chs 6 and 9; Bridget Hill, *Women, Work and Sexual Politics in Eighteenth-Century England* (Oxford, 1989).

33 Sonya Rose, *Limited Livelihoods: Gender and Class in Nineteenth-Century England* (London, 1992), p. 128.

34 Davidoff and Hall, *Family Fortunes*, chs 1–2.

35 A. James Hammerton, *Cruelty and Companionship: Conflict in Nineteenth-Century Married Life* (London, 1992), chs 3–4.

36 J.S. Bratton, *The Victorian Popular Ballad* (London, 1975), pp. 184–8.

37 William Cobbett, *Advice to Young Men* (London, 1926, first pub. 1830), p. 10.

38 Davidoff and Hall, *Family Fortunes*, pp. 229–34.

39 Keith McClelland, 'Some thoughts on masculinity and the "representative artisan" in Britain, 1850–1880', *Gender & History* 1 (1989), pp. 164–77 (repr. in Roper and Tosh, *Manful Assertions*, pp. 24–91).

40 Paul Willis, *Learning to Labour: How Working-Class Kids Get Working-Class Jobs* (London, 1977), pp. 52, 148.

41 Gregory Anderson, *Victorian Clerks* (Manchester, 1976).

42 On the mill-girls, see Ivy Pinchbeck, *Women Workers and the Industrial Revolution, 1750–1850* (London, 1930) and Jane Rendall, *Women in an Industrializing Society, 1750–1880* (Oxford, 1990). On women office clerks, see Anderson, *Victorian Clerks*.

43 Merry E. Wiesner, 'Guilds, male bonding and women's work in early modern Germany', *Gender & History* 1 (1989), p. 125.

44 Mary Ann Clawson, *Constructing Brotherhood: Class, Gender and Fraternalism* (Princeton, 1989); Mark C. Carnes, *Secret Ritual and Manhood in Victorian America* (New Haven, 1989).

45 Not all of these institutions were the exclusive preserve of men throughout the period; for example, women did appear in pubs and they had their own friendly society lodges in the early nineteenth century. But by the second half of the century the exceptions to male control were relatively few. See R.J. Morris, 'Clubs, societies and associations', in F.M.L. Thompson (ed.), *The Cambridge Social History of Britain 1750–1950* (Cambridge, 1990), vol. 3, pp. 430–6.

46 Eve K. Sedgwick, *Between Men: English Literature and Male Homosocial Desire* (New York, 1985), ch. 1.

47 Quoted in Jeffrey Weeks, *Coming Out: Homosexual Politics in Britain from the Nineteenth Century to the Present* (London, 1977), p. 21.

48 Cobbett, *Advice to Young Men*, p. 170.

49 See, for example, John Angell James, *The Family Monitor, or a Help to Domestic Happiness* (Birmingham, 1828), p. 22.

50 Frances Armstrong, *Dickens and the Concept of Home* (Ann Arbor, 1990), p. 155, n. 1.

51 J.A. Froude, *The Nemesis of Faith* (1849), as quoted in Walter E. Houghton, *The Victorian Frame of Mind, 1830–1870* (New Haven, 1957), pp. 345–6.

52 [Coventry Patmore], 'The social position of women', *North British Review* 14 (1851), pp. 521–2.

53 John Tosh, *A Man's Place: Masculinity and the Middle-Class Home in Victorian England* (London, 1999), pp. 172–82.

54 A. Conan Doyle, quoted in J.A. Hammerton (ed.), *Stevensoniana* (London, 1903), p. 243. On the appeal of adventure as a counterpoint to domesticity, see Martin Green, *Dreams of Adventure, Deeds of Empire* (New York, 1979).

55 This aspect of Scouting has yet to be analyzed, but for analogous work on Scouting in America, see Jeffrey P. Hantover, 'The Boy Scouts and the validation of masculinity', in Elizabeth and Joseph H. Pleck (eds), *The American Man* (Englewood Cliffs, 1980).

56 Anna Clark, 'The rhetoric of Chartist domesticity: gender, language and class in the 1830s and 1840s', *Journal of British Studies* 31 (1992), pp. 70–1.

57 McClelland, 'Masculinity and the "representative artisan"'.

58 Carl Chinn, *They Worked All Their Lives* (Manchester, 1988); Ellen Ross, *Love and Toil: Motherhood in Outcast London, 1870–1918* (New York, 1993). See also Nancy Tomes, 'A "torrent of abuse": crimes of violence between working-class men and women in London, 1840–1875', *Journal of Social History* 11 (1978), pp. 328–45. A striking account of the twentieth century is Pat Ayers and Jan Lambertz, 'Marriage relations, money and domestic violence in working-class Liverpool, 1919–39', in Lewis, *Labour and Love*, pp. 195–219.

59 For example, Lynne Segal, *Slow Motion: Changing Masculinities, Changing Men* (London, 1990).

60 For an unusual and illuminating instance, see Pamela Walker, ' "I live but not yet I for Christ liveth in me": men and masculinity in the Salvation Army, 1865–90', in Roper and Tosh, *Manful Assertions*, pp. 92–112.

61 Norma Clarke, 'Strenuous idleness: Thomas Carlyle and the man of letters as hero', in Roper and Tosh, *Manful Assertions*, pp. 25–43.

62 See esp. Michael Rosenthal, *The Character Factory: Baden-Powell and the Origins of the Boy Scout Movement* (London, 1986), ch. 3. Also Robert H. MacDonald, *Sons of the Empire: the Frontier and the Boy Scout Movement, 1890–1918* (Toronto, 1993), pp. 159–62.

63 Ross, *Love and Toil*.

64 Lyndal Roper, 'Blood and cod-pieces', in her *Oedipus and the Devil: Witchcraft, Sexuality and Religion in Early Modern Europe* (London, 1994).

65 John R. Gillis, *Youth and History*, 2nd edn (New York, 1981).

66 Alan Bray, *Homosexuality in Renaissance England* (London, 1982), ch. 4; Rictor Norton, *Mother Clap's Molly House: Gay Subculture in England 1700–1830* (London, 1992), esp. chs 3–5.

67 The notion of a distinctive construction of homosexuality in the late nineteenth century may have been overstated by recent historians following in the wake of Foucault, but a qualitative change at that time seems undeniable. The evidence is marshalled in Weeks, *Coming Out*, chs 1–6, 10; Weeks, *Sex, Politics and Society*, 2nd edn (1989), ch. 6; and Matt Cook, *London and the Culture of Homosexuality, 1885–1914* (Cambridge, 2003).

68 Hammerton, *Cruelty and Companionship*, pp. 65–7.

69 R.W. Connell, *Gender and Power* (Cambridge, 1987), esp. pp. 183–8; Tim Carrigan, Bob Connell and John Lee, 'Toward a new sociology of masculinity', in Harry Brod, *The Making of Masculinities* (Boston, 1987), pp. 63–100.

70 See esp. Judith Walkowitz, *City of Dreadful Delight: Narratives of Sexual Danger in Late-Victorian London* (London, 1992).

71 Rose, *Limited Livelihoods*; McClelland, 'Masculinity and the "respectable artisan"'.

72 These examples tend to presuppose a good income and social position. Working-class instances are more difficult to find. We need to know much more about those communities where almost all the available paid work was for women and the men performed the domestic labour. For suggestive comment on the potteries at the turn of the century, see Margaret Hewitt, *Wives and Mothers in Victorian Industry* (London, 1958), p. 193.

73 Shanley, *Feminism, Marriage and the Law*; Sheila Jeffreys, *The Spinster and Her Enemies: Feminism and Sexuality 1880–1930* (London, 1985), pp. 6–26; Frank Mort, *Dangerous Sexualities: Medico-Moral Politics since 1830* (London, 1987), pp. 103–36.

74 Hammerton, *Cruelty and Companionship*, pp. 82–133.

75 Geoffrey Pearson, *Hooligan: a History of Respectable Fears* (London, 1983). More generally, see Gillis, *Youth and History*.

76 Connell, *Gender and Power*, pp. 158–63; Michael S. Kimmel, 'The contemporary "crisis" of masculinity in historical perspective', in Brod, *Making of*

Masculinities, pp. 121–53; Arthur Brittan, *Masculinity and Power* (Oxford, 1989), pp. 25–35.

77 Elaine Showalter, *Sexual Anarchy: Gender and Culture at the Fin de Siecle* (London, 1991), esp. pp. 9–15.

78 Richard N. Price, 'Society, status and jingoism: the social roots of lower middle-class patriotism, 1870–1900', in Geoffrey Crossick (ed.), *The Lower Class in Britain* (London, 1977).

79 Anderson, *Victorian Clerks*, pp. 56–60; Meta Zimmeck, 'Jobs for the girls: the expansion of clerical work for women, 1850–1914', in Angela John (ed.), *Unequal Opportunities* (Oxford, 1986), pp. 153–77.

80 See my 'Manliness, masculinities and the New Imperialism, 1880–1900' (Chapter 9 below).

81 This has been the tendency in some recent American work, e.g. Mark C. Carnes and Clyde Griffen, *Meanings for Manhood: Constructions of Masculinity in Victorian America* (Chicago, 1990).

82 A very influential account of the psychic foundations of masculinity has been Nancy Chodorow, *The Reproduction of Mothering: Psychoanalysis and the Sociology of Gender* (Berkeley, 1978). For a general survey, see Segal, *Slow Motion*, esp. chs 4 and 5.

83 See esp. Newsome, *Godliness and Good Learning*, and J.R. de S. Honey, *Tom Brown's Universe: the Development of the Victorian Public School* (London, 1977).

84 Jane Rendall, *The Origins of Modern Feminism* (Basingstoke, 1985), esp. chs 2–3. See also Ruth Bloch, 'American feminine ideals in transition: the rise of the moral mother, 1785–1815', *Feminist Studies* 4 (1978), pp. 101–26.

85 Mary Benson to Fred (E.F.) Benson, 1 June 1880, Benson Deposit 3/66, Bodleian Library Mss.

86 This aspect of nineteenth-century family culture has been particularly emphasized in work on America. See esp. E. Anthony Rotundo, *American Manhood* (New York, 1993). It should be noted that the argument here is not about 'blaming mother': the mid-Victorian pattern of middle-class upbringing was as much the creation of fathers as of mothers.

87 H. John Field, *Toward a Programme of Imperial Life: the British Empire at the Turn of the Century* (Oxford, 1982).

88 John Barrell, *The Infection of Thomas de Quincey: a Psychopathology of Imperialism* (New Haven, 1991); Catherine Hall, *Civilising Subjects: Metropole and Colony in the English Imagination, 1830–1867* (Cambridge, 2002).

89 Dawson, *Soldier Heroes*, chs 6–8.

90 Barrell, *Infection of Thomas de Quincey*.

91 See Bristow, *Empire Boys*, esp. pp. 130–46.

92 Or, as Joanna de Groot has put it, men's power 'should be understood not just as a practical function but also as a process of defining the self and others'. Joanna de Groot, '"Sex" and "race": the construction of language and image in the nineteenth century', in Susan Mendus and Jane Rendall (eds), *Sexuality and Subordination* (London, 1989), p. 100.

93 Sally Alexander and Barbara Taylor, 'In defence of "patriarchy"', in Samuel, *People's History and Socialist Theory*, p. 372.

PART TWO

Changing masculinities

The old Adam and the new man: emerging themes in the history of English masculinities, 1750–1850

Historical work on English masculinities stands at something of a crossroads. A small body of high-quality and varied work has been carried out, but with a very uncertain sense of how the field is constituted, and how these specialist contributions might inform our received readings of the past. This uncertainty is not, however, due to intellectual timidity, but stems rather from the nature of gender itself. Feminist scholarship has demonstrated beyond question that gender permeates all cultural and social forms and all human experience. As the implications of that proposition have been explored, so women's history has fragmented, undermining the confidence with which only a few years ago scholars invoked 'patriarchy' or 'difference' as comprehensive conceptual frameworks.[1] Masculinity, like femininity, is historically expressed in complex and confusing variety, with comparable dangers to conceptual coherence. But there is a further problem which applies to masculinity specifically. Because men have historically been dominant in the public sphere, masculinity carries public meanings of great political moment, in addition to its bearing on personal conduct and self-imagining. Whereas femininity has often been defined to exclude women from economic activities and civic responsibilities, representations of masculinity have necessarily straddled the public/private divide, covering the entire spectrum from men's domestic

Reprinted with revisions from Tim Hitchcock and Michèle Cohen (eds), *English Masculinities, 1660–1800* (London, 1999), pp. 217–38.

conduct at one extreme, to the manly virtues which should characterize the body politic at the other. In tackling the subject of masculinity in such different ways, historians have shown no less than a proper respect for its complexity – and its multiple points of contact with the conventional content of their subject.

Recent work on the period 1750–1850 bears out this general picture. 'Masculinity' stands for a bewildering diversity of approaches: the gendering of public discourse about the state of the nation, the marking of class difference, the experience of sexuality, the exercise of household authority, the rise of the work ethic, and so on.[2] This diversity is, I repeat, necessary and welcome. But the point has perhaps been reached when a broader synthesis can be attempted, not least as a means of directing future work. The period 1750–1850 is one which invites a thematic overview with particular insistence. At the level of popular stereotype, no greater contrast could be imagined than that between the uninhibited 'Georgian' libertine and his sober frock-coated 'Victorian' grandson; if only at the level of social mores there are clearly significant changes to be explained. More centrally, this period is the focus for historical debates about the transition to modernity in England. Was there a shift in masculinity commensurate with the contemporary transformations in economy and politics? Can we speak of a 'new man' to match a new politics and a new kind of production? More broadly, we might consider what light this period sheds on the relative autonomy of gender in historical explanation. Were changes in the gender order merely contingent on higher-level changes determined elsewhere? Might it make more sense to conceive of gender as a structure of practices and attitudes which was particularly *resistant* to change?

Hitherto the attempt to identify major changes in masculinity during this period has followed one of two paths, with few signs of convergence. The first treats changes in masculinity as in some way related to changes in the class structure of England, in particular the transition from a landed to a commercial society. It charts the rise to ascendancy of a bourgeois masculinity which eclipsed – without ever entirely displacing – its aristocratic predecessor. The second path interprets masculinity in the context of a growing polarization of sexual difference, embracing body, mind and the gendering of social space. Science and the arts were at one in making the binary opposition between male and female a dominant idiom of culture, and this imposed new rigidities on the understanding of masculinity, as also of femininity. In this chapter I evaluate the claims of each of these perspectives to offer a viable history of masculinity. In each case I draw back from the more ambitious claims of transformative change advanced by some historians, while acknowledging that both perspectives address significant issues. I then turn to a third perspective, that of gender identity, which has been implicit rather than fully articulated in recent work. Here the key question is whether the period 1750–1850 marked a significant stage in the shift from masculinity as social reputation to masculinity as an interiorized sense of personal identity. Once again, the record turns out to be contradictory, indicating a greater scope for masculine individuality but not necessarily any greater freedom of choice in determining how that individuality should be defined. I conclude by suggesting that our historical understanding might be better served by recognizing the relative impermeability and endurance of many structures of gender, instead of expecting (or hoping) to bring to light dramatic trajectories of social transformation.

I

Analyzing masculinity through the lens of class is much the most established approach. The grand theme here is the transition from a genteel masculinity grounded in land ownership to a bourgeois masculinity attuned to the market. The new commercial society was made possible by, and in turn reinforced, a new manhood. The man of substance and repute came to be someone who had a steady occupation in business or the professions, instead of receiving rents or trading in stocks. In its most schematic form – in the writings of the sociologist R.W. Connell for instance – the change is from personal to bureaucratic authority, from sociability to domesticity, and from sexual licence to respectability.[3] In essentials this is the framework of the most significant analysis of masculinity to date, Leonore Davidoff and Catherine Hall's *Family Fortunes*. Their book is certainly not schematic or unduly linear – indeed much of its strength lies in its close attention to occupational and religious variation; but this very diversity on the ground serves only to throw into relief the two key elements of the new masculinity: the elevation of work as a 'calling', and the moralizing of home as the focus of men's non-working lives.[4] These were the constituents of an integrated gender code: domestic steadiness was conducive to success in business, while the rigours of bread-winning were rewarded by the comforts of home. The bourgeois character of this new configuration is neatly illustrated by the history of the term 'effeminacy'. In the eighteenth century one of the give-away symptoms of this condition was 'luxury' – the unbridled desire to acquire and spend; by 1850 this meaning of effeminacy had disappeared, suggesting a much easier relationship between normative masculinity and the values of commercial society.[5] According to this account, by the mid-nineteenth century, middle-class masculinity was firmly in the ascendant. The expansive sociability, luxury and sexual laxity associated with the aristocracy had become a vestige of the past, as more and more men from the landed classes conformed to the new pattern.

Lower down the social scale a comparable process is suggested by the much smaller corpus of work which has attended to the masculinity of the labouring classes. Anna Clark has shown how in London around the turn of century artisan culture was focused on the workshop and the tavern, at the expense of home and neighbourhood. Journeymen whose attainment of full masterhood was blocked by the conditions of trade continued to affect a bachelor style of life, including heavy convivial drinking, well after marriage. By the 1840s, however, artisan culture was well on the way to transforming itself 'from drunken misogyny to respectable patriarchy'. The 'moral force' wing of the Chartist movement staked the working man's claim to the vote on his sober and self-controlled domesticity. This reflected not only conditions in London, but the pattern of working-class masculinity in the mill towns of Lancashire where the responsibilities of the bread-winner were reflected in a high value on marriage and a demand for the 'family wage'. By 1850 the lineaments of a 'mature' (i.e. modern) working class were discernible. The growing gulf between working men who sub-scribed to domesticity and those who continued to adhere to what Clark calls 'pugilist and pub culture' anticipated the great Victorian divide between 'respectable' and 'rough'.[6]

Would that things were quite so simple. The application of a class ana-lysis to the history of masculinity during this period looks much less secure today than it did ten years ago. The fit between class and gender is more awkward. For a start, the 1780s seem somewhat less significant as a turning-point in the rise of bourgeois masculinity. Dutiful attention to business and a prioritization of home pursuits had been the standard – and in many cases the practice – of men of the middling sort since the early eighteenth century. Margaret Hunt shows how domesticity was favoured by these men not so much from home-loving sentiment as from a hard-headed aware-ness of the danger which the pleasures of the town posed to credit and reputation; 'rational domesticity' embodied many of the values which the Evangelicals would claim as their own a hundred years later.[7] As for the eighteenth-century gentry, Anthony Fletcher has reminded us that they were hardly the bearers of a uniform masculinity: at one extreme stood the boor-ish homosociality of the hunting squire; at the other the civility of the refined gentleman bent on improving his mind and his land.[8] This latter group has been the subject of an illuminating case study by Amanda Vickery. She demonstrates how in north-east Lancashire around the end of the century gender distinctions between commercial and landed families were less striking than their common attachment to domestic comfort, field sports and public service.[9] Revisionist work on the nineteenth century has also complicated the picture. Dror Wahrman, for example, has shown how in the 1820s the middle class had no monopoly of family values; the agitation on behalf of Queen Caroline traded on a popular equation of manliness with chivalry towards the 'weaker' sex, rather than a specifically middle-class sense of affronted propriety. Finally, the contrast between gentle and bourgeois modes of masculinity needs to be tempered by a recognition of the continuities between them, most notably the ethic of public service; as Stefan Collini points out, the Victorian elite's cult of 'character' stood in the eighteenth-century tradition of civic virtue.[10]

To say the picture has been oversimplified, however, does not mean that it is wrong. After *Family Fortunes* it is hard to deny that the maturing of the English middle class was a gendered process, in the sense of having been deeply conditioned by the structure of relations between men and women. Equally, the shift in the class alignment of the British elite between 1750 and 1850 caused the definition of masculinity to be understood in new ways. One which has been sadly neglected is the decline of bearing arms as a core attribute of masculinity. Along with the exercise of household authority, the bearing of arms had been the central attribute of manhood since feudal times. Military manliness was still at a premium during the Napoleonic Wars, but it rapidly lost ground after 1815.[11] With the abandonment of the duel, the growing professionalization of the armed forces and the reform of policing, the exercise of violence became specialized: as Connell puts it, 'Mr Gladstone did not fight duels, nor lead armies'.[12] The increasing popularity of fox-hunting among businessmen and professionals during the Victorian period qualifies the picture somewhat, particularly if we take seriously the argument – put forward by military men of the time – that riding to hounds was a preparation for a 'real' cavalry charge. But compared with fighting, hunting was a very inferior test of manhood: 'all the excitement of war with only half its danger', as the hunting journalist R.S. Surtees conceded.[13] The dominant forms of masculinity were becoming increasingly detached from military training and from the expectation of taking up arms. This is borne out by the vogue for medieval chivalry which, far from socializing men to military ways, displaced valour and danger into a safe haven of agreeable fantasy.[14]

The decline of arms as a facet of masculinity bears the unmistakable imprint of bourgeois values in the ascendant. It also depended on the unusually long period of peace between Waterloo and the Crimea. Notions of the heroic had to be adjusted accordingly. In Thomas Carlyle's immensely influential lectures *On Heroes* (1840) hardly any space was given to martial valour – the honours went to the man of letters, the prophet and the statesman. The first military figure to seize the public imagination since Wellington was Sir Henry Havelock of Indian Mutiny fame, and the impact of the new masculinity is clear; the public was moved as much by the edifying spectacle of an elderly man returning to duty in order to support wife and children, as by the race to relieve Lucknow.[15] Behind this redefinition of the heroic lies a shift in men's attitudes to weapons and combat which merits much closer attention.

On its own terms, then, the historiography I have been describing so far has much to commend it. But I have a more fundamental unease about it. In the last resort what it does is to present the gendered dimensions of a transition whose logic is determined elsewhere – in the economy, in elite politics, in religion. This is certainly much to be preferred to a reading of the past which is wholly innocent of gender. But is gender in the last analysis superstructural and epiphenomenal? Possibly it is, but if so the proposition must be subject to much more rigorous testing. In particular we need to consider very carefully those facets of masculinity which did *not* significantly change during the transition to bourgeois ascendancy. There were important aspects of gender which proved impermeable to the play of class politics at this time.

Take, first, the issue of household authority. The married state called for the exercise of what Boswell called 'manly firmness'.[16] Like the bearing of arms, this had been a touchstone of masculinity throughout Western history, but unlike the bearing of arms it remained fairly resilient during this period. Adult gender identity for men involved forming a household, maintaining it, protecting it and controlling it. As a socially validated status, masculinity depended on these attributes as strongly as ever. New patterns of work and leisure changed the context, but not the fundamental requirement. The theory of middle-class domesticity might be based on marital harmony achieved through complementary roles, but the reality had to take account of men's continuing insistence on mastery in the home. The courts were shocked by cases in which an angry husband usurped his wife's control over children and servants or threatened her with violence. But these cases were only the tip of the iceberg. As A. James Hammerton suggests, the conventions of domesticity imposed strains on masculine self-esteem which, if anything, increased rather than diminished the incidence of household tyranny.[17] Enough work has now been done on domestic violence at various periods between the late seventeenth and the mid-nineteenth centuries to point to some very enduring continuities.[18] Through the shifting relationship between class and gender during this period, masculinity remained deeply wedded to the exercise of private patriarchy.

My second instance of enduring masculinity is the sexual rite of passage of young men on the threshold of manhood. In terms of peer-group standing this was no less a badge of masculine status than the household headship which was meant to follow a few years later. In the mid-eighteenth century it would seem that sowing wild oats was often commended not only by a well-born young man's companions, but by his parents also.[19] The life of the libertine was grounded in the first instance in a period of youthful sexual experimentation which was widely condoned. The standards of nineteenth-century bourgeois masculinity were much less accommodating, but their impact on the conduct of the young needs to be questioned. By the 1850s libertinage had long ceased to be a culturally validated lifestyle, yet many of its governing assumptions still prevailed among young men. Except for those from devout families, they were under pressure to lose their virginity, and repeated 'conquests' were a form of display intended to impress other males. This is the main explanation for the vast scale of Victorian prostitution, with clients encompassing every variant of bachelorhood from the common soldier living in barracks to the well-heeled bourgeois awaiting the means to marry in style.[20] (The cheating husband was less to the fore than his posthumous notoriety suggests.) Repeated appeals to young men to turn to religion, to study, to sport, to business advancement, to 'manly science'[21] – in short to anything which distracted them from vice – testify to the undiminished appeal of the 'gay life'. In 1848 Ralph Waldo Emerson was shocked to hear Dickens and Carlyle accept as a matter of course the lack of chastity in England's young men; Dickens went so far as to express fears for the health of a young man who remained chaste.[22] This time-honoured feature of apprentice manhood was certainly proof against the morally challenging discourse of middle-class masculinity.[23]

Both these features of what might be called resilient masculinity were, of course, fundamentally to do with the assertion of men's power over women. Sexual mastery and household authority are surely at the very heart of face-to-face patriarchy. Their persistence prompts the reflection that recent historians may have overplayed the idea of masculinity as a variable discursive construction. The alternative is not an essentialist conception of sexual difference, but a recognition that some of the salient structures of gender are grounded in social arrangements and psychic needs which are particularly resilient: they are of course subject to change and modification, but on a time-scale which may not relate very closely to other historical trajectories. This is where Connell has made perhaps his most original contribution. The phrase 'hegemonic masculinity' is sometimes used to refer to the prescribed masculine attributes of whichever class happens to be dominant at a given time. Connell deploys the term in a more pointed way to highlight the reach and durability of the gender order. 'Hegemonic masculinity' in his account denotes those masculine attributes which serve to sustain men's power over women in society as a whole; and a vital measure of their success is that they elicit support and conformity regardless of economic or political status.[24] Household authority and sexual predation were in this sense facets of hegemonic masculinity, and they persisted through substantial changes in the class formation between 1750 and 1850. The work of Antony Simpson and Anna Clark shows how both these features loomed large in the masculinity of the labouring classes throughout the period. As regards the dominant masculinities of late Georgian and early Victorian England, we need to balance the implications for change of the new class order against those traditional attributes of masculinity which remained in essentials unchanged.[25]

II

Alongside the convergence of class and gender has developed a second broad strand of work on masculinity which places sexual difference at the heart of its analysis. There are three elements here. First, the emergence of a stable sexed opposition between the male and the female body, in place of a traditional Galenic continuum in which men's bodies were superior to, but not radically different from, those of women. Thomas Laqueur has been criticized for locating the transition from what he calls a 'one-sex' to a 'two-sex' model in the late eighteenth century, instead of taking account of the gradual undermining of the Galenic model over the previous two hundred years.[26] Yet Laqueur's chronology is apt, for the full implications of the revolution in anatomical knowledge were not registered until after 1750. Only then did the complementary notions of female sexual passivity and an all-powerful male libido become the received wisdom of educated society.[27] The intellectual victory of the two-sex model may have arisen from a need to redefine woman as fundamentally different, but the consequences were certainly not confined to women. The stage was set for men to locate the sexual energy required for both pleasure and procreation primarily in themselves, not only by demeaning the sexuality of women, but by prioritizing penetrative sex, and (less certainly) by increasing still further the odium attached to homosexual acts.[28] It was an appropriation which would become increasingly burdensome to men as sexuality itself became pathologized during the Victorian period.

The second dimension of the polarizing tendency, closely related to the first, concerned sexual character. With the two-sex model came an increasingly dichotomized notion of mind and temperament. For men this meant an intensified emphasis on rationality as against emotionality, energy rather than repose, constancy instead of variability, action instead of passivity, and taciturnity rather than talkativeness. In the light of this changed character alignment, several male activities had to be reassessed. The sedentary profession of letters was one; the libertine style of life was another.[29] Of much wider relevance, and very little discussed so far, was the role of father. Here the traditional masculine concern with instruction and discipline had to be balanced against the tendency of the new sexual economy to concentrate all nurturing qualities in the mother.[30] Underlying these dichotomies was a conviction of essential difference which structured the sexed mind as well as the sexed body.[31] As Mary Wollstonecraft complained, the writers of her day maintained that 'the sexes ought not to be compared' on the grounds that men were superior to women 'not in degree, but in essence'.[32] And if men were marked off by natural difference from women, it followed that their manliness was more secure – which helps to explain why the discourse of effeminacy was so much less prominent in the nineteenth century than the eighteenth.[33]

This framework has the great advantage of foregrounding the relational aspect of gender: within an insistent metaphor of polarization, masculinity can only be understood in relation to its 'other', and during this period the feminine became a much more pervasive 'other' than the child, the slave or the savage, each of which provided alternative reverse images of man. But while the conceptual implications of the 'two-sex' model continue to fascinate historians, it is worth pausing to ask whether sexual polarization was anything more than a discursive trope. Did it reflect the reality of relations between men and women? This question is particularly insistent when we turn to the third dimension of polarization, the development of separate spheres. The possibility that everyday social behaviour reflected new and fundamental beliefs about sexual difference has a tempting symmetry about it. But on closer inspection this is no more convincing than the assumed convergence of gender and class, with which I began. Recent critiques by

Amanda Vickery and Robert Shoemaker have focused mainly on the inconsistency between separate spheres ideology and the roles actually performed in public by middle-class women. Indeed it may be that the incessant flow of prescriptive texts on this subject was designed (vainly) to draw women back into the home.[34]

But the really interesting questions about separate spheres concern men. This is because the relationship between domesticity and masculinity has always been so ambiguous. A fine balancing of advantages and drawbacks recurs again and again in prescriptive accounts of men in the home from the early eighteenth century through to the late nineteenth, pointing to a real conflict of interests. In Margaret Hunt's account, domesticity among the eighteenth-century middling sort held out the prospect of comfort (dependent of course on attentive service), economy (as against the sometimes crippling cost of male conviviality) and respectability (especially as regards sexual reputation); 'rational domesticity' of this type was conducive to what Hunt calls the 'almost inhuman level of self-discipline' needed for success in the high-risk conditions of early capitalism.[35] It is also worth pointing out that the practice of domesticity by fathers served to moderate the fear that sons brought up in a feminine setting would prove deficient in manliness later in life.[36] All these arguments in favour of domesticity were recognized well before turn-of-the-century evangelicalism raised the profile of home as a moral refuge from the contamination of city life. The contrary arguments were fewer perhaps, but they were weighty. The danger of domesticity to true manliness applied not just to sons, but to the head of the household himself; the man who spent too much time in the company of wife and daughters might become effeminized, at the expense of both his manly vigour and his familial authority.[37] Furthermore, as we have seen, in real life male domesticity was often a recipe for marital conflict, since the husband who was constantly at home was more likely to impose himself in matters of domestic management and thus to antagonize his wife.

Above all, the home-loving man was losing out on all-male conviviality – both its social pleasures and the business contacts which it often oiled. Leonore Davidoff has recently commented that 'domesticity', unlike so many key-words, has no conceptual 'other'.[38] In broad terms this is correct, but from men's perspective there *is* a binary opposite – the somewhat infelicitous neologism 'homosociality'. ('Fraternalism' is an older and more attractive term, but it is best reserved for more institutionalized forms of male association based on an ideology of brotherhood.[39]) Passing time with male companions was the traditional leisure occupation of men at all levels of society, whether in the informal conviviality of an alehouse or in more elaborate craft associations and fraternities. This reflected the central role of peer approval in confirming masculine status, as well as the need for support networks for men who were seeking to survive and prosper in business or employment. The conflict between homosocial activities and the claims of home and family provided one of the staple themes of didactic writers from the mid-eighteenth century until the High Victorian period.[40] The era of domesticity did not of course sweep away these homosocial underpinnings, but it did necessitate some careful balancing. Henry Fox, we are told, dealt with the potential conflict by transplanting his club to his house, where he regularly entertained his cronies despite the intermittent jealousy of his wife.[41] One can see a scaled-down version of this procedure in the dining practices of wealthy bourgeois in the late eighteenth century. In urban Scotland, according to Stana Nenadic, the expensive mahogany dining-table made its appearance at this time, as middle-class men displayed their wealth and hospitality to their business associates, but in the early nineteenth century this was superseded by mixed-sex dining.[42]

The truth was that for men domesticity and homosociality were inherently in a state of tension, because they answered to different needs. It is a misreading of 'separate spheres' to see this situation as aberrant. Between 1750 and 1850 home and public space were subject to progressively sharper differentiation. The term 'separate spheres' is a convenient recognition of this trend, fully supported by the contemporary sense that the home was unique and indispensable. But this should not be allowed to prejudge the gender issue. How much time, and of what quality, men spent in the home is a separate question, not to be answered by collapsing separate spheres with gender polarization. At one extreme stood the middle-class suburbanite who needed reminding that public duty might from time to time require him to forsake his creature comforts.[43] If anyone lived out the dictates of 'separate spheres', it was the London journeymen at the other end of the spectrum; denied their due as masters, these artisans married just the same, but continued to act as if they were still bachelors, according to a fraternal ethos of drunken misogyny which kept them out of the home most of the time.[44] In between came the affluent public-spirited men of the established middle class – the ones who loom so large in the historiography of the Victorian bourgeoisie.[45] These men acknowledged the claims of both home and associational life. This double call certainly exposed them to competing demands on their time, but we are imposing an artificial contradiction if we suppose that it also transgressed an accepted principle of 'separate spheres'. The point is rather that men operated at will in *both* spheres; that was their privilege.

III

The third strand of my agenda is much less securely rooted in the current historiography. Issues to do with identity have attracted comparatively little attention from scholars, despite their central place in writing about contemporary masculinity.[46] Much of the best work on masculinity in our period has treated it primarily as a public discourse – a metaphor for the nation's virility in the case of the eighteenth century, and a set of prescriptions for the virtuous and profitable life in the nineteenth century. There has been much less interest in the terms on which individual men internalized the discourse. All that can be said with confidence is that a fundamental shift occurred between the seventeenth and twentieth centuries. In the sixteenth and seventeenth centuries masculinity was regarded as a matter of reputation; it had first to be earned from one's peers and then guarded jealously against defamation, in court or in combat. Domestic disorder, which later generations would regard as a personal predicament, was then seen as a serious blow to a man's standing in the community.[47] In the twentieth century, by contrast, masculinity has come to be experienced as an aspect of subjectivity, sensitive to social codes no doubt, but rooted in the individual's interiority; an 'insecure' masculinity is one which is assailed by inner doubt (particularly about sexuality) rather than by threats and aspersions from other men. These issues have been placed on the agenda by Anthony Fletcher, but very little work has been done.[48] We know little about the pace and timing of this change in the nature of gender identity. Does the apparent lack of prickliness in matters of honour on the part of the Victorians mean that their masculinity was more securely anchored within than that of their Georgian forebears? Was the period 1750–1850, so crucial for the development of class identities, also critical in the gradual transition from masculinity as reputation to masculinity as interiority?

The evidence of language should obviously not be ignored, but it offers no easy answers. It so happens that the word 'masculinity' itself entered the English language in the middle of the eighteenth century. But the term implied none of the interiority which is so strongly indicated today.[49] According to the *OED*, 'masculinity' was an importation from France, and its primary meaning was gender privilege, as in matters of inheritance. My impression is that the word was little used until the late nineteenth century.[50] Prior to the twentieth century, the only abstract nouns which did duty for masculinity were the traditional ones of 'manhood' and 'manliness'. From the perspective of gender identities, these are perplexing terms. Both of them – and particularly 'manliness' – embraced moral or cultural as well as physical facets of being a man: courage as well as virility (or 'vigour'), for example. The adjectival form 'manly' was used interchangeably with 'masculine', and with the same duality.[51]

This ambiguity reflects an important truth about early modern England. Reputation and honour may have been the measure of all things, but they did not rest on behaviour and appearance alone. They depended on the solid inner qualities which were always implicit in 'manliness', such as courage, resolution and tenacity. Ambiguities in the language reinforced this: not only manliness itself, but unequivocally physical labels like 'sturdy' and 'robust' acquired moral dimensions. It was the consistent aim of boys' education to internalize these moral qualities – to make them second nature so that they could be expressed in action instinctively and convincingly. Virtue was held to be inseparable from manliness.[52] The same applied to the code of civility which became dominant among gentlemen during the eighteenth century. For all the stress on social accomplishments, civility was widely recognized to depend on an inner moral sense.[53] Taciturnity, as Michèle Cohen shows, was increasingly valued as a pointer to the gentleman's 'self-discipline and his strength'.[54] In the last analysis honour and reputation were worthless without virtue and wisdom.

However, respect for inner qualities is not the same as interiority. Modern notions of masculinity (and femininity also) emphasize the inner consciousness of the individual. Masculinity may be culturally deter-mined, in the sense of featuring only a limited repertoire of traits, but it is also understood to be an expression of the self, and up to a point a matter of individual choice, tormenting or liberating as the case may be. Authenticity is the exacting standard by which contemporary gender iden-tities are judged. In the eighteenth century, on the other hand, the most authoritative forms of manliness and civility demanded the *repression* of the self.[55] The indulgence of the self which characterized so much youthful behaviour was seen as a passing phase, brought to a close when reason and intellect prevailed over impulse. Again and again control of the passions, restraint of the appetites and moderation in sex were emphasized. A man who would have authority over others must first master himself. The charge of effeminacy was laid against the man who relaxed all restraint and surrendered to his every desire.[56] Individual men certainly faced a choice, but it was cast in the stark binary form of manliness against effeminacy, self-indulgence against self-discipline – or vice against virtue, as in the Choice of Hercules, a popular theme in the visual arts of the period.[57] The only context in which something like a choice of identity was on offer was the molly-house homosexual sub-culture of the metropolis, with its own spaces, its own argot and its own dress-codes. While the molly-house presents some fascinating anticipations of modern sexual identity,[58] it seems to have been wholly exceptional, and it cannot be taken to signify that sexuality was widely understood to be the core of a man's identity: that proposition was probably entertained only in the literary circles influenced by Rousseau and other advanced thinkers.[59] Rank, marital status and honour were more significant than sexuality, and each of them was firmly rooted in external circumstance and social standing.

By the end of the period the traditional manifestations of the code of honour were in decline. In the upper levels of society duelling had virtually disappeared by the 1840s; and its plebeian equivalent of fist-fighting was also less common than it had been.[60] The curtailment of interpersonal violence was part of a broader reform of manners for which the Evangelicals claimed most of the credit. Since the Evangelicals also had an articulate sense of the values they wished to see prevail in the place of honour, their programme is particularly relevant here. Manliness in its popular form was high on their hit-list of corrupt practices. From the Evangelical perspective, the fatal flaw in traditional manliness was that it was built on the chimera of reputation; the world which judged a man's actions was not imbued with virtue and refinement, as the exponents of civility complacently assumed, but was mired in vice and hypocrisy. In place of reputation, the Evangelicals elevated *character* – by which they meant the inner resources of heart and mind transformed by God's saving grace. Instead of being guided by the opinion of others, the serious Christian was urged to listen only to the inward monitor of conscience, and to appear to the world as he really was. If this gave him authority, it was genuine authority from within, instead of the counterfeit currency of reputation. 'Manliness is superiority and power certainly,' conceded Isaac Taylor in 1820, 'but it is power and superiority of character, not of vociferation.'[61] All this could only be achieved by means of unremitting self-scrutiny through private prayer and contemplation. The inner man was represented as in constant struggle with the world and its expectations.[62]

One of the most significant expressions of the Evangelical sense of self was the moralizing of work. Traditionally work had very demeaning associations: it implied burdensome toil, or a servile dependence on patronage (as in 'place' or 'situation'). The new social morality emphasized 'independence'; that is, the autonomy which came from running one's own business, practising a profession, or (more tenuously) marketing a hard-won skill. Here Evangelical morality converged with the requirements of political economy which attributed economic vitality to the self-motivated, rational, independent actor. Work was now redefined as 'occupation' and – even more pointedly – as 'calling'. Entrepreneurs (no less than clergy) believed that they laboured under the direction of Divine Providence. The Bradford wool-comber Isaac Holden thought of himself first and foremost as a 'Man of Business', a phrase which implied a sanctified vocation and not merely knowledge of the mundane expedients required to run a mill. As the stormy history of his marriage shows, Holden's masculine self was in the last analysis constructed by his work, rather than his family or his Methodist faith.[63] The dignifying of occupation within an Evangelical world-view was surely the starting-point for the modern secular notion that a man's masculinity is vested in his working identity.[64]

Yet there were severe limits to the Evangelicals' respect for the masculine self. It is certainly true that they cultivated a greater awareness of the self than anyone else, but the desired outcome was not self-expression, but a repression of the self far more severe than anything laid down by the gentlemanly code of restraint. For the Evangelical, the self was the seat of all impure thoughts and vain ambitions; he was in a state of war with his inner impulses. Nowhere was this conflict more keenly felt than with regard to sexuality. The mores of the libertine were of course shunned, but so too was the sexual latitude permitted under the code of civility. Evangelicals were expected to marry, lifelong celibacy being regarded as popish deviance; but no experimentation and no deviation from the heterosexual norm were countenanced. Sexuality was a perilous impulse to be curbed – a burden, not a form of self-expression.

Nor did Evangelicalism set much of a premium on individual choice. Of course, becoming a serious Christian involved a decision, and much was made of the responsibility of the individual to turn to God. Yet, like the Choice of Hercules between vice and virtue, the approach to conversion did not open up a range of possibilities, only the sharp alternatives of salvation or perdition, true or counterfeit manliness. Once within the fold, the options for Evangelical men were very restricted. The worship of 'character' denoted not a generous appreciation of human diversity, but a narrow definition of carefully prescribed attributes. Nor did the new respect for the dignity of work introduce a significant element of individual choice of occupation. Evangelicalism did not undermine the father's right to endow the next generation with a station in life. It was still commonplace for sons to enter the family business, or to be placed by their fathers under kinsmen or business associates. The real turning-point here was the growing bureaucratization of the professions from the mid-nineteenth century onwards, which increased the range of practical choice open to young men, while restricting the scope for paternal influence. Prior to that point personal identity, in the sense of individual choice, was marginal to the working lives of middle-class men.

The paradox of Evangelicalism is that it imposed an almost impossibly demanding personal discipline and yet was credited with wide influence. It is certainly true that the Evangelical outlook spread far beyond those who recognized the full authority of 'serious religion'. But a condition of this influence was a dilution of the challenging – even confrontational – quality of the original message. This is especially true of the key concept of character, which quickly became sullied with just those associations of 'reputation' which the Evangelicals had fought so hard against. What had begun as a rallying-call for moral integrity became shorthand for the qualities which were at a premium in commercial society. 'Character' was in effect taking over some of the ground previously occupied by birth and rank as markers of social status. As Stefan Collini points out, 'to be known as a man of character was to possess the moral collateral which would reassure potential business associates or employers'; and he continues, 'character was an ascribed quality, possessed and enjoyed in public view'.[65] In practice 'character' was interpreted to conform with the much more self-serving and socially attuned requirement of 'independence'. Victorian manliness retained that blend of innate and ascribed qualities which had characterized all the most influential definitions of masculinity for centuries. It is hard to see compelling evidence for a new sense of interiority as yet. That would only come much later, with the decline of religious discipline and the further growth in urban individualism.

Masculine identity in this sense was very much a middle-class possession, available to the 'improving' upper echelons of the lower orders, but scarcely relevant to the broad mass of working people. Yet momentous changes were taking place at this level. Working-class men were relatively far removed from the discursive shifts that enveloped men of the middle class (many indeed were beyond the reach of organized religion); but they had been exposed to much greater disruption in their patterns of living and working. The ways in which a sense of manhood was invested in skill, in bread-winning and in fraternal solidarity arose from specific material conditions and were central to the whole process of class formation.[66] Drink, sex and resort to violence carried distinctive meanings. The suggestion has also been made that men who were forced off the land into the cities sought compensation for their lost status by demanding greater authority within the home.[67] What is far from clear is how much of this was new, and how much represented a reworking of established patterns. Much more comprehensive work on eighteenth-century plebeian masculinities will have to be carried out before this question can be tackled.

IV

For understandable reasons gender historians have sought to uncover major transformations and turning-points which will hold the same intellectual excitement as the better-known stories of economic and political change. Reviewing the work done so far on the period 1750–1850 suggests some of the limitations to this approach. There is certainly plenty in this period to support a dynamic interpretation. At a discursive level, gender was a flexible and effective idiom for arguments about human nature and national character, which changed quite sharply during this period.[68] In terms of social practice, major changes occurred in the gendering of work, which I have scarcely touched on here.[69] But, while being alert to the evidence of major change, we need to register the weight of those structures of gender which changed little and which obstructed or qualified changes in other areas. Masculinities were subject to less change than the shifting pattern of class hegemony would imply. Sexual polarization was much more characteristic of medical and prescriptive writing than of actual social relations. And the development of masculine interiority in place of the code of honour was contradictory, to say the least. At this stage in the debate, a certain caution in embracing ambitious models of change would be more consistent with respect for the place of gender in history.

This is a less defensive posture than it may seem at first sight. For allowing gender a deeper anchorage in the social fabric opens a route to understanding the ways in which gender transcends class. Here I am not primarily thinking of the 'two-sex' model which, in prioritizing sexual difference over other distinctions, implied that the essentialized masculinity shared by master and man might count for more than the division of rank between them.[70] Taken to such an extreme, two-sex thinking becomes an abstraction with little purchase on social experience. My argument is about persistence rather than change. For a period when so much social and discursive change was taking place, too little attention has been given to those structures of masculinity which were hegemonic in the sense that they moulded consciousness and behaviour at all levels of society. Predatory sexuality among the young and domestic patriarchy among the fully mature are two such structures. We need to know more about the culture and social practice of young unmarried men – the homosocial networks, the appropriated public spaces, the drinking and whoring, the balance between comradeship and competition, in short the apprentice culture which Joan Lane has reconstructed in outline for early modern England.[71] And we need much more content to our picture of domestic patriarchy, not only the incidence of marital violence but the dynamics of household authority which fuelled grievance, insecurity, provocation and assault.

The argument here is not that the troubling transition to adult masculinity, or the enforcement of domestic patriarchy, operated in precisely the same way everywhere, but that class distinctions only make sense when seen in the context of certain shared (and enduring) patterns of gendered behaviour.[72] Historians of gender have tended to feel uneasy with models of continuity, not only because they find change more alluring, but because persistence and stasis imply a trans-historical essentialism. But when anthropologists observe recurrent patterns, they do not leap to the conclusion that all societies are 'the same', or that the common traits they have uncovered are biologically programmed; as David Gilmore has shown, men almost universally perform the functions of protecting and providing for dependants, but manhood ideologies vary according to the social and material environment.[73] As historians we should be equally ready to recognize the embeddedness and durability of certain aspects of gender. Taking the measure of masculinities in England between 1750 and 1850 means engaging with the old Adam quite as much as the new man.

Notes and references

1 For a review of the different directions in women's history, see K. Offen and R. Pierson (eds), *Writing Women's History: International Perspectives* (Basingstoke, 1991).

2 Compare, for example, the deployment of masculinity in Leonore Davidoff and Catherine Hall, *Family Fortunes: Men and Women of the English Middle Class, 1780–1850* (London, 1987) with Kathleen Wilson, *The Sense of the People: Politics, Culture and Imperialism in England, 1715–1785* (Cambridge, 1995).

3 R.W. Connell, 'The big picture: masculinities in recent world history', *Theory & Society* 22 (1993), pp. 597–623. See also his *Masculinities* (Oxford, 1995), pp. 191–203.

4 Davidoff and Hall, *Family Fortunes*. The phrase 'new men' appears from time to time, e.g. p. 113.

5 John Barrell, *The Birth of Pandora and the Division of Knowledge* (London, 1992), pp. 64–5; M. Cohen, *Fashioning Masculinity: National Identity and Language in the Eighteenth Century* (London, 1996).

6 Anna Clark, *The Struggle for the Breeches* (Berkeley, 1995), pp. 25–34, 271. See also Michael Anderson, *Family Structure in Nineteenth-Century Lancashire* (Cambridge, 1971).

7 Margaret Hunt, *The Middling Sort: Commerce, Gender, and the Family in England, 1680–1780* (Berkeley, 1996).

8 Anthony Fletcher, *Gender, Sex and Subordination in England, 1500–1800* (London, 1995), pp. 325–9.

9 Amanda Vickery, *The Gentleman's Daughter: Women's Lives in Georgian England* (London, 1998).

10 Dror Wahrman, ' "Middle-class" domesticity goes public: gender, class and politics from Queen Caroline to Queen Victoria', *Journal of British Studies* 32 (1993), pp. 396–432; Stefan Collini, *Public Moralists: Political Thought and Intellectual Life in Britain 1850–1920* (Oxford, 1991), ch. 3.

11 Linda Colley, *Britons: Forging the Nation, 1707–1837* (London, 1992), pp. 178, 193.

12 Connell, 'The big picture', p. 609. On the end of duelling, see Donna T. Andrew, 'The code of honour and its critics: the opposition to duelling in England, 1700–1850', *Social History* 5 (1980), pp. 409–34.

13 Colley, *Britons*, p. 172; R.S. Surtees, quoted in Davidoff and Hall, *Family Fortunes*, p. 406.

14 Mark Girouard, *The Return to Camelot: Chivalry and the English Gentleman* (London, 1981). See also Michèle Cohen , ' "Manners" make the man: politeness, chivalry and the construction of masculinity 1750–1830', *Journal of British Studies*, forthcoming.

15 Graham Dawson, *Soldier heroes: British Adventure, Empire and the Imagining of Masculinities* (London, 1994), pp. 134–44.

16 J. Bailey (ed.), *The Shorter Boswell* (London, 1925), p. 26.

17 A.J. Hammerton, *Cruelty and Companionship: Conflict in Nineteenth-Century Married Life* (London, 1992), chs 3 and 4.

18 Elizabeth Foyster, 'Male honour, social control and wife-beating in late Stuart England', *Transactions of the Royal Historical Society*, 6th ser. VI (1996), pp. 215–24; Margaret Hunt, 'Wife-beating, domesticity and women's independence in eighteenth-century London', *Gender & History* 4 (1992), pp. 10–33; Clark, *Struggle for the Breeches*; Hammerton, *Cruelty and Companionship*.

19 Fletcher, *Gender, Sex and Subordination*, pp. 342–6.

20 I explore the relationship between prostitution and bachelorhood at greater length in ch. 6 of *A Man's Place: Masculinity and the Middle Class Home in Victorian England* (London, 1999).

21 A. Thackray, 'Natural knowledge in cultural context: the Manchester model', *American Historical Review* 79 (1974), p. 690.

22 *Journals and Miscellaneous Notebooks of Ralph Waldo Emerson*, vol. 10 (Cambridge, 1973), pp. 50–1.

23 Cf. Lyndal Roper, 'Blood and cod-pieces', in her *Oedipus and the Devil* (London, 1994), ch. 5.

24 R.W. Connell, *Gender and Power* (Oxford, 1987), pp. 183–8. Connell's concept of 'hegemonic masculinity' is also very illuminating with regard to the relationship between dominant and subordinate masculinities. See also J. Tosh, 'What should historians do with masculinity? Reflections on nineteenth-century Britain', *History Workshop Journal* 38 (1994), pp. 191–2 (repr. in Chapter 2 above); and see now my 'Hegemonic masculinity and the history of gender', in Stefan Dudink, Karen Hagemann and John Tosh (eds), *Masculinities in Politics and War: Gendering Modern History* (Manchester, 2004), pp. 41–58.

25 Antony Simpson, 'Masculinity and control: the prosecution of sex offenses in eighteenth-century London' (PhD thesis, NewYork University, 1984); Clark, *Struggle for the Breeches*.

26 Thomas Laqueur, *Making Sex: Body and Gender from the Greeks to Freud* (Cambridge, 1990); Fletcher, *Gender, Sex and Subordination*, pp. 34–43.

27 Interestingly, Trumbach points out that after 1750 men were no longer arrested for consorting with prostitutes; the implication is that men were considered less responsible for their sexual urges. Randolph Trumbach, 'Sex, gender and sexual identity in modern culture: male sodomy and female prostitution in Enlightenment London', *Journal of the History of Sexuality* 2 (1991), p. 195.

28 Tim Hitchcock, *English Sexualities, 1700–1800* (Basingstoke, 1997); Simpson, 'Masculinity and control'.

29 Norma Clarke, 'Strenuous idleness: Thomas Carlyle and the man of letters as hero', in M. Roper and J. Tosh (eds), *Manful Assertions: Masculinities in Britain since 1800* (London, 1991); Anna Clark, *Women's Silence, Men's Violence: Sexual Assault in England, 1770–1845* (London, 1987).

30 For a beginning, see J. Tosh, 'Authority and nurture in middle-class fatherhood: the case of early and mid Victorian England', *Gender & History* 8 (1996), pp. 48–64 (repr. in Chapter 6 below).

31 Fletcher, *Gender, Sex and Subordination*, pp. 390–400; Cohen, *Fashioning Masculinity*, pp. 79–83.

32 Mary Wollstonecraft, *A Vindication of the Rights of Woman*, ed. C.H. Poston (New York, 1988), p. 63.

33 For eighteenth-century effeminacy, see C.D. Williams, *Pope, Homer and Manliness* (London, 1993), and Wilson, *Sense of the People*, pp. 185–205.

34 Amanda Vickery, 'Golden age to separate spheres? A review of the categories and chronology of English women's history', *Historical Journal* 36 (1993), pp. 383–414; Robert W. Shoemaker, *Gender in English Society, 1650–1850: the Emergence of Separate Spheres?* (London, 1998).

35 Hunt, *Middling Sort*, pp. 202, 217.

36 See Williams, *Pope, Homer and Manliness*, p. 33.

37 Margaret Hunt, 'English urban families in trade, 1660–1800' (PhD thesis, New York University, 1986), p. 250; Williams, *Pope, Homer and Manliness*, pp. 36–8, 94.

38 Leonore Davidoff, *Worlds Between: Historical Perspectives on Gender and Class* (Cambridge, 1995), p. 228.

39 M.A. Clawson, 'Early modern fraternalism and the patriarchal family', *Feminist Studies* 6 (1980), pp. 368–91.

40 Tosh, *A Man's Place*, chs 2 and 6.

41 Stella Tillyard, *Aristocrats* (London, 1995), pp. 32–3.

42 S. Nenadic, 'Middle-rank consumers and domestic culture in Edinburgh and Glasgow, 1720–1840', *Past & Present* 145 (1994), pp. 122–54.

43 For an attack on this lifestyle, see John Angell James, *The Family Monitor, or a Help to Domestic Happiness* (Birmingham, 1828), p. 22.

44 Clark, *Struggle for the Breeches*, pp. 25–34.

45 R.J. Morris, *Class, Sect and Party: the Making of the British Middle Class, 1820–1850* (Manchester, 1990); H.L. Malchow, *Gentlemen Capitalists: the Social and Political World of the Victorian Businessman* (London, 1991).

46 A good example is R. Chapman and J. Rutherford (eds), *Male Order* (London, 1988).

47 The most comprehensive recent discussion is Fletcher, *Gender, Sex and Subordination*, chs 8–17.

48 Ibid., pp. 322–3.

49 Here I differ from Fletcher. Ibid., p. 322.

50 For a corresponding observation with regard to the USA, see Gail Bederman, *Manliness and Civilization* (Chicago, 1995), pp. 17–19.

51 *OED*, entries for 'masculinity', 'manliness', 'manhood', 'manly' and 'masculine'.

52 Fletcher, *Gender, Sex and Subordination*, ch. 15; G.C. Brauer, *The Education of a Gentleman* (New York, 1959).

53 Fletcher, *Gender, Sex and Subordination*, pp. 332–5. See also Cohen, *Fashioning Masculinity*, pp. 55–6.

54 Ibid., pp. 104–5.

55 The vogue for 'sensibility' among educated men around mid-century certainly validated a less severe code of living, but how far its influence extended from literary convention into social behaviour is unclear.

56 Fletcher, *Gender, Sex and Subordination*, p. 411; David Donald, *The Age of Caricature: Satirical Prints in the Age of George III* (London, 1996), p. 81.

57 R. Paulson, *Emblem and Expression: Meaning in English Art of the Eighteenth Century* (London, 1975), pp. 38–40, 73; Barrell, *Birth of Pandora*, pp. 65–6. Cf. Philip J. Greven, *The Protestant Temperament* (New York, 1977), pp. 243–50.

58 Alan Bray, *Homosexuality in Renaissance England*, rev. edn (London, 1995); Rictor Norton, *Mother Clap's Molly House* (London, 1992).

59 For a less conservative interpretation, see Ludmilla Jordanova, *Sexual Visions* (Hemel Hempstead, 1989), p. 12.

60 Anna Clark, 'The rhetoric of Chartist domesticity', *Journal of British Studies* 31 (1992), pp. 62–88, and *Struggle for the Breeches*.

61 Isaac Taylor, *Advice to the Teens: or Practical Helps Towards the Formation of One's Own Character*, 3rd edn (London, 1820), p. 93.

62 For the place of character and reputation in Evangelical thinking, see Marjorie Morgan, *Manners, Morals and Class in England, 1774–1858* (Basingstoke, 1994), pp. 63–71, 100–3, 107–8.

63 J. Tosh, 'From Keighley to St-Denis: separation and intimacy in Victorian bourgeois marriage', *History Workshop Journal* 40 (1995), pp. 193–206. See also below, pp. 153–7.

64 Davidoff and Hall, *Family Fortunes*, pp. 229–34.

65 Collini, *Public Moralists*, p. 106.

66 Keith McClelland, 'Masculinity and the "representative artisan" in Britain, 1850–80', in Roper and Tosh, *Manful Assertions*, pp. 74–91.

67 Simpson, 'Masculinity and control', esp. pp. 604–20. Cf. Andrew Tolson, *The Limits of Masculinity* (London, 1977), p. 31.

68 See, for example, Jordanova, *Sexual Visions*, chs 1–2; Wilson, *Sense of the People*; Mary Poovey, *Uneven Developments: the Ideological Work of Gender in Mid-Victorian England* (Chicago, 1988).

69 For an up-to-date review of the issues, see Shoemaker, *Gender in English Society*.

70 A. Clark discusses this implication of Laqueur's thesis. Clark, *Struggle for the Breeches*, p. 2.

71 Jane Lane, *Apprenticeship in England, 1660–1914* (London, 1996). Cf. Roper, 'Blood and cod-pieces'.

72 The argument here is not dissimilar to that of Judith Bennett with regard to the low skill and low status of women's work from the thirteenth to the nineteenth centuries. Judith M. Bennett, ' "History that stands still": women's work in the European past', *Feminist Studies* 14 (1988), pp. 269–83.

73 David P. Gilmore, *Manhood in the Making* (New Haven, 1990), pp. 222–5. See also Michelle Z. Rosaldo, 'Women, culture and society: a theoretical overview', in M.Z. Rosaldo and L. Lamphere (eds), *Women, Culture and Society* (Stanford, 1974).

CHAPTER 4

Gentlemanly politeness and manly simplicity in Victorian England

Politeness is not a quality we readily associate with Victorian men. In the light of the received picture of sober, dutiful earnestness, it strikes a trivial and anachronistic note. If Gladstone or Mill can be counted as 'polite' we feel that this was a superficial accomplishment, revealing little of the individual or the cultural values he espoused. Unlike the Georgians, the Victorians had little invested in the social virtue of politeness. The first casualty of the new seriousness was that paragon of Regency fashion, the dandy – the man who lived for appearances.[1] Fenimore Cooper reported in 1837 that the English dandy was no more: 'the men, as a whole, are simple, masculine in manner and mind'.[2] The second casualty was the conduct book – the dominant genre of advice literature in the late eighteenth and early nineteenth centuries – now supplanted by the etiquette manual. Whereas the conduct book had taught manners in a fundamentally moral framework, the etiquette book reduced the perplexities of behaviour in company to strict conformity to fashion. Viewed through the lens of etiquette, politeness was no more than a mask to facilitate and conceal the ambition of the social climber.[3] The idea of polite society, it appeared, had lost its power to civilize.

This contrast between Georgians and Victorians is so familiar that we may lose sight of there being something to explain. But it is not immediately obvious why politeness should have been so little esteemed by the Victorians. Those with a 'position' in society certainly valued progress in manners and refinement, while at the same time being disturbed by social climbing on an unprecedented scale. But beyond the ranks of 'polite society' politeness had diminishing leverage. Its place as a marker of social

Reprinted with minor revisions from *Transactions of the Royal Historical Society*, 6th series, 12 (2002), pp. 455–72.

and political virtue was taken by 'manliness', defined in terms which emphasized the departure from polite standards. My purpose in this paper is to analyze this process, in a necessarily somewhat schematic way, given the lack of detailed research in this area. My aim is to suggest a way forward by juxtaposing the consensus which has begun to emerge on eighteenth-century politeness with the very uneven literature on manliness during the early and mid-Victorian period.

I

The most familiar approach to the decline of politeness is to treat it as a shift in the culture of the governing elite. Lord Ashley (later the seventh Earl of Shaftesbury) succinctly identified the trend in 1844. Visiting Rugby School with his son's future in mind, he reflected on the poor light in which it placed Eton, the obvious choice for a man of his rank:

I fear Eton. . . . It makes admirable gentlemen and finished scholars – fits a man, beyond all competition, for the dining-room, the Club, St James's Street, and all the mysteries of social elegance; but it does not make the man required for the coming generation. We must have nobler, deeper, and sterner stuff; less of refinement and more of truth; more of the inward, not so much of the outward, gentleman.[4]

While Eton had changed little over the previous half-century, Rugby had experienced a transformation. Thomas Arnold (who had died two years earlier) had placed Rugby at the forefront of the reforming movement in the public schools. The school was now a by-word for 'serious' education, in which moral tone and a sense of demanding vocation in life were the pre-eminent goals. In short, Rugby promised that attention to the 'inward gentleman' which Ashley was looking for.

Of course the contrast with Eton expressed much more than a choice of schools. Arnold's achievement at Rugby represented one of the most significant fruits of the reform of manners since it began to impinge seriously on the propertied classes in the 1790s. And like the Evangelicals, Arnold had little time for the niceties of refined society. He had more weighty things on his mind. 'Gentlemanly conduct' featured second among Arnold's goals (after 'religious and moral principles' and before 'intellectual ability'), but he meant by that the translation of sound religion into action, not the perpetuation of a social code.[5] For Arnold the sense of pressing tasks to be accomplished allowed no time for leisure or sociability. One of his most devoted followers, Arthur Penrhyn Stanley, confessed to an impatience with those who did not 'take life in earnest': 'I want a sign, which one catches as by a sort of masonry, that a man knows what he is about in life – whither tending, and in what cause he is engaged.'[6] The implication was that he would not find it in polite society. This was the new gentlemanliness: extending far beyond the Evangelical circles in which it had begun, it became the characteristic mind-set of many in public service and political life. It might be described as the moral rearmament of the Victorian governing classes.

The limitation of this line of analysis is that it relates to only a tiny elite. In Arnold's time there were nine recognized public schools. The appearance of a further thirty-two schools between 1840 and 1860 represented a crucial phase in the development of the modern public school.[7] But this growth in absolute terms has masked the fact that the public schools continued to draw upon a very constricted social base. There was significant recruitment from the ranks of the professions, in addition to the traditional landed and clerical classes, but in this period the public schools made virtually no impact on manufacturing and commerce, which accounted for the majority of the middle class, including its 'coming men'. In order to register their concerns, we must turn to the alternative models of masculinity current among the non-gentle classes. These occasioned less debate at the time, and have attracted correspondingly less attention from modern historians, but their social reach was considerably greater.

A striking illustration comes from Elizabeth Gaskell's novel, *North and South*, of 1855. During an exchange between the vicar's daughter, Margaret Hale, and the mill-owner, John Thornton, Margaret remarks that to her mind the term 'gentleman' subsumes what John appears to mean by a 'true man'. John turns her proposition on its head: 'I take it that "gentleman" is a term that only describes a person in his relation to others; but when we speak of him as "a man," we consider him not merely with regard to his fellow-men, but in relation to himself – to life – to time – to eternity.' For John Thornton gentlemanliness is other-related in the negative sense of being caught up in considerations of status and appearance, whereas manliness has to do with interiority and authenticity; he applauds what he calls 'the full simplicity of the noun "man"'.[8] There is a resonance here with Ashley's inner man, defined by 'character' rather than the siren call of worldly reputation. There is also a comparable weight given to work. However, what drives John Thornton is not the elevated calling of the Evangelicals, but the single-minded attention to making money which has brought him from inauspicious beginnings as the son of a bankrupt and suicide, to be a prominent Manchester manufacturer. He speaks for the new entrepreneurial class of early Victorian England who neither claimed nor received the title of 'gentleman'. The standard by which they asked to be judged was 'manliness'.

II

My contention in this paper is that manliness and gentlemanliness were sharply distinguished in the early and mid-Victorian period, and that much of this distinction turned on their relation to politeness. While 'gentlemen' continued to value a certain refinement and sociability, manliness spoke to the virtues of rugged individualism, and this style of masculinity gained in social and political weight as the century proceeded. Politeness was a critical faultline between the gentlemanly and manly ideals. It summed up the exclusiveness and affluence of the former, in contrast to the open and unhierarchical character of the latter. One could be born a gentleman – in fact gentle birth gave one a clear edge in status over other brands of gentleman.[9] Manliness, on the other hand, was socially inclusive. Birth, breeding and education were secondary, compared with the moral qualities which marked the truly manly character. Manliness had to be earned, by mastering the circumstances of life and thus securing the respect of one's peers. It lay within the grasp of every man who practised self-help with single-minded discipline.

The association between politeness and gentlemanly status remained close. An exception was often made in the case of country squires who were said to make up in moral sturdiness what they lacked in polish – a social type that was certainly not new to the Victorians.[10] Otherwise 'politeness' continued to be synonymous with 'breeding' and leisure: polite behaviour remained the surest indicator of breeding and the indispensable lubricant of sociability. Opinions differed about how much weight should be attached to politeness, just as they differed with regard to the salience of birth or morality in the gentlemanly ideal. The advice books tended to claim more for politeness than daily experience was likely to bear out: to assert, in the words of one didactic writer, that politeness was 'the result of the combined action of all the moral and social feelings, guided by judgment and refined by taste',[11] went well beyond common understanding of the word. James Fitzjames Stephen took a more cynical view: 'when we speak of a gentleman,' he remarked, 'we do not mean either a good man, or a wise man, but a man socially pleasant.'[12] But whether merely pleasant or intimating moral worth, politeness was the hallmark of the gentleman.

Manliness is an even more slippery concept. In nineteenth-century England the word was used in an extraordinary variety of contexts and it was repeatedly pushed in fresh directions by religious writers and social theorists, often in mutually inconsistent ways. In the name of manliness Victorian men were urged to work, to pray, to stand up for their rights, to turn the other cheek, to sow wild oats, to be chaste, and so on. It is clear that the idea of manliness exercised a powerful hold over the Victorians, but the nature of that hold has been obscured by recent scholarship. One strand treats manliness as the special province of the public schools, with headmasters cast in the role of expert.[13] The other dominant approach, by resurrecting some of the more eccentric versions of the Tractarians, the Evangelicals and the muscular Christians, has created the misleading impression that manliness was a matter of applied theology.[14] But manliness was more than a subject of learned disputation, more even than an educational tool; it was a guide to life, deeply rooted in popular culture, and often resistant to the redefinitions proposed by didactic writers.

Viewed as an aspect of the 'common sense' of social relations, manliness comprised a set of core values which had characterized masculine culture long before the Victorians. The main thrust is accurately conveyed by the *Oxford English Dictionary*, which gives 'the possession of manly vigour' before 'those virtues characteristic of a man'. Manly vigour included energy, virility, strength – all the attributes which equipped a man to place his physical stamp on the world. Next came the moral qualities which enabled men to attain their physical potential – decisiveness, courage and endurance. These virtues had traditionally had a strong military resonance; now they were considered applicable as much to the struggle of life as to the battlefield. These qualities of physique and character – what Carlyle called 'toughness of muscle' and 'toughness of heart'[15] – were in turn yoked to some notion of social responsibility – whether loyalty to one's peers or chivalry towards women. The desired outcome was the 'independent man' – one who was beholden to no one, who kept his own counsel and who ruled his own household. These were the English characteristics which Hippolyte Taine summarized in the 1860s as 'the need for independence, the capacity for initiative, the active and obstinate will'.[16]

One other attribute was critically important in distinguishing manliness from gentlemanliness: frank straightforwardness, not only in action (about which there could be no disagreement in principle), but also in speech. The touchstone of polite conversation was the anticipated impression made on the listener. The manly man was someone who paid more attention to the promptings of his inner self than to the dictates of social expectation. Manly speech was therefore direct, honest and succinct. Its purpose was not to please, or to shield listeners from the disagreeable, but to convey meaning without equivocation. The result might not be 'socially pleasant'. It came from the heart, unbridled by fear of reprisal or ridicule. What James Fitzjames Stephen called 'plain, downright, frank simplicity' was 'the outward and visible sign of the two great cognate virtues – truth and courage'.[17] It was also the outward sign of 'independence', since conformity in speech was the most telling indication of subservience or deference. Directness and sincerity might well cross the boundary of propriety and appear brusque or even rude. When a man had nothing to say from the heart, the right course was silence. Hence, in complete distinction from the conventions of politeness, manliness often meant taciturnity. Here again it is hard to avoid quoting Carlyle. Manliness was for him exemplified by the man of action, the man of few words: he hailed 'the silent English'[18] and Oliver Cromwell as the 'emblem of the dumb English'.[19] No question here of allowing one's conversation to be moulded by ladies.

Robin Gilmour has written of manliness as 'a key Victorian concept', connoting 'a new openness and directness, a new sincerity in social relations'.[20] He overestimates its novelty. Since the days of Addison and Steele objections to the artificiality inherent in polite manners had been cast in terms of an appeal to honesty and authenticity. Taciturnity verging on the brusque had long been considered by foreign visitors to be an English trait.[21] The virtues of 'sincerity' had been a major theme of social moralists in the closing decades of the eighteenth century. With different emphases, both Gerald Newman and Michèle Cohen have shown how the rise of sincerity was a reaction against the indiscriminate imitation of fine manners by social climbers in mid-eighteenth-century urban society, and how it became subsumed in a redefinition of Englishness.[22] What was new in the mid-nineteenth century was the consolidation of sincerity into the dominant gender ideal for middle-class men. This was the ideal of 'manly simplicity', continuously reinforced by general precept and commended in the lives of individual men.[23] Here was the very antithesis of the refinement and artifice of polite society.

Reporting on a visit she had received in 1853 from Charles Kingsley, the proponent of muscular Christianity, Elizabeth Barrett Browning found herself pleasantly surprised: she had steeled herself to receive a manly person of the type she detested, but instead encountered geniality and 'almost tender kindliness'. Barrett Browning was measuring Kingsley not against his own rarefied vision of divine manhood, but by the standards of manliness as commonly understood.[24] Energy, assertiveness, independence, directness and simplicity were its core attributes. They were manifest less in formal treatises than in the texture of social existence. They were certainly much older than the nineteenth century. Interestingly, in a recent attempt to distil the essence of manliness as a Western cultural tradition, Harvey Mansfield stresses its individual quality, biased in favour of action, and characterized by struggle, stoicism and independence.[25] These characteristics can be confirmed again and again in the bestselling novelists of the Victorian period, Trollope and Wilkie Collins being perhaps the clearest guides.[26]

III

The cultural prestige of these manly ideals must be seen in the context of the increasing irrelevance of politeness. In several crucial respects, it had become redundant. Eighteenth-century politeness had expressed a faith in the improving effects of leisure, sociability and social mixing between the sexes. But each of these was downplayed in the social perspective of the Victorians. Leisure was the most fundamental precondition of politeness, the mark of the gentleman being either a man living on private means, or someone on whom business did not weigh too heavily. The squire drawing rent from his tenant farmers, the rentier living off investments, the man of letters and the professional with some private capital behind him – all could be accommodated to the traditional model of the leisured gentleman who valued sociability both for its own sake and as a means of contributing to the public good. The emphasis among the Victorian middle class was different. For men who had built up a business from small beginnings or had made their way up a professional ladder, the demands of work loomed much larger. Leisure often amounted to no more than a few snatched moments away from factory or counting-house. Lives were disfigured by excessive attention to business. The mill-owner Isaac Holden was continually distracted from the company of his wife and from the claims of the Methodist community by his 'dear old combing machines'; he appears to have taken all too literally the newly minted motto of the town of Bradford, *Labor vincit omnia* (work overcomes everything).[27] Edward Benson, the first head of Wellington College, filled every hour of the day with work: any time left over from his official duties was devoted to a lifelong scholarly study of the Early Church father, St Cyprian.[28] In their different ways both men shared the profound belief that self-realization comes from purposeful work, not from the enjoyment of society.

The conditions for men's sociability had also altered. The rationale of eighteenth-century politeness had been to counter social and sectarian division through the civilizing effects of company: hence the high value placed on the arts of conversation, guided by restraint of the self and respect for others.[29] In Victorian society, on the other hand, individualism counted for more than sociability. This was partly a reflection of the competitive conditions in which businessmen and professional men worked. Self-improvement, instead of depending on the leavening effect of polite society, was seen as a solitary endeavour. Not surprisingly the institutions of male sociability were at a low ebb during this period. There were fewer clubs in London than there had been in the eighteenth century, or than there would be after about 1870, and in other cities clubs were slow to develop.[30]

Judged against the requirements of politeness, these clubs offered a problematic form of sociability, in that their membership was confined to men. The civilizing properties of women had been especially valued in the heyday of politeness. Assembly rooms, public balls and theatres had encouraged relations of easy informality between the sexes, allowing the rough edges of masculine behaviour to be smoothed down. By the 1830s the assembly rooms were in decline. The associational life of men and women tended to run in separate grooves – for example in philanthropy, where men and women staked out their distinctive responsibilities, with their own organizing committees.[31] The only context in which easy relations between the sexes were applauded without qualification was the family, where the demands of domesticity on men were pitched at a higher level during the early and mid-Victorian period than at any time before or since. Domesticity is commonly associated with the Evangelicals, who redefined the home as the site of spiritual exercises and the shrine of angelic woman-hood.[32] In fact only a minority fully subscribed to the views of Hannah More and John Angell James, but the Evangelicals were nevertheless running with the spirit of the times rather than against it. Shorn of its religious hyperbole, their notion of domesticity became the accepted wisdom of the respectable classes. Home was experienced as a vital refuge from the alienation of the market and from the degradation of urban life; or in James Anthony Froude's words, as a respite from 'the struggle in the race of the world'.[33]

Yet the sociability offered by domesticity was essentially private. Social intercourse with neighbours was not casual and spontaneous, but increasingly regulated by invitation and calling rituals. Home offered middle-class men not so much a route into neighbourhood society as a substitute for it. Moreover the authority vested in the head of the household – and the priority accorded to his needs – meant that his interaction with wife and children was not likely to be easy or equal. All too often boys were given by their parents a very discouraging model of intellectual companionship. For that growing proportion of middle-class boys who were sent away to boarding school, this negative impression was intensified by exposure to the casual misogyny of all-male institutions.[34] The ability to relate to members of the opposite sex on terms of equality was much less common among the Victorian middle class than their Georgian predecessors.

IV

Whereas politeness was increasingly redundant and irrelevant, the core values of manliness directly addressed the middle-class life experience. This was true in three respects particularly. Manliness exemplified the polarized conception of sexual character which underpinned the tendency of Victorian men and women to seek the company of their own sex; it fully validated the work ethic; and it set standards of self-discipline for men who faced life as embattled individuals.

Victorian manliness was premised on a powerful sense of the feminine 'other', with each sex being defined by negative stereotypes of the other. The separation of the sexes was not of course just an overliteral reflection of natural difference; it was the outcome of a powerful discursive trend over the previous century which is familiar from the work of Thomas Laqueur. According to his book *Making Sex*, a transformation in biological thought occurred in the late eighteenth and early nineteenth centuries, from sexual difference understood in incremental terms, to a two-sex model which exaggerated the anatomical differences between the two sexes. Women were now typecast as sexually passive, men as consumed by an all-powerful libido.[35] Whatever objections to Laqueur's thesis in relation to the seventeenth and eighteenth centuries, there is little dispute that early nineteenth-century medicine emphasized the biological differences between men and women to a greater extent than ever before. With this came an exaggeration of secondary differences, particularly as regards sexual character. Manly independence was dramatized by feminine dependence, manly action by feminine passivity, and so on. Both body and mind were now sexed.[36] As the educational reformer Emily Davies sadly noted, 'whatever is manly must be unwomanly, and vice versa', leading to 'the double moral code, with its masculine and feminine virtues'.[37] Manliness claimed the active virtues for men, naturalizing the privilege by dwelling on their female opposites:

dependence, caprice, emotionality and timorousness. All too many of both sexes were fully convinced that the attributes of manliness were either natural or God-given. Hence the charge of effeminacy was more damaging than ever, and for this reason it was perhaps less often levelled than in the past.

Logically the implication of this must be that manliness was exclusive to men. In actual fact women were occasionally described as 'manly', suggesting some confusion between what was human and what was specific to the male sex. Yet, applied to women, 'manly' was a rare compliment, and they were doomed always to fall short of total achievement. Thus when Samuel Smiles addressed the writer Eliza Lynn Linton as 'beloved woman, most manly of your sex', he meant that she had surpassed the capacities of women, not that she equalled those of men.[38] The only exponents of manliness who believed that women were on an equal footing with men were writers from the Evangelical camp: the subsuming of manliness in the Christian virtues clearly had androgynous implications, as Claudia Nelson has demonstrated.[39] But common usage respected the assumed polarity between male and female. Manliness was as much to do with separating from the feminine as with affirming the masculine. This sense of a yawning gender divide was reinforced by education: while the promise of intellectual achievement was always extended to middle-class boys (however patchy the actual provision), their sisters were all too likely to be trained in 'accomplishments' which confirmed their inferior standing. The outcome was a significant increase in the cultural obstacles to easy social intercourse between the sexes. Victorian men frequently assumed that female company would be unimproving and unstimulating. The young Mandell Creighton admitted: 'I find ladies in general are very unsatisfactory mental food: they seem to have no particular thoughts or ideas, and though for a time it is flattering to one's vanity to think one may teach them some, it palls after a while.'[40] That remained his view until, three years later, he met his future wife in the intellectually bracing atmosphere of a lecture by Ruskin. It was hardly an auspicious frame of mind in which to cultivate the society of the opposite sex.

Secondly, Victorian manliness was closely identified with work. 'It is by work, work, work – constant, never-ceasing work – work well and faithfully done . . . that you are to rise out of things into men,' declared William Landels in 1859.[41] Such passages can be read as a somewhat crude attempt to socialize young men in the habits of discipline. But the work ethic was much more deeply inscribed in middle-class masculinity than that. It not only served to keep men at a punishing pitch of self-discipline; it also justified the priority they attached to money-making and personal advancement by elevating work as a good in itself. No one conveyed this message with more rhetorical force than Thomas Carlyle (and no one made less effort to master the niceties of polite behaviour). His own compulsion to keep despair at bay by ceaseless activity produced a secular gospel of work, in which salvation lay in the spirit in which the work was undertaken rather than its outcome, and in which idleness represented a threat to the self. 'Consider how, even in the meanest sorts of Labour, the whole soul of man is composed into a kind of real harmony, the instant he sets himself to work! . . . The man is now a man.'[42] The immense popular success of *Past and Present* (1843) testifies to the deep resonance these ideas had with men making their way in life.[43] From this perspective, the gentleman's material ease was corrupting rather than empowering. What had been seen in the eighteenth century as the prerequisite for public life was now thought to undermine moral vigour. It was not unknown for a middle-class man to reject a gentlemanly suitor for his daughter precisely *because* he enjoyed 'prospects', lest she should find herself yoked to a man without energy or self-reliance.[44] Manliness upheld the work ethic; gentlemanliness had a distinctly ambivalent relationship with it.

Thirdly, manliness represented the quintessence of individualism. This is something of a paradox. In one sense Victorian manliness was no different from other models of masculinity in requiring the young male to conform to the expectations of the peer group by adjusting his behaviour and self-image to the approved model of manhood. But in commercial and professional society individualism *was* the approved model. Some of that approval emanated from religious sources. Confronted by what they regarded as the scandalous state of youthful morality, Evangelical writers in the earlier part of the century had aimed to moralize manliness as a vital part of their programme of social regeneration. In their view the problem with manliness lay in its undue respect for the worldly standards implied in the notion of 'reputation'; in its place they strove to establish 'character', by which they meant the internal urgings of a man's conscience.[45] The voluminous religious advice literature addressed to young men at this time represents the achievement of manhood almost entirely as a solitary quest, with other men regarded as a temptation to idleness or worse.[46]

But the material underpinning for this individualism was also very strong. The Victorian bourgeois world was highly competitive, and it placed a premium on the virtues of self-reliance and personal autonomy. The strongest metaphors of manliness were drawn from the battlefield (life was 'a battle and a march', insisted Carlyle[47]); manliness therefore fitted the uphill struggle of outsiders far more closely than the life of those with an assured social position. Success was viewed as a personal achievement, and adversity could only be overcome by calling on personal reserves of character. As Stefan Collini has put it, 'the classic scenes of character-testing are essentially private – facing the discouragement of an empty order-book, coping with the failure of one's inventions and projects, studying deep into the night to acquire by hard labour what seemed to come so easily to the expensively-educated'.[48] Ordeals of that kind were more likely to produce a prickly autonomy than a complaisant ease of manner. Indeed the drive to self-reliance almost eclipsed the idea of sociability. Far from being honed in society, manliness was regarded as a personal possession, achieved and maintained through adversity: in Charles Kingsley's phrase, 'all true manhood consists in the defiance of circumstances'.[49] Growing up to manhood was less about cultivating easy relationships with one's peers than about learning to stand on one's own two feet – and stay standing amid the buffets of fortune. At the age of twenty the future publisher Daniel Macmillan told his brother: 'I do not feel bound to follow in the footsteps of any of my relations. I am here to act for myself. . . . The most important things must be done by myself – alone.'[50]

V

Thus far I have presented manliness as essentially the code of middle-class men. A case can be made for the proposition that manliness was merely the gendered face of class consciousness. Davidoff and Hall, for example, analyze a form of manliness which proved highly functional in bourgeois terms, and since they give scant consideration to other class forms, it is reasonable to conclude from their work that gender, while undoubtedly the subject of a distinctive social language, was subordinate to other forms of status.[51] But there is an important sense in which manliness transcended class, owing its discursive power precisely to its detachment from the strongest social divisions of the day. In common culture manliness stood for those qualities which were respected by men without regard to class – by men *as men*. It provided a language for commending (or disparaging) one's fellows across the boundaries of class. In order to gauge the strength of the reaction against politeness, it is necessary to recognize that many of the manly values which prevailed among the bourgeoisie also had a purchase on the upper reaches of the working class. (The same could hardly be said of politeness; as one working-class writer put it in 1861, the word was rarely used and was taken to mean 'some supposed affectation of "fine" behaviour'.[52])

Significant differences of emphasis were to be found between working-class and middle-class versions of manliness. The lives of most working men made much heavier calls on their physical strength than was the case in the middle class, and bodily vigour was thus even more at a premium. The manly way to settle a dispute or defend one's honour was with the fists – a convention which did not persist much beyond the schooldays of the middle-class boy. Working-class independence meant not freedom from patronage, but security against penury and the associated indignities of charity and the workhouse. Given the prevalence of women's wage-earning, polarized notions of sexual difference carried less weight among workers than among the bourgeoisie. Equally, middle-class values of individualism were less relevant to a working-class culture permeated by the fraternalism of friendly societies, working men's clubs and trade unions.

But the common ground of manliness was important. One vital element was a strong masculine investment in work. Partly this was because diligence and self-discipline seemed to hold out to working men the promise of upward social mobility (of the kind of which Samuel Smiles provided so many invigorating anecdotes). Partly also intense commitment to work was for most workers a precondition of maintaining a household: this was the period when the word 'bread-winner' entered the language, and when the 'family wage' became a key objective of organized labour.[53] But in the upper reaches of the working class there existed a version of the 'work-for-its-own sake' ethos in the valorization of skill. Masculine self-respect was bound up with apprenticeship and the successful practice of hard-won skill thereafter – as is demonstrated by the craft pride of a community such as the carpet-weavers of Kidderminster described by Sonya Rose.[54] Above all, respect for physical vigour, courage and independence were manly values which transcended class, and which informed the standards by which one man judged another, whatever class he belonged to.

This convergence of gender ideals had considerable political significance. Manly discourse was socially inclusive, uncluttered by class baggage. It elevated attributes which all men admired, which were potentially within the grasp of every man, and which therefore served to diminish the moral gulf between classes. Thackeray saluted the person 'who can look the world honestly in the face with an equal manly sympathy for the great and the small'.[55] There was a decided implication of social levelling. In the final analysis manliness was more than an indicator of social mores; it had potentially democratic implications, pointing to a politics of social inclusion.

It was John Vincent who first observed that manliness was 'the great moral idea of liberalism'.[56] By this he meant that liberalism stood for a rejection of all forms of patronage – in other words it elevated manly independence to be a vital prerequisite of responsible political agency. Liberalism's image of the citizen was someone who stood on his own two feet, responsible for his opinions and answerable to no one. Such a person could safely be entrusted with the franchise because his freedom from obligation would ensure that he would not be susceptible to pressure. Indeed his resistance against pressure was proof of his political virtue, which helps to explain why many liberals were reluctant to legislate for the secret ballot.[57] The rhetoric of independence was an important dimension of the debates on parliamentary reform prior to 1832,[58] and as the focus of debate about the franchise shifted to the working man, independence became an even more critical determinant of political virtue, especially during the run-up to the 1867 Reform Act. The most effective working-class political organizations did not demand manhood suffrage, since that would have extended the vote to many categories of men who lacked either the moral or the material resources to cast their vote responsibly. The nub of the reformers' case was that the 'independent working man' met the essential criteria for admission to full citizenship; he came within the pale of the constitution no less than those sections of the middle class granted the vote in 1832. The discourse of reform was, as Keith McClelland has put it, characterized by 'the play of independence and dependence'.[59]

But the political purchase of manliness extended well beyond the benchmark of independence. It also served as a marker to distinguish the broad mass of citizens from the privileged and idle. What 'the people' had in common was what made them socially useful – the dignity of labour. In popular culture this was one of the foundations of true manliness, and it distinguished the people from the aristocracy. In answer to the question 'In what does manhood consist?', one working-class campaigner responded in 1873, 'Well, certainly not in walking the streets with a cigar and a silver-headed cane.' The men who possessed the rights of citizenship, he continued, were 'the men who swept the streets or shaped the wood, or hammered the iron, or hewed the coal' – a telling indication of the potential scope of manly discourse.[60] One explanation for the high profile of manliness, then, is that its values corresponded with the individualism and the suspicion of privilege which were widespread in popular political culture between the first and third Reform Acts. Manliness worked well as the common profession of a masculine representative democracy whose members, even before 1867, included a great swathe of voters who could never have claimed the name of 'gentleman' or sought admission to polite society.

The seal was set on the decline of politeness as a political reference point by the emergence of 'the plain man' as the ideal citizen. This was not an entirely original conceit, but it was advanced with an entirely new intensity and conviction by the most acclaimed leaders of the Liberal Party. John Bright came from a wealthy factory-owning family, but in speech and dress he played up to the image of a man of the people, and the simplicity of his family life at home in Oldham was widely commended.[61] When he retired from politics in 1870 – ironically from a nervous disorder which his robustness of manner belied – Walter Bagehot remarked, 'There is an evident sincerity and bluff *bona fides* about him, which goes straight to the hearts of Englishmen'.[62] An even more striking reinvention was achieved by W.E. Gladstone. His education at Eton and Christ Church had been designed to turn him into the consummate polite gentleman. It has been said of Gladstone that 'he accepted the manners of the landed class, not merely without demur, but with enthusiasm' on account of the Welsh estates he acquired through marriage.[63] By the 1860s, however, Gladstone was 'the people's William', and later the 'Grand Old Man'. His honest manliness was symbolized by his much publicized tree-felling at Hawarden – the perfect symbol of full masculine vigour.[64] His career can stand for the triumph of manliness over politeness in English political culture. Manliness provided a major discursive resource against the exclusive pretensions of gentlemanly status by suggesting that all that was needed to make a good citizen was to be a good man. In that sense it was well suited to a political discourse which spoke with increasing authority in terms of 'the people'.[65]

VI

What then was the relationship between gentlemanly politeness and manly simplicity during the High Victorian era? The discussion between Margaret Hale and John Thornton turned on the issue of which could be subsumed in the other. Margaret accepted the ascription of all worthy qualities to the gentleman, including what passed for manly ones. John dismissed gentlemanliness as no more than a code for ordering social relations, which did not touch the inner man. Given the inclusive character of manliness, it would be surprising if there were not substantial convergence. Michael Curtin has observed, for example, that the manly independence and rejection of patronage which were valued so highly by the middle and working classes 'were easily compatible with the characteristics of the ideal gentleman'.[66] Respect for martial fitness and athletic prowess was also shared. The moral qualities of courage and stoicism were common to both. Independence mattered to the gentleman no less than the businessman or professional man, though it was measured in rents rather than profits or fees. Even the inner integrity in which Thornton took such pride was also appropriated by definitions of gentlemanliness. Writing in the *Contemporary Review* in 1869, J.R. Vernon commented: 'A gentleman is a MAN. And he realizes what is contained in that word – the high descent, the magnificent destiny. So in the presence of his God and of his fellow-men he is never abject; he is always manly, always keeps self-respect.'[67]

But this was special pleading. The difference between gentlemanliness and manliness was critical, and it turned on the dichotomy between politeness and authenticity. This was the nub of John Thornton's hostility towards the fine gentleman. His views were matched from the other side of the social divide by Thomas Hughes through the character of Tom Brown's father. When Squire Brown declares his belief that 'a man is to be valued wholly and solely for that which he is in himself, for that which stands up in the four fleshly walls of him', he is identifying with 'manly' values and distancing himself from the birth and fine breeding habitually associated with men of his class.[68] The practical force of this distinction was accurately conveyed by the Revd Harvey Newcomb: a growing boy, he counselled, should strive to be 'both a man and a gentleman'. By aiming for the latter he would gain courtesy and propriety; by the former he would acquire courage, energy and perseverance. The desired outcome was 'a solid, energetic, manly character, combined with true gentility of manners'.[69] Manliness represented the common aspiration of men in all walks of life; gentlemanliness was a refinement which marked the boy out as one of a social elite.

Gentlemen had traditionally prided themselves on their refined manners, which served the double purpose of easing interpersonal relations and putting down a marker of social exclusiveness. That rationale still counted for something in the mid-Victorian era, but in a world where the basis of economic and political power was being steadily expanded, gentlemen were compelled to place much greater emphasis than in the past on their moral claims to pre-eminence, appealing to values which were shared throughout 'respectable' society and beyond. The notions of polite society and of polite conduct were increasingly devalued. James Fitzjames Stephen fairly summed up the meaning of politeness in a phrase which reflects its marginal status in Victorian culture: gentlemen, he said, were 'only picked and polished specimens of the material of which the nation at large is composed'.[70]

Notes and references

1 Robin Gilmour, *The Idea of the Gentleman in the Victorian Novel* (London, 1981); Ellen Moers, *The Dandy: Brummell to Beerbohm* (London, 1960).

2 J. Fenimore Cooper, *England* (London, 1837), p. 195.

3 Michael Curtin, *Propriety and Position: a Study of Victorian Manners* (New York, 1987).

4 Lord Ashley, diary for 21 Nov. 1844, quoted in Edwin Hodder, *The Life and Work of the Seventh Earl of Shaftesbury*, 2 vols (London, 1886), II, p. 77.

5 A.P. Stanley, *The Life and Correspondence of Thomas Arnold*, 8th edn, 2 vols (London, 1858), I, p. 100.

6 A.P. Stanley, quoted in James Eli Adams, *Dandies and Desert Saints: Styles of Victorian Masculinity* (Ithaca, 1995), p. 61.

7 Figures from J.A. Banks, *Prosperity and Parenthood* (London, 1954), pp. 228–9.

8 Elizabeth Gaskell, *North and South* (London, 1855), ch. 20 ('Men and gentlemen').

9 'A gentleman by birth remained a cut above other gentlemen'. Mark Girouard, *The Return to Camelot* (London, 1981), p. 263.

10 Anthony Fletcher, *Gender, Sex and Subordination in England 1500–1800* (London, 1995), pp. 325–9.

11 Charles Duncan, *The Gentleman's Book of Manners or Etiquette* (London, 1875), p. 7.

12 [James Fitzjames Stephen], 'Gentlemen', *Cornhill Magazine* V (1862), p. 331.

13 David Newsome, *Godliness and Good Learning* (London, 1961), pp. 195–227; J.R. de S. Honey, *Tom Brown's Universe: the Development of the Victorian Public School* (London, 1977).

14 Norman Vance, *The Sinews of the Spirit: the Ideal of Christian Manliness in Victorian Literature and Religious Thought* (Cambridge, 1985); Boyd Hilton, 'Manliness, masculinity and the mid-Victorian temperament', in *The Blind Victorian: Henry Fawcett and British Liberalism*, ed. L. Goldman (Cambridge, 1989), pp. 60–70; David Alderson, *Mansex Fine: Religion, Manliness and Imperialism in Nineteenth-Century British Culture* (Manchester, 1998).

15 Thomas Carlyle, *Past and Present* (Oxford, 1934), p. 144.

16 Hippolyte Taine, *Notes on England*, trans. E. Hyams (London, 1957), p. 268.

17 Stephen, 'Gentlemen', p. 336.

18 Carlyle, *Past and Present*, p. 142.

19 Quoted in Raphael Samuel, *Island Stories: Unravelling Britain* (London, 1998), p. 286.

20 Gilmour, *Idea of the Gentleman*, p. 18.

21 Paul Langford, *Englishness Identified: Manners and Character, 1650–1850* (Oxford, 2000), pp. 306–9.

22 Gerald Newman, *The Rise of English Nationalism: a Cultural History 1740–1830* (New York, 1997), pp. 128–55; Michèle Cohen, 'Manliness, effeminacy and the French: gender and the construction of national character in eighteenth-century England', in *English Masculinities, 1660–1800*, ed. T. Hitchcock and M. Cohen (London, 1999), pp. 44–61.

23 David Newsome, *The Parting of Friends* (London, 1966), p. 59; Newsome, *Godliness and Good Learning*, pp. 195–6; Gilmour, *Idea of the Gentleman*, pp. 58, 69.

24 F.G. Kenyon (ed.), *Letters of Elizabeth Barrett Browning*, 2 vols (London, 1897), II, p. 134.

25 Harvey Mansfield, 'The partial eclipse of manliness,' *TLS*, 17 July 1998.

26 On Trollope, see Gilmour, *Idea of the Gentleman*; on Collins, see Bruce Haley, *The Healthy Body and Victorian Culture* (Cambridge, 1978), pp. 223–6; Alderson, *Mansex Fine*, pp. 62–4.

27 John Tosh, *A Man's Place: Masculinity and the Middle-Class Home in Victorian England* (London, 1999), pp. 76–7.

28 David Newsome, *History of Wellington College* (London, 1959), pp. 92, 151.

29 John Brewer, *The Pleasures of the Imagination: English Culture in the Eighteenth Century* (London, 1997), pp. 99–112.

30 Peter Clark, *British Clubs and Societies, 1580–1800* (Oxford, 2000); Brian Harrison, *Separate Spheres: the Opposition to Women's Suffrage in Britain* (London, 1978), ch. 5.

31 Leonore Davidoff and Catherine Hall, *Family Fortunes: Men and Women of the English Middle Class, 1780–1850* (London, 1987), pp. 436–45; F.K. Prochaska, *Women and Philanthropy in Nineteenth-Century England* (Oxford, 1980).

32 See Davidoff and Hall, *Family Fortunes*, chs 1–2; and Tosh, *A Man's Place*, pp. 34–9.

33 [J.A. Froude], *The Nemesis of Faith* (London, 1849), p. 113.

34 This point was repeatedly made by women didactic writers. See for example: Sarah Lewis, *Woman's Mission*, 7th edn (London, 1840), p. 32, and Sarah Ellis, *The Mothers of England* (London, 1843), p. 77.

35 Thomas Laqueur, *Making Sex: Body and Gender from the Greeks to Freud* (Cambridge, 1990).

36 On these dichotomies, see Mary Poovey, *Uneven Developments: the Ideological Work of Gender in Mid-Victorian England* (Chicago, 1988).

37 Quoted in Claudia Nelson, 'Sex and the single boy: ideals of manliness and sexuality in Victorian literature for boys', *Victorian Studies* 32 (1989), p. 530.

38 Quoted in A. Smiles, *Samuel Smiles and His Surroundings* (London, 1956), p. 67.

39 Claudia Nelson, *Boys Will be Girls: the Feminine Ethic and British Children's Fiction, 1857–1917* (New Brunswick, 1991).

40 Quoted in Louise Creighton, *Life and Letters of Mandell Creighton*, 2 vols (London, 1904), I, p. 33.

41 William Landels, *How Men are Made* (London, 1859), p. 43.

42 Carlyle, *Past and Present*, p. 177.

43 Walter Houghton, *The Victorian Frame of Mind, 1833–70* (New Haven, 1957), pp. 242–62.

44 See, for example, John Heaton to Helen Heaton, 17 May 1874, Heaton MSS, private collection, Cornhill-on-Tweed.

45 Marjorie Morgan, *Manners, Morals and Class in England 1774–1858* (Basingstoke, 1994), pp. 63–71, 100–3, 107–8.

46 For example: H.S. Brown, *Manliness* (London, 1858); J.B. Figgis, *Manliness, Womanliness, Godliness* (London, 1861); Thomas Hughes, *The Manliness of Christ* (London, 1879).

47 Quoted in Houghton, *Victorian Frame of Mind*, p. 206.

48 Stefan Collini, 'The idea of "character" in Victorian political thought', *Transactions of the Royal Historical Society*, 5th series, 35 (1985), p. 40.

49 Quoted in Adams, *Dandies and Desert Saints*, p. 110.

50 Daniel Macmillan to Malcolm Macmillan, 15 June 1833, quoted in Thomas Hughes, *Memoir of Daniel Macmillan* (London, 1882), p. 17.

51 Davidoff and Hall, *Family Fortunes, passim*.

52 J. Shepherd, in *Social Science: Being Selections from John Cassell's Prize Essays by Working Men* (London, 1861), p. 187.

53 Wally Seccombe, 'Patriarchy stabilized: the construction of the male bread-winner norm in nineteenth-century Britain', *Social History* 11 (1986), pp. 53–76.

54 Sonya Rose, *Limited Livelihoods: Gender and Class in Nineteenth-Century England* (London, 1992), pp. 128–30.

55 W.M. Thackeray, *Vanity Fair*, ch. 62, quoted in Gilmour, *Idea of the Gentleman*, p. 69.

56 John Vincent, *The Formation of the Liberal Party* (London, 1966), p. 14.

57 James Vernon, *Politics and the People: a Study in English Political Culture, c. 1815–1867* (Cambridge, 1993), pp. 102, 158, 314.

58 Work in progress by Matthew McCormack.

59 Keith McClelland, ' "England's Greatness, the Working Man" ', in C. Hall, K. McClelland and J. Rendall, *Defining the Victorian Nation: Class, Race, Gender and the British Reform Act of 1867* (Cambridge, 2000), pp. 97–101.

60 Thomas Beckwith, quoted in Eugenio Biagini, *Liberty, Retrenchment and Reform: Popular Liberalism in the Age of Gladstone, 1860–80* (Cambridge, 1992), p. 286.

61 Patrick Joyce, *Democratic Subjects: the Self and the Social in Nineteenth-Century England* (Cambridge, 1994), pp. 116–24.

62 Walter Bagehot, 'Mr Bright's retirement' (1870), repr. in *Historical Essays*, ed. N. St-J. Stevas (London, 1971), p. 226.

63 Vincent, *Formation of the Liberal Party*, pp. 212–13.

64 On Gladstone's tree-felling, see Biagini, *Liberty, Retrenchment and Reform*, pp. 396–400.

65 It would be interesting to evaluate Conservative politicians from the same perspective. Matthew McCormack has pointed out to me that Disraeli, of course, was a vivid throwback to the dandy tradition.

66 Curtin, *Propriety and Position*, p. 290.

67 J.R. Vernon, 'The grand old name of Gentleman', *Contemporary Review* 11 (1869), p. 564.

68 Thomas Hughes, *Tom Brown's Schooldays* (1857; repr. Oxford, 1989), p. 52.

69 Harvey Newcomb, *Youth and its Duties: a Book for Young Gentlemen, Containing Useful Hints on the Formation of Character* (London, 1873), p. 11.

70 Stephen, 'Gentlemen', p. 340.

CHAPTER 5

Middle-class masculinities in the era of the women's suffrage movement, 1860–1914

I n late twentieth-century Britain male support for the cause of women's liberation has included some quite searching critiques of masculinity. Writers and activists have drawn the conclusion that, however overdue attention to women's demands may be, sexual inequality will remain intact unless the spotlight is turned onto the dominant sex as well. Men have been fully involved in this endeavour, producing critiques of surprising harshness, as well as more celebratory forms of self-appraisal.[1] Before 1914, however, this aspect of male solidarity with the women's cause was conspicuously absent. Much has been made in recent years of Edward Carpenter, socialist, homosexual and supporter of women's rights. In *Love's Coming of Age* (1896) Carpenter argued that 'woman the serf' and 'man the ungrown' were two sides of the same coin of bodily and spiritual denial, and that human progress depended on a radical reform of both.[2] But Carpenter was one of the very few male polemicists seriously to address these issues. Other supporters of women's rights tended to justify their crossing of gender lines in ways which left their own gender unscrutinized. For example, in the Men and Women's Club, a small group of progressive intellectuals of both sexes who met in London in the 1880s, female members complained that the subject of male sexuality was ignored while the men repeatedly directed attention to woman's nature.[3] Women were still 'the sex', and men the unstated standard by which the world was judged. Compared

First published as 'The making of masculinities: the middle-class in late nineteenth-century Britain', in Angela V. John and Claire Eustance (eds), *The Men's Share? Masculinities, Male Support and Women's Suffrage in Britain, 1890–1920* (London, 1997), pp. 38–61. Reprinted here with minor revisions.

with present-day debates on sexual politics, masculinity seems to have been almost invisible in the classic era of women's suffrage.

In the light of this reticence it is perhaps understandable that the actions of male suffragists still tend to be interpreted in terms of their personal relationships or their adherence to general (and gender-free) political principle. Yet if there is one conclusion on which all recent work on masculinity concurs, it is its relational quality. Neither masculinity nor femininity is a meaningful construct without the other; each defines, and is in turn defined by, the other. Men do not decide to work for a major change in the position of women without experiencing a modification in their own gender identity. Some male suffragists interpreted their role as one of protection due to the other sex, which might be weaker in physical terms but was superior to men on moral grounds.[4] This required a reworking of the traditional ideal of chivalry. Others like Laurence Housman saw women's disfranchisement as symptomatic of a wider malaise which distorted men's natures too. They looked for a dissolution of sexual difference, for comradeship in place of patriarchy. Whatever their conception of the women's cause, male supporters from John Stuart Mill to Frederick Pethick Lawrence had to court the charge of sexual treason; in Housman's words, they dared 'to be thought unmanly and cowardly'.[5] No man could maintain his public support for women's suffrage without reflecting on what his manhood really consisted of.

Historical analysis requires a comparable focus. What manhood really consisted of, both in social practice and in cultural representation, is an essential starting point for setting in context the male suffragist, as well as his opponent. And manhood cannot be considered apart from the gender order as a whole. Just as women's position was disclosing dramatically new possibilities during this period, so too some of the most fundamental constituents of masculinity were called into question, in many cases as a direct result of changes in the position of women. The crisis over women's suffrage between 1905 and 1914 was the latest and most dramatic stage in a destabilizing of gender boundaries which had been gathering pace since the 1870s. The issue of votes for women had been a focus of debate throughout that time, but seldom the dominant one; in practical terms far more had been achieved with regard to women's education, employment, lifestyle and marital status. Many men were disturbed and threatened by these changes. Others experienced them as liberating. But all participants in the struggle for women's suffrage were marked by that experience. Masculinity, no less than femininity, had shifted ground as a result.

Changing codes of manliness offer one clearly marked point of entry into this neglected field. Masculinity may have been scarcely visible in critical discourse, but its approved forms were endlessly proclaimed. The voluminous late nineteenth-century literature on 'manliness' is testimony to that: it documents some significant shifts in thinking over the period, and has provided the most accessible material for historians of masculinity.[6] But there is a limit to how much we can learn from a fundamentally didactic body of texts. For this period they tell us more about the rise of secular imperialism at the expense of religion than about masculinity itself. A deeper and more comprehensive enquiry is needed which engages with men's gender identity at three levels. First, and most fundamentally, masculinity is formed within the family, in intimate relations of desire and dependence. How those relations are structured affects both the gender conditioning of boys and their subsequent attitude to family life as adults. Secondly, from puberty (and often earlier) masculine identity is developed, and partly vailidated, through participation in male peer-groups, school usually being the first arena in which boys are exposed to a competitive masculine ethos. Winning recognition from one's fellows is critical to socially valid masculinity, which partly explains why male bonding continues to be such an important feature of men's adult lives, notably at the workplace or in leisure activities. Thirdly, masculinity is constructed by a perception of women, not so much as individual family members, but as a social category bound by patriarchal relations to the dominant sex. In most societies the exercise of patriarchal power, both individually and collectively, is so inseparable from masculine identity that changes in the structure of sexual relations usually have a very direct – and sometimes undermining – impact on masculinity. The later nineteenth century saw significant changes in each of these areas: in family life, in schooling and associational life, and in relations between the sexes. In this essay I consider these changes as they affected men in the middle class, from which the majority of men prominent in the suffrage movement were drawn.

I

The most fundamental, but also the least understood, trend affecting domestic relations in this period was the reduction in family size. Beginning in the 1860s among doctors and clergy, family limitation soon spread to professional people in general, followed by the commercial and industrial classes. Upper- and middle-class couples who married during the 1880s were having 3.5 children on average, compared with 6.4 for those married in the 1850s.[7] There has been much debate among historians as to where the initiative for this process came from, and what were the respective inputs of husband and wife.[8] Wives were influenced by the continuing perils of childbirth and by the anticipated gain in the quality of mothering if concentrated on fewer recipients. Sometimes husbands co-operated out of deference to their wives' wishes. But they were also keenly aware of the rising cost of providing each child with the socially appropriate level of domestic comfort and schooling. The man holding the purse-strings was likely to be highly susceptible to the argument that fewer children would avert the dangers of spreading family resources too thinly.[9] Yet what made good economic sense exacted an emotional cost too. Virility was a traditional test of masculinity, and men who had no children suffered definite loss of reputation.[10] As Peter Gay has pointed out, to limit the number of one's offspring raised insistent, if largely unconscious, doubts about the capacity to make children.[11] Becoming a father was no less central to traditional notions of household headship. Both attributes were most effectively demonstrated by fathering a quiverful of children. The alternative construction, which saw reduced fertility as a mark of manly self-reliance, probably had more meaning for working-class husbands with a tenuous hold on respectability than for their middle-class counterparts.[12] Having fewer children might also modify the power dynamic within marriage. A wife with fewer burdens of childbirth and childcare was in a stronger position to extend the scope of her parenting and to contest her husband's authority in other ways.[13] But given the extreme reticence of the Victorians on sex within marriage, little more than speculation is possible here.

We are on firmer ground in assessing the changing appeal of domesticity. In late Victorian Britain the sanctification of home was alive and well across a wide swathe of society. To live in domesticity continued to be a compelling aspiration for men on the margins of 'respectable' society who were anxious to better their social status. The non-working wife, the terraced house and the front room were becoming the hallmarks of the skilled working man, with rhetoric to match from his trade union.[14] Much the same was true of the rapidly expanding ranks of clerks and office workers among the lower middle class – like the fictional Mr Pooter who struggled so hard to make reality conform with his vision of domestic decorum.[15] But higher up the social ladder the situation was different. Men of the middle and upper classes expressed mounting reservations about the proper place of domesticity in their lives. Reluctance to marry was a demographic fact. The age of first marriage rose gradually but steadily in the second half of the nineteenth century; for professional men it had reached 31.2 years by 1885.[16] Many well-established families, like the Gladstones or the Rhodeses, faced possible termination of the family name because of their sons' preference for bachelorhood.[17] Thousands of young men avoided their marital fate by embarking on careers in the colonies as single men. Much was made by contemporaries of the deterrent effect of the rising cost of marriage, defined as the level of expenditure needed to set up a household in accordance with the bride's expectations.[18]

Rejection of domesticity was also strongly written into the culture of the period, suggesting a deeper alienation from the married state. The arrival of Robert Louis Stevenson and H. Rider Haggard on the London literary scene in the mid-1880s signalled the rapid rise of a new genre of men-only adventure fiction, in which the prevalent concern of the English novel with marriage and family was quite deliberately cast aside in favour of a bracing masculine fantasy of quest and danger, a world without petticoats.[19] What Arthur Conan Doyle called 'the modern masculine novel' accounted for many bestsellers.[20] The bachelor had become, in Eve Kosofsky Sedgwick's phrase, 'the representative man' in English literature.[21] The same tendencies were at work on the persona of the popular hero. The new paragons of imperial manliness, like Gordon, Kitchener and Baden-Powell, were represented as men without female ties, in contrast to Nelson's passionate private life or Henry Havelock's acute sense of family duty.[22] Domesticity, in short, had a much more equivocal place in the lives of English middle-class men by the 1890s than had been the case in the High Victorian era.

This ambivalence only makes sense if we register the full extent of what the late Victorians were reacting against. Their grandfathers had made a bigger investment in family life than their counterparts in any other country. In all settled communities family and household furnish the beginnings of masculine identity; but in Victorian England, foreign observers were agreed, home life had a place in the construction of men's lives without parallel in, say, France or America. The Englishman was perceived as a home-loving soul who preferred the tender ministrations of wife and children to life on the town. It was because public men drew so much of their identity from the familial sphere that R.W. Emerson regarded domesticity as the 'taproot' of the English nation.[23]

Domesticity had conferred many benefits on the early Victorian bourgeois or professional man. The home was a protected zone for the exercise of masculine authority over those defined as inferior on account of sex, age or class, at a time when authority relations in society as a whole were being redrawn in unpredictable ways. There was the possibility of greater intimacy within marriage, in conformity with the companionate and romantic ideals which had grown up since the late eighteenth century. Above all, for the many men who were alienated or exhausted by their labours in the counting-house or the factory, home was touted as the one place where they could fully express their humanity. 'We cease the struggle in the race of the world, and give our hearts leave and leisure to love', was how J.A. Froude put it.[24] The centrality of home in Victorian culture reflects its heightened meanings for men, as much as its exclusive claim on the priorities of women.[25]

At the same time, however, home was always an ambivalent marker of masculinity. Traditionally the man who withdrew from male conviviality and spent his time at home in the company of women was exposed to the charge of effeminacy. Worse still, his capacity for independent action might be undermined and his governance of the home surrendered to his wife or daughter. Evangelicalism, which had such a profound influence on early Victorian family life, gave a new twist to this fear of female control by emphasizing woman's superior moral nature and her role as Angel Mother. But this higher profile for women was offset by the more traditional Protestant idea that the household head stood in place of God to his family and was charged with responsibility for their moral and spiritual progress – an ideal symbolized by the father presiding over daily family prayers. As Leonore Davidoff and Catherine Hall have shown, it was primarily the teachings of Evangelicalism which enabled middle-class men to be both domesticated and manly. Time spent at home was compatible with manhood, provided the man was in command.[26]

In the 1880s the prevailing social conditions which had accounted for so much of the appeal of domesticity in the 1830s had not significantly shifted. It may be that urban spaces now appeared a little less threatening as commercial and leisure amenities improved.[27] But the working life of most middle-class men continued to be as stressful and alienating as before – indeed probably more so in view of the economic anxieties current during the Great Depression of the 1880s and early 1890s. The domestic conventions inherited from the early Victorians were still sustained by the doctrine of separate spheres, now freshly decked out in the fashionable garb of evolutionary science.[28] But among men the consensus in favour of those values was no longer so overwhelming. There was mounting evidence of frustration and *ennui*. What W.R. Greg in 1869 called 'the decent monotony of the hearth' had long been an occupational hazard of domesticity for men.[29] But this complaint became more pronounced in the 1880s, with observers tending to notice the boredom rather than the bliss of the married state – like the anonymous man-about-town who remarked, 'I would sooner dine in public, with a play of life and character around me. . . . I consider the domestic dinner gruesome'.[30]

Much of the boredom was no more than the acceptable face of sexual antagonism. Men resented what they perceived as a negative shift in the balance between female service and female authority, and their evaluation of domesticity changed accordingly. It has often been pointed out that Victorianism became more rigid and formulaic with every decade, and this was certainly true of the middle-class home, where ceremonial diversified and rigidified. Since the wife had the management of these routines, her role came to seem more obtrusive. She controlled the increasingly elaborate domestic rituals, from the dinner table to the Christmas tree. Her ascendancy within the home was most evident in the drawing-room, perhaps most of all in the institution of five o'clock tea, which the journalist T.H.S. Escott called 'the symbol of the ascendancy of the softer over the sterner sex'.[31] Of course, as Edward Carpenter correctly deduced, there was a mockery about this drawing-room homage, in that the lady's sovereignty was more apparent than real, but even the appearance of masculine inferiority was galling, not to mention the time expended on sustaining the fiction.[32] Men therefore sought avenues of escape. The nineteenth century was, according to Mark Girouard, the great age of the smoking-room and the billiard-room in country houses – men-only sanctums where husbands and bachelors alike could indulge in masculine pleasures.[33] Wealthy London bourgeois husbands often maintained bachelor pads in places like the Inns of Court or the Albany.[34] Lower down the social scale husbands were urged to set aside a 'den' to be reserved for their old mementoes and photographs – and for a quiet pipe. 'The tired master should have one place secure from the seamy side of domesticity', as one advice book writer put it.[35] Thus at the very time that young middle-class women were revolting against the stifling conventions of the drawing-room, their fathers and brothers were in many cases making their own, less obtrusive protest. Some were staking out autonomous territory in or near the home, while others were postponing marriage indefinitely.

Reactions of this kind were themselves partly conditioned by family upbringing. One of the deepest though most intangible influences on masculine identity in the late nineteenth century was the sharp divide experienced in childhood between the roles of mother and father. The culture of separate spheres meant not only a strong demarcation of gendered spaces; it also tended to polarize the character traits of men and women, and in the home this was a crucial aspect of gender conditioning. While making due allowance for the variety of both character and parenting styles, the structure of bourgeois family life tended to push parental roles in opposite directions of love and discipline. Sons often experienced from their mothers warmth, affection and a degree of emotional openness – qualities which were fully validated by the mystique of the Angel Mother. But fathers, whether or not they spent much time in the home, were constrained by different priorities. Their most pressing concern was to prepare their sons for an adult world which many saw as more challenging and dangerous than they themselves had ever faced as young men. The moral qualities required for survival in this world were summed up by the word 'manliness', which meant courage, resolution, tenacity and self-government or 'independence'. How far these qualities could be instilled in a domestic environment was a question which much troubled Victorian fathers, but whether or not they opted for boarding education for their sons, their own role was clear: guidance and discipline must be clearly laid down, and emotional closeness avoided in the interests of instilling manly independence.[36] Of course by no means all fathers acted according to these austere principles, and family memoirs of the period recall many instances of openly affectionate fathers or ineffectual ones who had virtually abdicated their parental authority.[37] But the reproduction of masculinity was a serious business, and fathers tended to be over-serious in consequence. Edmond Demolins, who visited England regularly in the 1890s, noted that, whereas French parents continued to treat their sons as children long after it was appropriate, English parents sought to hasten their emancipation: 'a father's conversation with his children bears on serious, real, manly topics . . . they vaunt the Struggle for Existence and Self-Help.'[38]

In a domestic regime where the mother stood for love (and often indulgence) while the father represented the discipline needed for survival in the outside world, growing sons often experienced a gulf between the characters of father and mother. They identified readily with the stern and undemonstrative father and learned to associate tenderness and emotional support exclusively with women. The display of affection – even the awareness of inner feeling – became incompatible with a masculine self-image, and while a son might sentimentalize these qualities in his mother he could not express them in his own demeanour. This was the background which produced some of the characteristic masculine traits of the period. The stereotype of the 'stiff upper lip' approximates pretty well to the emotional repression which marked so many men of the upper and middle classes at this time – 'man the ungrown' in Carpenter's telling phrase. Lord Kitchener, son of a martinet and of an adored mother who died when he was fourteen, fits the mould; as a colleague later recalled, 'He loathed any form of moral or mental undressing. He was even morbidly afraid of showing any feeling or enthusiasm, and he preferred to be misunderstood rather than be suspected of any human feeling.'[39]

Then there were those who craved more emotional warmth than their fathers had ever given them, and who found it in intensely homosocial settings, and sometimes homosexuality. The three surviving sons of Edward Benson (born between 1862 and 1871) had experienced a particularly acute temperamental divide between mother and father; all of them conducted their adult lives outside the normal confines of domesticity in bachelor quarters or collegiate communities, and all of them were drawn to 'Uranian' notions of love between males.[40] Other men – an increasing number in this generation – were drawn to a career in the colonies not only for economic reasons but also because of the freedom it offered from home ties. Their response, and that of countless others, to the distorting emotional field of the conventional bourgeois family was to renounce domesticity, including the patriarchal privileges that went with it.

This trend must not be exaggerated. The reproduction of patriarchy did not grind to a halt. Large numbers of men continued to contemplate matrimony happily, and many were satisfied with the results. But even their conventional contentment was played out against a new backdrop. From the 1880s, as never before, the merits of the married state were open to question. The fact that they were vociferously denied in some quarters, while legal judgments and media comment pointed to more exacting standards for husbands, caused a great deal of heart-searching among the young. Marriage could certainly not be taken for granted. For an unprecedented proportion of upper- and middle-class men, avoidance of marriage was a real option, and bachelorhood a recognized pattern of life.

II

The socialization of boys and young men by their peers can take many forms. In the past it had been associated with apprenticeship, often a by-word for rowdy group behaviour of a precocious and exaggerated kind. In the late nineteenth-century urban working class, peer-group discipline was imposed in the street. But for middle- and upper-class boys school was the critical arena of peer-group recognition, and more and more the boarding public school. The overwhelming dominance of these schools over the education of boys from 'good families' was a recent phenomenon. At the beginning of the century, seven public schools had catered mainly for the landed aristocracy and squirearchy. By 1890 their number had leaped to some seventy-two, and they attracted boys from the professional classes, and a rising number from the business classes.[41] The private tutor was now a rarity, and attendance at day school among the affluent middle class was the exception. For the public service and professional elites, public school had become the defining initiation into manhood. This function was directly addressed by the official ethos of the schools. Thomas Arnold of Rugby, who had a huge posthumous influence on the new foundations around mid-century, aimed to push boys into moral and intellectual maturity as quickly as possible, so that they would leave school with a fully formed sense of Christian public duty and the inner discipline to fulfil it. By the 1880s the initiation was seen differently. The schools' job was to mould and direct a phase of life now seen as fundamentally healthy. Under the influence of evolutionary biology educationalists developed a new respect for the instinctual aspects of boyhood. Boys were admired for their animal spirits, their testing of physical limits, their primitive loyalties and their presumed sexual innocence. Whereas Arnold had aimed to compress the transition from child to man by forcing the pace of maturation, public-school headmasters at the end of the century thought nothing of indulging 'boyishness' until the age of nineteen or twenty. In practice this meant encouraging team games and physical toughness at the expense of intellectual and moral growth.[42]

But the importance of the public schools to the construction of late Victorian masculinity lay not so much in the programme of the educators as in the values instilled in each other by the boys themselves. The schools were ruled by peer-group pressure with a vengeance. A boy's standing – often his access to food and whatever physical comforts the school provided – was at the mercy of his fellows. This was what explained the enduring appeal of the public schools through all the changes of fashion from the eighteenth century onwards. A middle-class father's decision to adopt the expensive expedient of sending his son to public school might be influenced by academic or professional ambitions, or by the hope that the boy would acquire the patina of a gentleman, but the bedrock of the schools' appeal was the training which they provided in self-government and self-reliance. Learning to stand on one's own feet, to rub shoulders with all sorts, to have the guts to stand out against the crowd – these qualities were integral to manliness, and they were not likely to be acquired at home. Provided the worst excesses were avoided, hard knocks and salutary neglect at school were acceptable to parents as the best means of teaching their son to 'shift for himself'.[43] Analogies with ancient Sparta drew attention to this aspect of the public schools.[44]

The boy culture of the public schools despised intellectual ability and aesthetic sensibility; it elevated athletic prowess to become a fetish; and it cultivated a strong but somewhat mechanical group loyalty, easily adapted to an unthinking patriotism and a secular sense of public duty.[45] Two attitudes proved particularly relevant to men's responses to women's suffrage. In the first place, public school enforced a crude pecking order of privilege by seniority and by muscular might. Anti-suffrage men placed great weight on the contention that, since government rested on the use or threat of force, it could not concern the weaker sex.[46] Pro-suffrage activists like Laurence Housman who struggled to counter this 'physical force' argument were well aware that undue respect for force was one of the most pernicious legacies of a school culture which taught boys to endure cruelty and then inflict it on those weaker than themselves.[47] Secondly, the public schools intensified a preference for the company of males. Women were confined to the humble servicing role of matron or maid. Mother and sisters were not to be spoken of, or displayed in photographs. Those who breached this convention were branded as weak and effeminate. For every boy who pined for home there were others for whom the home and its female inmates seemed increasingly unreal and who would never adapt to a conventional domestic environment. Behaviour associated with the opposite sex succumbed to the same fate. This was particularly true of emotional disclosure. Already, as we have seen, the gender polarization of many middle-class homes discouraged the display of feeling in boys; school tended to make the ban absolute. Sir Francis Younghusband recalled of his days at Clifton in the late 1870s, 'to betray any sort of sentiment was a crime'.[48] In the words of a colonial educationalist in 1903, 'the manly man is to stand like a bluff headland unshaken by the waves of emotion'.[49]

The dominant code of manliness in late Victorian Britain accurately expressed the public-school values of the time. Chivalry towards women was *de rigueur*, but it was secondary. Manliness was essentially a code which regulated the behaviour of men towards each other. It extolled action rather than reflection, duty to one's country rather than one's conscience, and physical pluck rather than moral courage. The manly ideals propagated in the 1880s and 1890s made less allowance for the inner man or for transparency in personal relations; they emphasized instead conformity of opinion and correctness of behaviour – or 'good form'. Of course the public school did not just produce an elite of rigid conformists. More critical spirits who survived its rigours were ready for anything, as the career of Frederick Pethick-Lawrence testifies: at Eton in the 1880s 'the very fact that I stood then against the stream strengthened my spirit of independent judgement and gave me self-reliance'.[50] But Carpenter's estimate of public-school manliness was surely right: a narrow and conventional sense of honour, which might comprehend the call to duty, and even self-sacrifice, but was deaf to the dictates of the heart.[51]

Beyond public school lay a range of openings which beckoned the young man inured to men-only living. The universities and the armed services maintained their traditional appeal; colonial administration and public schoolmastering both offered many more openings during this period; while settlement houses and Anglican celibate orders were entirely new. All of these occupations provided a total homosocial environment reminiscent of public school. But this was also the golden age of the gentleman's club, especially in London's West End. Here bachelors could conduct social life on their own terms, and married men could find a reassuringly masculine refuge from the overfeminine ambience of home. Closer to the margins of respectable society, London also spawned its own version of Bohemia, composed of artists and writers who were either too poor to marry or too fearful that domesticity would sap their talent. As Brian Harrison has put it, the period before the First World War was 'an age of bachelors, or of married men who spent a large part of their lives as though they were bachelors'.[52]

This preference for bachelor living begs important questions about the ties between men. Advocates of Social Purity attacked the public schools as dens of homosexual vice where boys were corrupted by their seniors into a life of perversion. London and other big cities had their rent-boy sub-culture which was well patronized by men of the governing classes, and the colonies offered further exotic (and inexpensive) possibilities. But relations between men of the same class were much more inhibited. As Eve Kosofsky Sedgwick has pointed out, a fine but critical line separates being 'a man's man' from being 'interested in men': male friendship in an institutional setting strengthens patriarchy, but exclusive sexual relationships between men introduce division and jealousy, as well as undermining the vital reproductive mechanism of marriage. According to Sedgwick, it was during the second half of the nineteenth century that this schism between friendship and sex in homosocial relations became absolute. Darwinism rehabilitated the healthiness and normality of sex in the scheme of evolution, while branding non-reproductive forms of sex as pathological. Concern about the evidence of a declining rate of population growth from 1881 tended to the same effect. Imperial concerns also lent their weight: an educated class reared on the classics was sensitive to the argument that empires are brought low as much by moral canker within as by barbarian incursions from without. By the 1880s protests against vice of all kinds, especially in the young, were reaching a crescendo, and in 1885 homosexual acts in private were outlawed by the Criminal Law Amendment Act.[53]

These were the conditions for homosexual panic, causing men not only to proscribe homosexual behaviour in others, but to anxiously scrutinize their own emotional life for signs of illicit desire. When Oscar Wilde was convicted in 1895 under the 1885 Act, the journalist W.T. Stead (not a homosexual himself) presciently remarked to Edward Carpenter: 'A few more cases like Oscar Wilde's and we should find the freedom of comradeship now possible to men seriously impaired to the permanent detriment of the race.'[54] Close relations between men were much more circumscribed than in the early Victorian period. Too much effusiveness or physicality was open to misinterpretation. A steady stream of idealistic young men from Oxford and Cambridge was attracted to settlement houses and churches in slum areas, where they could enjoy an extension of common-room comradeship with their fellow graduates, and at the same time savour the rough manliness of working-class lads.[55] But decorum was usually observed. For some, residence in an all-male institution was only a phase, to be followed by marriage and domesticity. For others it became a permanent commitment and the focus of their emotional life. But even these men usually behaved as 'asexuals'. Middle-class men of this generation often yearned for 'man-talk and tobacco'. They did not, by and large, conduct erotically explicit friendships. They were probably happier with Kipling's image in *The Light That Failed* (1891) of 'the austere love that springs up between men who have tugged at the same oar together'.[56]

III

Growing up male is not only about establishing one's standing in the company of men and learning the appropriate codes of masculine behaviour; it is also about taking one's place in a social order designed to deliver power and privilege to men at the expense of women. For most, but not all, men patriarchy is an immediate personal agenda, a standard by which relations of dominance with wife, daughters or female employees are to be measured. But whether or not they share their everyday lives with women, all men benefit collectively from the structure of sexual inequality and thus have a vested interest in the maintenance of patriarchal values. The stake which men have in patriarchy is materially so valuable and culturally so pervasive that one may indeed question the extent to which masculinity can exist apart from patriarchy: not that it is entirely subsumed in patriarchy, but that it would be a radically different kind of identity in a situation of sexual equality.[57]

The suffrage movement was shocking because it openly challenged public patriarchy. When after 1905 militant suffragettes literally invaded the public sphere, the threat was even more disturbing. But this was not the first time that women had stepped out of their allotted role and challenged the conventional separation of spheres. In fact the suffrage campaigns would be hard to imagine without the earlier assault on the Contagious Diseases Acts in the 1870s and early 1880s, when the Ladies National Association attacked medical and state power as men's power, in public meetings where both the platform and audience were female. The movement also drew attention to the double standard of sexual conduct, relentlessly exposing the damage which young men of loose morals did to prostitutes and to their brides-to-be. After the temporary repeal of the Contagious Diseases Acts in 1883, this second aspect of the movement's agenda was developed by Social Purity feminists (in alliance with leading Evangelicals) into a call for the state repression of brothels. The Criminal Law Amendment Act of 1885 raised the age of consent to sixteen and outlawed brothel-keeping, leading to a massive increase in prosecutions against brothels. As a restraint on the traditional sexual freedoms of young men, the Act was a good deal more significant than the repeal of the Contagious Diseases Acts.[58]

Sexual behaviour on the street was not the only aspect of masculinity to be regulated by the state. The structure of family life came under critical scrutiny in ways which could be interpreted as fulfilling a feminist agenda at the expense of men. Despite the protests of *laissez faire* purists, the wall of domestic privacy was breached in important ways during this period, and limits were set on the sway of private patriarchy. First came the change in the law of divorce. The reform enacted in 1857 was certainly not intended to make for a more equal balance between husbands and wives. It upheld the traditional double standard which required wives to prove other offences (such as cruelty, incest or desertion) besides infidelity, while husbands could secure a divorce on grounds of adultery alone. But the greater accessibility and lower costs of the new Divorce Court, as compared with the old ecclesiastical courts, encouraged more wives to initiate proceedings: between the 1860s and 1911 the percentage of women petitioners gradually rose from 38 to 46.[59] As A. James Hammerton has movingly shown, the plight of wives who sought redress in the courts against years of abuse or neglect made a deep impression on judges – and on newspaper readers. Judges responded by extending the existing grounds of physical cruelty to include mental cruelty as well. The newspaper-reading public, who were given every detail of the more lurid cases, reacted in effect by subscribing to higher minimum standards for husbands – a tendency also reflected in the copious advice literature on marriage which now placed the greater responsibility for marital harmony on the husband rather than the wife.[60]

The reform in the law on married women's property was in some ways even more profound. Accomplished in two main stages, it was the second Act in 1882 granting 'separate property' to wives in the form of capital which meant most to the middle and upper classes. It was conceived by the Liberal government as a reform of anomalies in the relationship between equity and common law, but contemporaries were agreed that the social consequences were likely to be profound. The Act's opponents were wide of the mark in predicting an open season for domestic tyranny by wives. But feminists were right to hail the principal outcome – wives' control of their own property – as the end of one of the key props of patriarchy. Moreover, as many commentators pointed out at the time, separating out wives' property was not merely a financial matter; it was bound to enlarge the individuality and autonomy of wives in general.[61] Equally, greater legal constraints on husbands' authority influenced the way men weighed up the advantages of marriage. The suggestion made by one last-ditch opponent of the 1882 Act that the application of the measure be postponed for two years 'in order to give people who were contemplating matrimony time to change their minds when they find the law altered' may have been facetious, but it voiced real doubts about the attractions for men of marriage under the new dispensation.[62] It was in psychological dimensions of this kind that marriage changed most, adding to the dignity of wives while bringing time-honoured patriarchal assumptions into question. That process was extended by the widening scope of feminist critiques of marriage. Initially targeted in the 1870s at the economic subordination of the wife compared to her spinster sister, by the 1890s the attack was breaching the taboo on discussing sex in marriage.[63]

A different kind of challenge to patriarchy was thrown down by the New Woman. This label did not primarily denote an active feminist politics, though many who fitted the description certainly joined the ranks of the suffragists or the social purists and became 'platform women'. The term 'New Woman' originated as a media invention of the 1890s,[64] but it referred to trends which had been discernible since the 1880s. The New Woman was usually a young middle-class woman who enjoyed a measure of personal independence in ways which affronted patriarchal propriety. Behind the smoking and cycling which identified her in public was someone who lived on her own, or with other young women. She usually worked for her living, often in teaching or journalism. Somewhat lower down the social scale, the large numbers of women who were recruited into office work at this time – over 20 per cent of all clerks in some cities by 1901 – scarcely rated as 'middle class', but they posed a direct threat to the men who had monopolized clerical jobs hitherto.[65] The New Woman also asserted her freedom to be unchaperoned both in private and in public. She was increasingly likely to attend secondary school, and even university, and to play in the competitive team sports which these institutions encouraged. In these and other aspects of her lifestyle, the New Woman was highly visible – perhaps more so than her actual numbers warranted. Her claim to both intellectual and economic equality was highly provocative. Above all, in rejecting men's protection, the New Woman was refusing to lead her life by the patriarchal rules.[66]

Late nineteenth-century culture was permeated by images which expressed a fear of female power. Beneath the ridicule heaped on the New Woman by the press lay the anxiety instilled by women who flouted paternal authority and refused or postponed marriage. This was expressed in the almost morbid fear of women's sexuality which characterized the visual arts of the period, with their recurrent images of predatory seduction.[67] In avant-garde literature, the stories published in *The Yellow Book* between 1894 and 1897 reflected keen anxiety about women's assertion within marriage.[68] As Elaine Showalter has pointed out, the novels of masculine quest in the 1880s and 1890s, like those of Rudyard Kipling, Rider Haggard and Joseph Conrad, expressed acute fears of 'manly decline in the face of female power'.[69] Their analogue was the New Women novelists, whose merciless portrayal of venereally diseased husbands and sexually assaulted wives only intensified male anxieties. The changing character of manliness conformed to the same pattern: as Peter Gay has argued, the more strident tone of manly discourse towards the end of the century was, in part at least, a defence mechanism designed to bolster men against increasing female intrusion into 'their' sphere.[70]

IV

The question that remains is just how pervasive and undermining this sense of masculine insecurity was. Surveying the political scene in 1888, the editor of the *Spectator*, Meredith Townsend, expressed his unease as follows:

Whether for good or evil, a great change is passing over Englishmen. They have become uncertain of themselves, afraid of their old opinions, doubtful of the true teachings of their consciences. They doubt if they have any longer any moral right to rule anyone, themselves almost included. An old mental disease, the love of approbation, has suddenly risen among them to the height of a passion. . . . That is the real root of the great change which has passed over the management of children, of the whole difficulty in Ireland, of the reluctance to conquer, and of the whole of the new philanthropic social legislation.[71]

This ascription of specific national problems to a general failure of will and a weakening of backbone speaks the language of gender crisis. When men grow soft, the body politic disintegrates. Similar responses were sparked by the physical unpreparedness of British manhood for the Boer War.[72] And, like the lax management of children, craven concessions to women and the canker of homosexuality were both seized on as part metaphor, part cause, of the unsettled face of public life. The *fin de siècle* is now in fact commonly seen as a period of crisis in masculinity, when evidence from many different directions seemed to confirm that men were under threat and losing control of themselves and others. The consequence was a growth of irrational and paranoid responses in both society and culture.[73]

Against this must be set the plentiful evidence of unruffled masculine composure. The British upper and middle classes continued to boast a large number of men who were secure in their wealth and positions of power, untroubled by wifely independence and unreflecting in their enjoyment of club life. So far as their personal circumstances were concerned, patriarchy operated as smoothly as before. But the notion of 'crisis' does not mean that all men were personally confronted by a collapsing gender order – in the way that, for example, some sections of the lower middle class were by the rise of female clerical workers. What counted was the perception of social instability mediated in cultural terms. Here it was increasingly difficult to retain a confident sense that men's position was strong or unchanged. New social actors were at large, voicing new challenges. The hierarchy of family life was more openly questioned than at any time within living memory and had been partly modified by legislation. The spotlight had been thrown on the covert conventions of patriarchal sexual practice, and significant restraints imposed by law. Public spaces, including the workplace and educational institutions, were more open to women, and public life itself was subject to periodic female incursions. The journals of the day were open to radical feminist polemic, aided by feminist novels of sexual discontent and sometimes frank sexual antagonism.

Men's responses to the campaign for women's suffrage were firmly located in this context. At one extreme stood the rigid upholder of the patri-archal order, convinced that the suggested extension of the franchise was the most serious infringement of separate spheres yet proposed, with appalling consequences likely in each. In the domestic sphere, Frederic Harrison warned, the truth and spirituality of woman would be swept aside 'by gruesome cant about equal rights and adult suffrage'.[74] The whole struc-ture of woman's moral mission was in jeopardy. As for the public sphere, votes for women would introduce feminine susceptibilities into the heart of government where a masculine mind was most needed – they would, in other words, compound the very problem of collapsing backbone that Townsend had identified. Imperialists like Curzon and Cromer were particularly drawn to this argument.[75] They found plentiful support in the ranks of the public-school educated, and among the denizens of Clubland, a terrain which of course included both Houses of Parliament.

At the other extreme were those men whose personal experience and social principles had led them to regard conventional forms of masculinity as a cruel constraint rather than a support. Gender identities as polarized as late nineteenth-century manliness and femininity were bound to pro-duce a counter-discourse of androgyny. Many pro-suffrage writers of both sexes rejected the straitjacket of 'tough' manhood and 'soft' womanhood, either by reclassifying all the gendered virtues as 'human' or by recommending that each sex incorporate some of the qualities associated with the other.[76] Many men felt they had been personally damaged by the separation of spheres in family and education. Some, like Thomas Hardy and George Gissing, wel-comed the possibilities of greater openness in relations between men and women since the 1870s, and they saw women's suffrage not only as an over-due entitlement for women, but as a step towards the reform of sexual mores. For Laurence Housman and Edward Carpenter, support for militant suffragism amounted to a rejection of the stifling conventions of bourgeois family life. Others believed that votes for women would achieve a transformation in British political culture. The majority of leading pro-suffragists were anti-imperialists, and many (like Richard Pankhurst and Henry Nevinson) fervently hoped that women's suffrage would sound the death-knell of imperialism and militarism – even of capitalism itself.[77]

Both the inflexibility of the reactionary and the visionary optimism of the enthusiast were in their different ways the consequence of a generation of change in gender relations. Each was grounded not just in a narrow read-ing of the suffrage issue, but in a consciousness of shifting gender relations over a broad front. Historically men's power *vis-à-vis* women has partly depended on maintaining a veil over masculinity itself. The fact that so many of the constituents of masculinity, by becoming the subject of public discourse, were made visible during this period affected the gender identity of all men who had access to that discourse. Their reactions to the campaign for women's suffrage were framed accordingly.

Notes and references

1 This strand is best represented by the magazine *Achilles Heel* (1978–), and by the writings of Victor Seidler. See especially his *Rediscovering Masculinity* (London, 1989).

2 Edward Carpenter, *Love's Coming of Age* (London, 1914, first pub. 1896). Recent examinations of Carpenter include Sheila Rowbotham and Jeffrey Weeks, *Socialism and the New Life* (London, 1977), and Tony Brown (ed.), *Edward Carpenter and Late Victorian Radicalism* (London, 1990).

3 Lucy Bland, *Banishing the Beast: English Feminism and Sexual Morality 1885–1914* (London, 1995), pp. 40–1; Judith Walkowitz, *City of Dreadful Delight: Narratives of Sexual Danger in Late-Victorian London* (London, 1992), p. 146.

4 Angela V. John, 'Men, manners and militancy: literary men and women's suffrage', in A.V. John and C. Eustance (eds), *The Men's Share? Masculinities, Male Support and Women's Suffrage in Britain, 1890–1920* (London, 1997), pp. 88–109.

5 Laurence Housman, 'Militancy: and no mistake', *Votes for Women*, 15 March 1912.

6 This approach to the study of masculinity is best represented by J.A. Mangan and James Walvin (eds), *Manliness and Morality: Middle-Class Masculinity in Britain and America, 1800–1940* (Manchester, 1987). For a critique, see editors' introduction in Michael Roper and John Tosh (eds), *Manful Assertions: Masculinities in Britain since 1800* (London, 1991), pp. 1–4.

7 These figures are adapted from those of the registrar-general in 1911 by J.A. Banks, *Victorian Values: Secularism and the Size of Families* (London, 1981), pp. 40, 98. See also Michael Anderson, 'The social implications of demographic change', in F.M.L. Thompson (ed.), *Cambridge Social History of Modern Britain*, vol. 2 (Cambridge, 1990), p. 44.

8 For an authoritative review of these and related debates, see Simon Szreter, *Fertility, Class and Gender in Britain, 1860–1914* (Cambridge, 1996). See also F.M.L. Thompson, *The Rise of Respectable Society* (London, 1988), pp. 51–68.

9 This is the argument of J.A. Banks, *Prosperity and Parenthood* (London, 1954).

10 Ruskin and Mill are well-known examples.

11 Peter Gay, *The Bourgeois Experience*, vol. 1 (New York, 1984), p. 274.

12 Wally Seccombe, 'Starting to stop: working-class fertility decline in Britain', *Past & Present* 126 (1990).

13 A. James Hammerton, *Cruelty and Companionship: Conflict in Nineteenth-Century Married Life* (London, 1992), p. 165.

14 Keith McClelland, 'Masculinity and the "representative artisan" in Britain, 1850–80', in Roper and Tosh, *Manful Assertions*, pp. 74–91.

15 George and Weedon Grossmith, *Diary of a Nobody* (London, 1894). For a perceptive commentary, see A. James Hammerton, 'Pooterism or partnership? Marriage and masculine identity in the lower middle class, 1870–1920', *Journal of British Studies* 38 (1999), pp. 291–321.

16 Anderson, 'The social implications of demographic change', p. 34.

17 Pat Jalland, *Women, Marriage and Politics 1860–1914* (Oxford, 1986), p. 97; Robert I. Rotberg and Miles Shore, *The Founder: Cecil Rhodes and the Pursuit of Power* (New York, 1988), pp. 21, 92.

18 Banks, *Prosperity and Parenthood*, chs 3–4.

19 Elaine Showalter, *Sexual Anarchy: Gender and Culture at the Fin de Siecle* (London, 1991), ch. 5.

20 Arthur Conan Doyle, quoted in J.A. Hammerton (ed.), *Stevensoniana* (London, 1903), p. 243.

21 Eve Kosofsky Sedgwick, *Epistemology of the Closet* (Berkeley, 1990), p. 247.

22 Graham Dawson, *Soldier Heroes: British Adventure, Empire and the Imagining of Masculinities* (London, 1994), pp. 134–51.

23 R.W. Emerson, *English Traits* (London, 1856), pp. 62, 71–2, 164. See also Hippolyte Taine, *Notes on England* (trans. Edward Hyams) (London, 1957), esp. pp. 5, 61, 78.

24 J.A. Froude, *The Nemesis of Faith* (London, 1849), p. 113.

25 For the above two paragraphs, see John Tosh, *A Man's Place: Masculinity and the Middle-Class Home in Victorian England* (London, 1999), esp. ch. 2.

26 Leonore Davidoff and Catherine Hall, *Family Fortunes: Men and Women of the English Middle Class, 1780–1850* (London, 1987), ch. 2.

27 Walkowitz, *City of Dreadful Delight*, pp. 46–50.

28 Cynthia E. Russett, *Sexual Science: the Victorian Construction of Womanhood* (Cambridge, 1989).

29 W.R. Greg, *Why are Women Redundant?* (London, 1869), p. 21.

30 'One of us', 'Why we men do not marry', *Temple Bar* 84 (1888), p. 219.

31 T.H.S. Escott, *England: Its People, Polity and Pursuits*, 2nd edn (London, 1885), p. 309.

32 Carpenter, *Love's Coming of Age*, pp. 44–5. See also Edward Carpenter, 'The drawing-room table in literature', *The New Age*, 17 March 1910, p. 464.

33 Mark Girouard, *Life in the English Country House* (London, 1980), pp. 292–8.

34 See, for example, Alan Crawford, *C.R. Ashbee: Architect, Designer and Romantic Socialist* (New Haven, 1985), p. 6; Barbara Caine, *Destined to be Wives: the Sisters of Beatrice Webb* (Oxford, 1986), p. 137.

35 Mary Haweis, *The Art of Housekeeping: a Bridal Garland* (London, 1889), pp. 33–4.

36 Lee Krenis, 'Authority and rebellion in Victorian autobiography', *Journal of British Studies*, 18 (1978), p. 117.

37 John Tosh, 'Authority and nurture in middle-class fatherhood: the case of early and mid-Victorian England', *Gender & History* 8 (1996), pp. 48–64 (see below, Chapter 6); Caine, *Destined to be Wives*, ch. 8.

38 Edmond Demolins, *Anglo-Saxon Superiority: To What It Is Due* (London, 1898), p. 100.

39 Edward Cecil, *The Leisure of an Egyptian Official* (London, 1921), p. 184.

40 John Tosh, 'Domesticity and manliness in the Victorian middle class: the family of Edward White Benson', in Roper and Tosh, *Manful Assertions*, pp. 59–68.

41 Banks, *Prosperity and Parenthood*, pp. 189, 228–9.

42 J.R. de S. Honey, *Tom Brown's Universe: the Development of the Victorian Public Schools* (London, 1977); J.A. Mangan, *Athleticism in the Victorian and Edwardian Public School* (Cambridge, 1981).

43 Honey, *Tom Brown's Universe*, pp. 209–17.

44 Walter Pater, *Plato and Platonism* (London, 1893), pp. 200–2; Robert Baden-Powell, *Rovering to Success* (London, 1922), p. 24.

45 See for example Harold Nicolson's reminiscences of Wellington in Graham Greene (ed.), *The Old School* (Oxford, 1934), esp. pp. 91–2.

46 Brian Harrison, *Separate Spheres: the Opposition to Women's Suffrage in Britain* (London, 1978), pp. 73–8.

47 Laurence Housman, *Articles of Faith in the Freedom of Women* (London, 1910), p. 15.

48 Quoted in George Seaver, *Francis Younghusband* (London, 1952), p. 10.

49 John E. Adamson, *The Theory of Education in Plato's Republic* (London, 1903), p. 51.

50 F.W. Pethick-Lawrence, *Fate Has Been Kind* (London, 1943), p. 29.

51 Carpenter, *Love's Coming of Age*, p. 29.

52 Harrison, *Separate Spheres*, p. 97.

53 Eve Kosofsky Sedgwick, *Between Men: English Literature and Male Homosexual Desire* (New York, 1985), p. 89. See also her *Epistemology of the Closet*.

54 Quoted in Jeffrey Weeks, *Coming Out: Homosexual Politics in Britain from the Nineteenth Century to the Present* (London, 1977), p. 21.

55 Seth Koven, 'From rough lads to hooligans: boy life, national culture and social reform', in Andrew Parker *et al.* (eds), *Nationalisms and Sexualities* (New York, 1992), pp. 365–91.

56 Rudyard Kipling, *The Light That Failed* (Harmondsworth, 1988, first pub. 1891). pp. 58, 89.

57 This theoretical discussion draws heavily on R.W. Connell, *Gender and Power* (Cambridge, 1987).

58 Edward J. Bristow, *Vice and Vigilance: Purity Movements in Britain since 1700* (Dublin, 1977), pp. 154–74; Bland, *Banishing the Beast*, pp. 95–110.

59 G. Rowntree and N.H. Carrier, 'The resort to divorce in England and Wales, 1858–1957', *Population Studies* 11 (1958), table 2, p. 201.

60 Hammerton, *Cruelty and Companionship*, ch. 4.

61 Lee Holcombe, *Wives and Property* (Oxford, 1983), pp. 201, 218. See also Mary Lyndon Shanley, *Feminism: Marriage and the Law in Victorian England, 1850–1895* (London, 1989).

62 Holcombe, *Wives and Property*, p. 201; Shanley, *Feminism, Marriage and the Law*, p. 124.

63 Bland, *Banishing the Beast*, ch. 4.

64 David Rubinstein, *Before the Suffragettes: Women's Emancipation in the 1890s* (Brighton, 1986), pp. 12–34.

65 Gregory Anderson, *Victorian Clerks* (Manchester, 1976), pp. 56–60.

66 Rubinstein, *Before the Suffragettes*, chs 2–4; Walkowitz, *City of Dreadful Delight*, esp. ch. 2.

67 Bram Dijkstra, *Idols of Perversity* (Oxford, 1986).

68 Fraser Harrison (ed.), *The Yellow Book: an Anthology* (Woodbridge, 1982).

69 Showalter, *Sexual Anarchy*, p. 83.

70 Peter Gay, *The Cultivation of Hatred* (London, 1994), ch. 1.

71 Meredith Townsend, 'Will England retain India?', *Contemporary Review* 53 (1888), p. 811.

72 Anna Davin, 'Imperialism and motherhood', *History Workshop Journal* 5 (1978), pp. 9–65.

73 Showalter, *Sexual Anarchy*, pp. 9–15; Regenia Gagnier, *Idylls of the Marketplace: Oscar Wilde and the Victorian Public* (Stanford, 1987), p. 98. See also Michael S. Kimmel, 'The contemporary "crisis" of masculinity in historical perspective', in Harry Brod (ed.), *The Making of Masculinities* (London, 1987), pp. 121–53.

74 Frederic Harrison, 'Family life' (1893) in his *On Society* (London, 1918), pp. 45–6.

75 Brian Harrison, *Separate Spheres*, pp. 60, 75–6.

76 See for example Laurence Housman, *What Is Womanly?* (London, 1914), and Jane E. Harrison, *'Homo Sum': Being a Letter to an AntiSuffragist from an Anthropologist*, National Union of Women's Suffrage Societies (London, 1913).

77 John and Eustance, *The Men's Share?*; Sylvia Strauss, *'Traitors to the Masculine Cause': The Men's Campaigns for Women's Rights* (Westport, 1982), pp. 195–202, 224–5.

PART THREE

Family

Authority and nurture in middle-class fatherhood: the case of early and mid-Victorian England

Three images sum up the conflicting ways in which Victorian fatherhood has been represented in recent times. First, and most hackneyed, is the unsmiling domestic tyrant, probably the most enduring of the negative stereotypes which the first generation of post-Victorians foisted on posterity. A favoured theme of elite autobiography, as witness both the recollection of heavy-handed control and those family photographs of grim decorum, the domestic tyrant has been given a more common touch in the rogues' gallery of oppressive husbands culled from the Divorce Court records by A. James Hammerton.[1]

The second image arises from a desire to pinpoint the origins of the modern phenomenon of the 'absent father' whose time and energies are spent at work and elsewhere, removing him from the emotional cross-currents of family life. So far from being repressive, such a father is unable to perform the father's role at all, apart from paying the bills. Recent work on American families has unequivocally placed the origins of absent fatherhood in the first half of the nineteenth century.[2] British historians have been more hesitant. But there is in fact no shortage of evidence to point in this direction. The social content of middle-class family life was similar in the two countries, notably the growing separation of home from workplace. And the complaint that fathers were not pulling their weight was no less vociferous in Britain: one only has to listen to Sarah Ellis's concern about the 'almost double responsibility' borne by mothers, or follow the discussions

Reprinted with revisions from *Gender & History* 8 (Blackwell Publishing, 1996), pp. 48–64.

around mid-century in *The British Mothers Magazine* as Barbara Leavy has done.[3]

The third image is not strictly speaking Victorian at all, since it belongs to the early part of the nineteenth century; but why it recedes from view thereafter is an important question for Victorian studies. I refer to the engaging picture of the 'nursing father', immortalized by William Cobbett's fond recollection of his time as a young father 'divided between the pen and the baby'.[4] Few things in *Family Fortunes* surprised non-specialist readers more than Leonore Davidoff and Catherine Hall's very sympathetic portrayal of middle-class fathers. Family materials showed that Cobbett was far from being the glowing exception which he rather complacently claimed to be. In *Family Fortunes* fathers are characterized by a loving interest in their children's lives and a willingness to share the long watches of the night.[5] We are reminded that pleasure in children has always been a reason for having them, and that love in action (as well as in words) is no respecter of the sexes.

These three images owe their power over late twentieth-century readers to continuing anxieties about the place of both authority and nurture in fathering: the first image because it raises the spectre of paternal authority beyond reason, the second because it evokes a context in which neither nurture nor authority can be provided, and the third because of its reassuring implication that the active, loving father has been a historical reality and not just a contemporary aspiration of egalitarian sexual politics. Like all discourse about parenting, images of this kind are in one sense about the needs and experiences of children in the home, and perceptive historical work has examined nineteenth-century fatherhood from this perspective.[6] But these images also raise questions about the meaning of fatherhood for men, which have aroused less curiosity among historians.[7] What place did authority and nurture have in the lives of Victorian middle-class fathers, and how did they bear on contemporary notions of manhood?[8]

I

Recent historians have emphasized how bourgeois domesticity imposed conflicting expectations on Victorian middle-class men. On the one hand marriage was expected to be companionate, marked by attention to domestic concerns and regular fireside evenings. At the same time the ideology of separate spheres was founded on a clear functional distinction between the bread-winner and the home-maker, and usually presupposed a gulf between the characters of the two sexes.[9] Fatherhood was squarely situated in the midst of these contradictory pressures. It can be seen as the epitome of domesticity, or as a decidedly residual parenting role at odds with the separation of spheres. The issue of absent fatherhood is crucial in this context. Given the pressures of the workplace and the growing practice of commuting, the effective removal of the father for six days a week was clearly on the increase in Victorian England. Bread-winning could exact a heavy price; the father who 'elects to perform his parental duties entirely in the counting-house' was a type familiar to the historian J.R. Seeley.[10] But two important qualifications must be made. First, commuting was far from universal. Profes-sional men, farmers and clergy worked at home, and a significant minority of businessmen still did so as late as 1851.[11] These men were more available for paternal duties than the 'absent father' model would suggest. Secondly, while work was increasingly removed from the home, the opposite was true of leisure. Middle-class men of the early and mid-Victorian period were much less likely than their forebears to spend their time in the homosocial ambience of tavern and club. This aspect of middle-class mores struck foreign observers forcibly; Hippolyte Taine remarked in 1862 that the happiness of men of this class appeared to consist in 'home at six in the evening, an agreeable faithful wife, tea, four or five children clambering over their knees, and respectful servants'.[12] This was a much milder form of 'absent fatherhood' than prevailed in the cafe culture of France, or in America, where the hold of club-life and fraternities was so strong.[13] In the British context the 'absent father' model serves to highlight the sometimes high cost of attending to the basic duty of providing; but it is unhelpful if it implies that providing was *all* the middle-class father was able or willing to do.[14]

In order to understand what functions the father performed beyond bread-winning, a gendered analysis is essential. It is a curious fact that Victorian fatherhood, so often taken to be the epitome of the gender order which has crumbled within living memory, has been so little studied from a gender perspective. One reason may be that to do so satisfactorily requires an attention to both sexual difference and generational difference, a combination which makes for considerable complexity. At one level fatherhood is centrally a question of gender because it cannot be considered apart from motherhood. Both sexes have strong but divergent investments in having children, and how the balance of responsibilities between father and mother is struck in practice is unlikely to be stable or uncontested for long. In the nineteenth century, as in earlier periods, fatherhood was fundamental to middle-class masculinity because it contributed so markedly to a man's immediate social standing. It testified to his virility;

it lent greater substance to his role as sustainer and protector of family dependants (assuming economic disaster was kept at bay); and it provided an enlarged and privileged sphere for the exercise of personal authority. The first two of these three aspects of masculine reputation did not imply an interactive role for the father, but the third unquestionably did. Partly for this reason, masculine investment in fatherhood proved very sensitive to changes in the status of motherhood and in household organization.

But fatherhood was played for higher stakes than status and gratification in the present. Less often remembered is that it embodies fears and hopes about the future: as Charles Kingsley reminded his wife, their firstborn was 'the next link in the golden chain of generations'.[15] Fatherhood offered men the promise of a place in posterity, while at the same time leaving open whether that place would be one of credit or infamy. This was essentially an anxiety about sons who would carry the name and extend the line. For this reason (and not because of any lack of evidence) sons feature more prominently in this discussion than daughters. There is, as we shall see, abundant evidence that in the nineteenth century the trans-mission of masculine attributes to the next generation was taken extremely seriously by the middle class. Education and moral training in its broadest sense were central to a father's concerns. The masculinity of a household head was contingent on the masculine prospects of his sons – that is to say, their manly character and their future place in a man's world. The more sociological literature about the history of fatherhood focuses on questions of immediate social standing, while psychoanalytically oriented studies are more likely to explore intergenerational projections and conflicts.[16] But the problems of masculine identification which fatherhood posed for Victorian middle-class men cannot be fully grasped unless we pursue these two approaches together, and recognize that raising children carried a double burden for fathers: it had major implications for both masculine status in the present and the reproduction of masculinity in the future.

II

Masculinity was centrally about being master of one's own house, about exercising authority over children as well as wife and servants. Traditionally children were subject to their father because he provided for them, and because they had not yet attained reason. The fact that children were now more sharply distinguished from servants and were less likely to work under the father's direction certainly modified the character of their subordination, but daughters were still expected to serve their father and sons to obey him. Patriarchy in this most literal sense was unquestioned. John Stuart Mill deplored the uncompromising way in which paternal authority was too often applied, as if, he complained, a man's children were 'literally, and not metaphorically, a part of himself'.[17] Yet Mill seems primarily to have had in mind domestic violence among the labouring classes. Although voices were raised against the use of corporal punishment,[18] so far as the middle class was concerned the most contentious issue was to do with moral authority rather than physical power. Fatherhood was commonly reckoned to carry responsibility for the moral supervision and training of children. Since the Reformation all strands of Protestantism were agreed in allocating ultimate responsibility for the spiritual and moral welfare of household members to the father. A practical element of moral guidance was also inescapable, given that the father's standing was bound up with how his children – especially his sons – carried themselves in the world at large. The convention of the admonitory letter to a son at school or under apprenticeship is proof enough of that.[19]

In some ways the Victorian era was one of strengthened paternal moral authority. As Davidoff and Hall have carefully documented, the late eighteenth and early nineteenth centuries had seen a revival of the Puritan idea that the father was not only accountable for the religious welfare of the family but stood in place of God to his children.[20] At first a distinctively Evangelical position, this notion quickly shed some of its more sectarian associations and had far wider currency by mid-century. Didactic writers emphasized how vital the father's example and moral teaching were to the child's development.[21] The revival of the practice of family prayers emphasized his moral authority in the family.

But was that authority more than a court of last resort so far as his children were concerned? The evidence suggests that on balance it was not. For running counter to the tradition of paternal authority was a much stronger current valorizing the mother's moral role. The early Victorians stood at the end of two generations during which the status of mother had steadily risen in Britain, as in other Western societies. However murky the dynamics of that process may still be, the outcome is clear: motherhood stood on a new pinnacle of esteem, not only because greater value was placed on breast-feeding, but also because the mother was endowed with a unique moral role which stemmed from her reproductive function.[22] Sarah Lewis described maternal love as 'the only purely unselfish feeling that exists on this earth', a revelation of divine love with a unique power to regenerate mankind. Such sentiments became commonplace during the 1830s and

1840s.[23] There was no secret about what this meant for fathers. Child-rearing advice literature in the eighteenth century had commonly been addressed to the father, on the assumption that he exercised the chief responsibility for his children's upbringing once the nursing stage was over; now it tended to be written for mothers alone, or for parents in such a way as to exclude fathers.[24] Elizabeth Sandford said of the mother: 'None can supply her place, none can feel her interest; and as in infancy a mother is the best nurse, so in childhood she is the best guardian and instructress.'[25] Sarah Ellis was blunter: as wife, woman must accept second place to her husband, but as mother she could not 'be too dignified, or be treated with too much respect'. Indeed in Ellis's view there was a compelling symmetry about the allocation of parental roles: fathers lacked 'the nicety and tact to manage the minute affairs of domestic life, and especially those of individual feeling'; they were out of their depth because they lacked the moral resources for the job.[26]

Furthermore, there was a decided question mark over the father's role as disciplinarian. The early nineteenth century was a critical period in shifting attitudes towards the use of physical force in all relationships of power. Legislation against parental cruelty towards children was not passed until 1889, but one of the reasons why the law could be changed was that by then the common wisdom had moved so far away from corporal punishment in the home (though not yet in the school). No doubt many parents remained wedded to the Puritan agenda of breaking the will by the rod, but as Linda Pollock has shown there was a gradual but marked shift away from beating as a routine punishment.[27] The majority of texts assumed that the purpose of parental discipline was to bend and mould, not to crush. The desired outcome was not a broken spirit, but a capacity for self-government.[28] Yet the moral force implicit in bending and moulding required not decisive intervention, such as fathers had traditionally supplied, but the application of carefully graded emotional pressures, subtly attuned to the character of each child. This was widely assumed to be beyond the capacities of a working father. Most didactic writers both male and female, from Lant Carpenter in 1820 through to Sarah Sewell in 1869, took the view that moral influence, as distinct from physical correction, was the mother's exclusive sphere.[29]

One should obviously be wary of accepting prescriptive literature as evidence of practice, and there are plenty of pointers the other way. Jeanne Peterson has shown that maternalism is certainly not to be taken for granted in professional households at this time.[30] In more fashionable circles, the demands of society tended to draw women away from motherly duties, and there were repeated appeals to parents to train their daughters in moral qualities rather than feminine accomplishments. Practice was obviously much more diverse than the tract-writers would have liked. But this does not mean that their discourse had no moorings in experience. The Angel Mother, after all, was not only central to the Victorian image of the moral society; poetry and painting testified to her seductive psychosexual power for men. She features constantly in recollections of childhood, like those of the new entrepreneurs of mid-century Bradford whose early moral training had nearly always been the mother's charge.[31] She is also to be found in letters and diaries, where there is not the same danger of retrospective sentimentalization.[32] The enlargement of the mother's role which Nancy Cott and Mary Ryan have emphasized so strongly for the United States at this time was certainly less pronounced in Britain, but the circulation of the same ideas, indeed often the same texts, in the two countries suggests considerable convergence.[33] In the 1840s Horace Bushnell, the American authority on child-rearing, highlighted the transition from the mother's 'soft imperative' in infancy to 'the stiffer tension of the masculine word' and the 'father's masculine force' applied to the older child. But by the time Bushnell's work was published in England in 1861, this traditional distinction was under considerable pressure and the father's authority over older children was in doubt.[34]

Legally, it is true, paternal power was unimpaired. The father's sole rights of custody and guardianship were not seriously eroded until the Infant Custody Act of 1886, and his freedom to neglect or abuse his children was only curtailed in 1889 with the passing of the Prevention of Cruelty to Children Act.[35] At present we know far too little about how the courts applied the common law prior to the reforms of the 1880s.[36] But the significant point is that the law was changed because the legal powers of the father were thought to be glaringly out of step with the actual importance of mothers. As the *Glasgow News* declared in 1884 when supporting a bill for reform of the custody law, 'In principle and in fact the training of the mother is in nine cases out of ten the foundation of character, and to allow this to continue not only ignored, but denied, is an anomaly.'[37] Moral motherhood, in short, probably commanded greater prestige and practical observance in Britain between the 1830s and the 1880s than at any other time.

III

The area in which the higher status of motherhood created most difficulty for married men was the upbringing of their sons. One of the main expectations of a father was that he prepare his sons to take their place in society as fully masculine adults. Traditionally this had primarily been a matter of endowing them with a business or profession. Boys had been either trained up to the business under the father's eye or apprenticed to his choice of master. This pattern was still to be found in family firms, particularly in manufacturing, banking and commerce, as the careers of countless Victorian businessmen attest.[38] But elsewhere it was becoming an anachronism, as middle-class employment diversified and patronage declined. The days when a public servant like James Mill could ease his son into a junior appointment at India House were over. A father might push his son in a certain direction, and even demand that he follow his own profession, but the chances that the son would comply were not good. Time-honoured expectations of occupational endowment were at odds with both the new professional climate and tentative aspirations to filial autonomy. As a result a father was less likely to have a clear vision of his son's future, and he was less likely to enjoy the close day-to-day contact which arose from supervising a novice's first years in work.

What remained was the father's responsibility to train up his sons to carry themselves like men in the world – in a word, to acquire a proper manliness of bearing and character. There was nothing new in treating boys as apprentices to adult masculinity, or in agonizing over their progress. Eighteenth-century gentry families were often exercised by symptoms of 'effeminacy' in their male offspring.[39] But the Victorians regarded the process of training in manliness as fraught with difficulty. Rightly or wrongly, they believed that the marketplace was not only more bracing and demanding than it had ever been but also more dangerous in a moral sense. Preparing a boy to make his way in the world with honour and self-respect therefore went beyond any notion of parenting as routine. Manliness was clearly in part about physical capacities like athleticism and endurance, but the moral elements were given particular emphasis by the Victorian middle class. They included absolute virtues like 'frankness' and 'purity', and their application in 'self-government'. This last was perhaps the most crucial, as Steven Mintz has rightly emphasized.[40] He argues that, as the inherited certainties of social hierarchy and revealed religion began to crumble, so a greater burden was placed on the responsibility and discipline of the individual. Self-government was the key to life on an even keel in times of adversity and doubt.

This imperative explains the prevalence of a characteristic paternal stance which does not feature much in modern images of the Victorian patriarch, the overanxious father. The anxiety did not just focus on the health and survival of the children, for which indeed there continued to be good cause. It was above all about the prospects of the children in adulthood. Unease about children's future, combined with an acute sense of personal responsibility, was a common attribute of Victorian fatherhood. The novelist Thomas Hughes, looking back on a lifetime of family concerns, treated the contrast between a mother's love and a father's 'anxious affection' as a truism hardly worth discussing.[41] Expressions of anxiety were in nearly every case focused on sons, not daughters, and were usually concerned with the anticipated vicissitudes of their future lives. In 1838 the Revd John Breay wrote, 'The best mode of attempting the formation of character occupies much of my thoughts. With respect to the girls, the path appears to me comparatively clear; but the boys, who must eventually mix with a variety of characters, occasion me much anxiety.'[42] Writing in his diary in 1847, the Hertfordshire brewer William Lucas had more worldly concerns in mind: he had no desire to see his seven sons rise above 'the middle rank of life', but he still felt 'an inexpressible anxiety' that they turn out well; of his two daughters there is no mention.[43]

These and many other expressions of paternal concern demonstrate how fears about the direction of social change had greatly raised the stakes as to how and by whom boys should be brought up. Traditionally 'breeching', the moment when boys donned breeches in place of children's clothes, had marked their passage from the nursery into the tutelage of men. The change in appearance still occurred, usually at about the age of six, but it no longer carried the same meaning. Maternal influence over boys continued well beyond breeching, often into their teens. By the 1880s mothers were being encouraged to undertake their sons' sex education as well, previously regarded as a father's preserve.[44] In fact there is evidence that some mothers saw training in manliness as their responsibility. For example, Mary Benson was married to a bishop who regarded himself as an expert on the subject, but it was she who in 1879 admonished their son: 'I want you to be manly and all that we have ever talked of tends to this. . . . Stir yourself up then, my boy, and be a man' – this to a twelve-year-old caught in a minor infringement of the school rules.[45]

The tension in the position of many Victorian fathers arose, in part at least, from the contradiction between the greater priority attached to manliness for boys and the greater role of mothers in teaching it. There is some convergence here with recent work on middle-class fatherhood in America. The argument there is that the unprecedented role of women in moulding boys both at home and at school led to a generation of men alert to the dangers of the feminine within and anxious to compensate by identifying with unequivocally masculine symbols and lifestyles.[46] The parallel is not exact, since in Britain there was not the same prevalence of female schoolteachers nor was 'absent' fatherhood so pronounced, but the American analysis is helpful in bringing out the tensions inherent in domestic training in manliness. And it helps to explain the appeal in Britain of an expensive but increasingly common solution, the boarding public school. No doubt these schools attracted social climbers and those for whom sons were simply too much trouble to keep at home. But they also offered the advantage of removing teenage boys from their mother's influence, while submitting them to a crash course in manliness. The decision to send a boy to public school nearly always represented a decisive intervention by the father. But to resort to the employment of surrogates on this scale was a tacit admission of paternal failure. Manliness, it seemed, could not be taught at home.[47]

IV

Moral authority, then, represented one aspect of fatherhood which raised searching questions about masculinity for Victorian men, particularly as regards sons. The other area in which concerns about present and future were inextricably linked was nurture and play. Most of the examples we have of fathers intimately involved in the care of infants pre-date the Victorian period. Cobbett's nostalgic tone in his *Advice to Young Men* (1830) was derived from his awareness that the 'nursing father' was already a figure of the past. This change was evidently a consequence of one of the most significant trends between the 1760s and the 1830s, the growth of child-centredness. It is of course misleading to speak of 'child-centredness' if this implies (as it does today) that children called the tune. But the phrase is apt if we accept its literal meaning – that children's needs (as perceived and supplied by adults) should be at the centre of home life. This recognition began at birth with the increasing popularity of breast-feeding. The 'nursing father' who fed his children by hand and watched over them when ill was better able to express his nurturing impulses in the new child-centred climate.

This same child-centredness also led to the rearing of infants in a nursery secluded from the rest of the household, and in affluent families staffed by specialist servants. The nursery was not a place where men felt at their ease. Randolph Trumbach has pointed out that among the aristocracy the nursery had long been regarded as 'the kingdom of the dependent ruled by the dependent, . . . the rule of the irrational by the irrational'.[48] The spread of the specialized nursery to the middle class seems to have had the effect of instilling similar attitudes there as well. While 'men of sense' in the eighteenth century had confidently laid down the bases of infant care, few now followed the Prince Consort's example in drawing up a nursery regime for his children. Fewer still lowered their dignity by spending much time with infants. One exception was the Lincolnshire farmer Cornelius Stovin, who in the 1870s bottle-fed his babies and carefully recorded their progress. But it is an exception that proves the rule, for Stovin stresses that on account of his slender means and the coarseness of the servants his children could not be 'imprisoned in a nursery'.[49] Infants who were segregated in that way saw comparatively little of their fathers.

Stovin was also an extremely playful and tender father, and in this respect he was rather more typical. He describes himself leaping round the kitchen with a two-year-old, allowing him the run of the dining-room, encouraging his 'original and spontaneous remarks' and indulging his mischievous tricks.[50] The 'nursing father' may have been on the way out, but the playful father remains very much in evidence – and not only with toddlers. William Gaskell indulged in holiday pranks with his daughters in the 1850s; Dr John Heaton of Leeds enjoyed the tunes his ten-year-old son played on his stethoscope in the 1870s; even Dr Arnold of Rugby allowed his children the run of the study and conveyed 'a spirit of pure fun'.[51] The grim tales of upbringing recounted by Edmund Gosse and Samuel Butler made good copy in an iconoclastic age, but they are seriously misleading if they suggest that common tenderness was beyond the Victorian father.[52] The growing separation of home from work is often assumed to have reduced the Victorian father to a marginal figure, 'a worldly stranger to domestic life' in John Gillis's phrase.[53] But for many fathers time spent with children was a vital dimension of the healing power of home in a world of harsh entrepreneurial values. In Stovin's case, a romp round the dining-room offered welcome relief from the endless anxieties about the finances of his farm and the state of his wife's health. Romantic notions of the transformative power of childhood in the lives of adults had a continuing appeal which was rooted in the material tensions of bourgeois life.[54]

On a gender-polarized reading, nurture and playfulness might be regarded as 'feminine' traits in an adult man. But there is little trace of this kind of gender anxiety. When William Lucas, an inhibited and anxious father, sadly reflected that he lacked 'the art of winning children and getting free with them', he was acknowledging the importance of an everyday aspect of fatherhood.[55] Nor does the didactic literature of the day suggest a more ambivalent attitude. One would expect some discussion of the issue in advice books on parenting and in the many texts on manliness which addressed the gender insecurities of men in their domestic life. But the father as carer and as playmate is almost entirely absent. In Dinah Craik's bestseller, *John Halifax, Gentleman* (1856), on the other hand, he is brought to the foreground: John can weep at the sight of his firstborn and be 'patient as a woman' with a sick child, without his steadiness under adversity or his public resolution being placed in doubt; his domestic sensitivity is presented as an enhancement rather than a qualification of his manliness.[56] The figure of John Halifax is hopelessly idealized, and it is impossible to estimate how prevalent his model of parenting was. But Sarah Ellis, in writing off fathers as emotional illiterates best kept out of the way,[57] may well have been preparing women for the worst rather than characterizing the common run.

There is, however, an important qualification to be made, which relates once more to the reproduction of masculinity in the next generation. Sons and daughters experienced the paternal attributes of tenderness and authority in differing proportion. While nursery infants were played with (or ignored) without distinction of sex, the breeching of boys introduced discrimination. Because most middle-class girls were intended for a lifetime of dependence in the domestic sphere, there was less reason for the father to impose constraint or distance on a daughter. He could be tender and demanding, offering unstinted affection while at the same time expecting her care and her sympathy. In the 1850s ten-year-old Catty Tait used to wipe away her father A.C. Tait's tears as he recalled the lapses of his youth and other painful subjects; when she died, he lamented how his 'dear little comforter' had been taken from him.[58] Special intimacy could develop between a father and the daughter destined to care for him in old age. Beatrice Webb, who performed this role for her widowed father, Richard Potter, for seven years, recalled the 'tie of extraordinary tenderness' she had enjoyed with him when she was a girl in the 1870s, and he appears to have been fond and loving with each of his nine daughters.[59] Barbara Caine calls Potter 'in many ways a most unusual father';[60] he was probably more intimate and confiding than most, and certainly a better correspondent, but his easy unaffected pleasure in their company was not unusual.

With sons the dictates of masculine training pointed to less intimacy. For the early and mid-Victorians emotional warmth might still have a place among the attributes of a grown man, but this was much less readily conceded in relations between father and son. In 1849 the biographer James Stephen commended William Wilberforce not only as a great humanitarian, but also as a paragon of paternal virtue who had displayed tenderness and attentiveness towards his sons; but he hastened to add that these qualities had never degenerated into 'fondness' or caresses.[61] Conventional wisdom held that the regime for sons should be much more bracing than for daughters. It was not that a father should apply a hands-off approach: homilies, surveillance and correction were required in order to balance the mother's authority. But, as Lee Krenis has emphasized, too great an emotional closeness with sons would undermine their self-reliance and moral autonomy, that manly independence which was expected to be evident by the age of twelve or so.[62] This combination of intrusion and detachment exactly characterizes Edward Benson, whose four sons were growing up in the 1870s and early 1880s. They remembered his frowns and his heavy-handed criticism, but had to wait until they read his diary after his death to recognize his tender love for them. They correctly surmised that this regime had not only been oppressive for them as children but had deeply scarred their father's psyche too, driving underground much of his passionate nature.[63] The satisfactions Benson derived from being a father were heavily qualified by his conception of the bleak environment for which his sons had to be prepared. In such instances the sense of loss could be intense. Potter and Benson doubtless represent extremes in their demeanour towards daughters and sons respectively, but the gender distinction was critical, both for growing children and for their fathers.

V

Procreation, provision, authority and nurture comprise the main elements of fatherhood. In concentrating on the last two, I have attempted to bring into focus the ways in which the traditional expectations of Victorian middle-class fathers were most subject to change. On the one hand, the balance of moral authority within the family had tilted quite sharply in favour of the mother, not only because middle-class men were spending more time away from home at work, but also because motherhood itself enjoyed higher status. Paternal authority in the material sense probably changed little, given the unquestioned centrality of the bread-winner role in bourgeois ideology. But the moral lead was now less likely to be taken by the father, as all questions relating to the upbringing of children were increasingly resolved by the mother. On the other hand, attitudes to both paternal nurture and paternal authority were subtly changed by the anxieties induced by a rapidly changing (or, as many saw it, a rapidly *deteriorating*) social and religious environment. The task of endowing the next generation with the inner and outer attributes of masculinity was accordingly perceived to be one of unprecedented difficulty. The task was made no easier by the enhanced role that mothers now had in moulding the masculinity of their sons. This had the positive appeal of entrusting moral training to those deemed best qualified to provide it, leading hopefully to a sound moral backbone in their charges; but it also reawakened the old fear that excessive maternal influence would produce sons who were soft and effeminate.[64]

The cumulative effect of the changes I have described was to undermine fatherhood as a badge of masculinity in the present and as a means of reproducing masculinity in the future. Given that so much of men's experience of fatherhood turns on the particularity of the persons involved, one must be cautious about speaking of a crisis or a general malaise. But by the mid-nineteenth century the odds were more heavily loaded against sustaining a secure masculine identity through the years of active fatherhood. Two of the images with which I began demonstrate the more extreme ways of reacting to these tensions. In the case of the 'absent father' everything was left to the wife and the servants, although the claims of domesticity might still be observed as regards the marriage itself. Authority and nurture went by default, as in Sarah Ellis's sorrowful portrayal of the father outside the emotional currents of the family. From the point of view of women advice-writers, there was something to be said for a father who did not blunder in and upset his wife's delicate childcare regime, but on any scale of masculinity opting out was scarcely a solution. It made the husband something less than master of his own home. He became entirely dependent on his wife for the upbringing of his children, and was placed in an unacceptably passive position.[65]

The tyrannical father represents the opposite reaction: the man who reacted to the shifting balance of familial authority by making an issue out of those areas he could still control, such as the household budget, family prayers and the heavier forms of discipline. Men whose work was based at home and who were thus continuously exposed to the challenge implicit in the wife's enhanced status often behaved in this way; Samuel Butler's clerical father is a well-documented example.[66] But the pattern was more prevalent than that. In the most disturbing cases, such as those recounted by Hammerton, the harshness and inflexibility suggest an almost pathological failure to see familial relations in anything but terms of authority. One must concede that these extreme responses come over with greater clarity in the literature than do the more subtle (and successful) adjustments made by many fathers; but the fact that both the absent father and the tyrannical father are so well documented is some measure of the disarray in familial relations in the Victorian middle class.

One of the reasons why it has been so difficult to recognize Victorian fatherhood as part of social history, instead of an incoherent montage of snapshot images, is that historians have tended to see fathers through the memories of their children, which were inevitably partial in both meanings of the word. Fatherhood consequently dissolves into individual quirks and eccentricities and becomes separated from other aspects of men's experience. Our understanding of both masculinity and family life is thereby impoverished. Some years ago Peter Filene expressed his regret that 'fathers were banished [by historians] to the waiting-rooms of history'.[67] For this situation to be rectified, two things are necessary: that we pay much more attention to the documentary evidence produced by fathers themselves; and that in structuring and interpreting their experience, we register more carefully the gendered meanings of fatherhood itself.

Notes and references

1 A. James Hammerton, *Cruelty and Companionship: Conflict in Nineteenth-Century Married Life* (London, 1992), pp. 82–101, 106–18.

2 Mary P. Ryan, *Cradle of the Middle Class: the Family in Oneida County, New York, 1790–1865* (Cambridge, 1981); E. Anthony Rotundo, *Manhood in America* (New York, 1993).

3 Sarah Stickney Ellis, *The Mothers of England* (London, 1843), p. 108; Barbara F. Leavy, 'Fathering and *The British Mothers Magazine*, 1845–64', *Victorian Periodicals Review* 13 (1980), pp. 10–16.

4 William Cobbett, *Advice to Young Men* (1830; repr. London, 1926), p. 176.

5 Leonore Davidoff and Catherine Hall, *Family Fortunes: Men and Women of the English Middle Class, 1780–1850* (London, 1987), pp. 329–35.

6 See, for example, Lee Krenis, 'Authority and rebellion in Victorian autobiography', *Journal of British Studies* 18 (1978), pp. 107–30; Philip Greven, *Spare the Child* (New York, 1992); Anna Davin, *Growing Up Poor* (London, 1995).

7 Two distinguished exceptions are: David Roberts, 'The paterfamilias of the Victorian governing classes', in *The Victorian Family*, ed. A.S. Wohl (London, 1978), pp. 59–81, and Davidoff and Hall, *Family Fortunes*, esp. pp. 329–35.

8 The argument of this essay is more fully expounded in my *A Man's Place: Masculinity and the Middle-Class Home in Victorian England* (London, 1999), chs 4 and 5.

9 Davidoff and Hall, *Family Fortunes*, pp. 111–13, 319, 450–1; Hammerton, *Cruelty and Companionship*, pp. 150–3.

10 J.R. Seeley, *Lectures and Essays* (London, 1870), p. 271.

11 Davidoff and Hall, *Family Fortunes*, pp. 231–2.

12 Hippolyte Taine, *Notes on England*, trans. Edward Hyams (London, 1957), p. 5.

13 Mark C. Carnes, *Secret Ritual and Manhood in Victorian America* (New Haven, 1989).

14 This is the context in which male advice-writers called for an equal and complementary distribution of parental duties. John Angell James, *The Family Monitor, or a Help to Domestic Happiness* (Birmingham, 1828), pp. 128–9; S.S. Pugh, *Christian Home-Life* (London, 1880).

15 Charles Kingsley to Fanny Kingsley, 7 Nov. 1844, quoted in Susan Chitty, *The Beast and the Monk* (London, 1974), p. 98.

16 On the first, see Davidoff and Hall, *Family Fortunes*; on the second, see Bruce Mazlish, *James and John Stuart Mill: Father and Son in the Nineteenth Century* (London, 1975), and Lee Krenis, 'Authority and rebellion'.

17 John Stuart Mill, *On Liberty* (Harmondsworth, 1974), p. 175.

18 On this issue, see Linda Pollock, *Forgotten Children: Parent–Child Relations from 1500 to 1900* (Cambridge, 1983), pp. 173–87. See also David Grylls, *Guardians and Angels: Parents and Children in Nineteenth-Century Literature* (London, 1978).

19 Roberts, 'The paterfamilias of the Victorian governing classes', pp. 68–9. A classic example of paternal admonition appears in David Newsome, *Godliness and Good Learning* (London, 1961), pp. 161–84; for another instance in a more secular vein, see Thomas Hughes, *Memoir of a Brother* (London, 1873), pp. 49–58.

20 Davidoff and Hall, *Family Fortunes*, pp. 89, 108–10.

21 John Angell James, *The Family Monitor* (Birmingham, 1828), p. 129; Theodore Dwight, *The Father's Book* (London, 1834), *passim*. (Dwight was an American, but his didactic writings circulated in England too.)

22 For the general context, see Ruth H. Bloch, 'American feminine ideals in transition: the rise of the moral mother, 1785–1815', *Feminist Studies* 4 (1978), pp. 101–26.

23 Sarah Lewis, *Woman's Mission*, 7th edn (London, 1840), pp. 132–3. See generally Jane Rendall, *The Origins of Modern Feminism* (Basingstoke, 1985), pp. 74–96.

24 For example, Jacob Abbott, *Parental Duties in the Promotion of Early Piety* (London, 1834).

25 Mrs John Sandford, *Woman in Her Social and Domestic Character*, 6th edn (London, 1839), p. 219.

26 Ellis, *Mothers of England*, pp. 27, 160, 366.

27 Pollock, *Forgotten Children*, pp. 173–87. See also Steven Mintz, *A Prison of Expectations: the Family in Victorian Culture* (New York, 1983), pp. 30–9.

28 Mintz, *Prison*, pp. 35–8.

29 Lant Carpenter, *Principles of Education, Intellectual, Moral and Physical* (London, 1820), pp. 201–2; Sarah A. Sewell, *Women and the Times We Live In* (Manchester, 1869), pp. 52–4.

30 M. Jeanne Peterson, *Family, Love and Work in the Lives of Victorian Gentlewomen* (Bloomington, 1989), pp. 103–8.

31 Theodore Koditschek, *Class Formation and Urban Industrial Society: Bradford 1750–1850* (Cambridge, 1990), p. 187.

32 For example, Elizabeth Gaskell, *My Diary* (privately printed, London, 1923); Jean Stovin (ed.), *Journals of a Methodist Farmer 1871–1875* (London, 1982); A.C. Tait, unpub. diaries, Lambeth Palace Library MSS.

33 Nancy F. Cott, *The Bonds of Womanhood* (New Haven, 1977); Ryan, *Cradle of the Middle Class*.

34 Horace Bushnell, *Christian Nurture* (London, 1861), p. 206. The book was first published in America in 1843.

35 Mary L. Shanley, *Feminism, Marriage and the Law in Victorian England, 1850–1895* (Princeton, 1989), ch. 5; George Behlmer, *Child Abuse and Moral Reform in England, 1870–1908* (Stanford, 1982).

36 Megan Doolittle, 'Missing fathers: assembling a history of fatherhood in mid-nineteenth-century England' (PhD thesis, University of Essex, 1996).

37 *Opinions of the Press on the Law Relating to the Custody and Guardianship of Children and on the Infants Bill, 1884* (Manchester, 1884), p. 7.

38 Anthony Howe, *The Cotton Masters, 1830–1860* (Oxford, 1986), pp. 50–4, and Howard Malchow, *Gentlemen Capitalists: the Social and Political World of Victorian Businessmen* (Basingstoke, 1991).

39 Anthony Fletcher, *Gender, Sex and Subordination in England, 1500–1800* (London, 1995), chs 17–18. See also Paul Langford, *A Polite and Commercial People* (Oxford, 1989), p. 606.

40 Mintz, *A Prison of Expectations*, pp. 27–39.

41 'An Old Boy' [Thomas Hughes], *Notes for Boys (and their Fathers) on Morals, Mind and Manners* (London, 1885), p. 91.

42 Quoted in Davidoff and Hall, *Family Fortunes*, pp. 332–3.

43 William Lucas, *A Quaker Journal* (London, 1934), vol. 2, p. 395.

44 Elizabeth Blackwell, *Counsel to Parents on the Moral Education of their Children in Relation to Sex*, 2nd edn (London, 1879); Lucy Bland, *Banishing the Beast: English Feminism and Sexual Morality, 1885–1914* (London, 1995), pp. 139–43.

45 Mary Benson to Fred (E.F.) Benson, 1 June 1880, Benson Deposit 3/66, Bodleian Library MSS.

46 Ronald Byars, 'The making of the self-made man: the development of masculine roles and images in ante-bellum America' (PhD thesis, Michigan State University, 1979); Rotundo, *American Manhood*, pp. 29–30, 264–74.

47 On the relationship between public school and parental attitudes, see J.R. de S. Honey, *Tom Brown's Universe: the Development of the Victorian Public School* (London, 1977), pp. 203–17.

48 Randolph Trumbach, *The Rise of the Egalitarian Family* (New York, 1978), p. 248.

49 Stovin, *Journals*, esp. pp. 107, 149, 152, 190. See also Chapter 7 below.

50 Stovin, *Journals*, pp. 177, 190, 195.

51 Jenny Uglow, *Elizabeth Gaskell: a Habit of Stories* (London, 1993), pp. 301, 497; John D. Heaton to Fanny Heaton, 12 Oct. 1877, Heaton Papers, private collection, Leeds; Thomas Arnold, *Passages in a Wandering Life* (London, 1900), p. 9.

52 Edmund Gosse, *Father and Son* (London, 1907); Samuel Butler, *The Way of All Flesh* (London, 1903).

53 John R. Gillis, 'Gender and fertility decline among the British middle classes', in *The European Experience of Declining Fertility*, ed. J.R. Gillis, L.A. Tilly and D. Levine (Oxford, 1992), p. 43. See also John R. Gillis, *A World of Their Own Making: Myth, Ritual, and the Quest for Family Values* (Cambridge, 1996), ch. 9.

54 For an instructive American parallel, see Stephen M. Frank, *Life with Father: Parenthood and Masculinity in the Nineteenth-Century American North* (Baltimore, 1998).

55 Lucas, *Quaker Journal*, pp. 395, 474.

56 Dinah M. Craik, *John Halifax, Gentleman* (London, 1856), vol. 3, pp. 120–2, 138–9, 260. See also Catherine Hall, *White, Male and Middle Class* (Cambridge, 1992), pp. 261–2.

57 Ellis, *Mothers of England*, pp. 160, 366.

58 A.C. Tait, diary, 10 May and 21 May 1856, Lambeth Palace Library MSS; W. Benham (ed.), *Catherine and Crauford Tait* (London, 1879), pp. 294, 358.

59 Beatrice Potter, diary, 26 Nov. 1889, quoted in Richard Meinertzhagen, *Diary of a Black Sheep* (Edinburgh, 1964), p. 124. See also Deborah Gorham, *The Victorian Girl and the Feminine Ideal* (London, 1982), ch. 3, and Davidoff and Hall, *Family Fortunes*, pp. 346–8.

60 Barbara Caine, *Destined to be Wives: the Sisters of Beatrice Webb* (Oxford, 1986), 15.

61 James Stephen, *Essays in Ecclesiastical Biography* (London, 1849), pp. 272–3.

62 Krenis, 'Authority and rebellion', pp. 117–18.

63 John Tosh, 'Domesticity and manliness in the Victorian middle class: the family of Edward White Benson', in *Manful Assertions: Masculinities in Britain since 1800*, ed. Michael Roper and John Tosh (London, 1991), pp. 59–65.

64 For eighteenth-century fears in this regard, see Michèle Cohen, 'The Grand Tour: constructing the English gentleman in eighteenth-century France', *History of Education* 21 (1992), pp. 249–50.

65 Leavy, 'Fathering and *The British Mother's Magazine*'.

66 Philip Henderson, *Samuel Butler: the Incarnate Bachelor* (London, 1953); Peter Raby, *Samuel Butler: a Biography* (London, 1991).

67 Peter Filene, 'The secrets of men's history', in *The Making of Masculinities*, ed. Harry Brod (London, 1987), p. 110.

CHAPTER 7

Methodist domesticity and middle-class masculinity in nineteenth-century England

I

The history of the family, at least for the nineteenth century, has reached a certain maturity. Though not yet incorporated into mainstream history – that would be too much to expect – it now boasts a considerable specialist literature and some useful general surveys.[1] Undoubtedly the driving force has been the aspiration of women's history to reconstruct the lives of women in the past. Now that the personal records of women are being studied with such attention, there is a wealth of insights into their experience as daughters, wives and widows. Jeanne Peterson's account of the Paget family and their circle in Victorian England is a typical example.[2] For the nineteenth-century women's historian, there is the added bonus that this was the period when the claims of women to have the dominant influence in the family were taken most seriously – as witness the persistent appeal of the Angel Mother. Hence to research the history of the Victorian family promises results which will feature women as agents, and not merely as victims of patriarchal oppression.

In many ways, the most impressive thing about the history of the family is the speed and confidence with which it has moved beyond this initial position. The family is not only a women's concern. It is the

Reprinted with revisions from R.N. Swanson (ed.), *Studies in Church History* 14, Ecclesiastical History Society (Woodbridge, 1998), pp. 323–45.

most important context for the study of childhood (still enormously under-researched); and it is fundamentally about men as well: in the psychological sense that they are emotionally formed by their early domestic experience, and in the social sense that it is men who take the initiative in establishing a family and who must usually shoulder the burden of maintaining it. In short, the family must be seen as a whole, embracing all its members – as a field which is constructed in relational terms around generation and sexual difference. That is essentially what the history of gender means when applied to the family. It is already a well-established genre, chiefly as a result of the path-breaking work of Leonore Davidoff and Catherine Hall on the English middle class. In their book *Family Fortunes* the family is seen not merely as a private sphere reserved for women and children, but as a central ingredient of men's class identity and of an emerging middle-class culture.[3]

One important aspect of *Family Fortunes* is its close attention to religious issues. The authors convey a real sense that the lives of middle-class men and women between 1780 and 1850 were embedded in a religious culture. If historical understanding depends on entering (in some sense) the mentality of our subjects, then this approach to the history of class formation is surely indispensable. It has, however, been rather lost sight of in more recent work. Jeanne Peterson considers the church as a career which engaged wives as well as husbands, but not the meanings which religious allegiance conferred on family life. James Hammerton's fine study of cruelty and divorce in Victorian marriage tends to understate the influence of religion, in order to do justice to the play of conflicting legal principles.[4] But placing religion on the sidelines in this way is simply not an option for the Victorian historian. All denominations in this period placed a heavy emphasis on the family. More important for my purpose, they saw the family as a whole, with prescribed and interlocking roles for every member. Of course these roles were not necessarily followed, not least because the various religious traditions taught conflicting lessons. Yet the fact remains that, in the middle class at least, an avid reading public was steeped in a public discourse on family which was articulated almost entirely in religious terms.

That discourse is one obvious focus for research. Sermons and advice literature can tell us much – as Davidoff and Hall showed in their absorbing account of the Congregationalist minister John Angell James, the so-called 'Bishop of Birmingham'.[5] The highly influential writings of Sarah Ellis, married to a member of the London Missionary Society, are another rich source on family mores.[6] Didactic literature of this kind can supply an analytical frame for studying the history of the family, and it is not difficult to track its influence in particular homes. The problem with this approach is that family experience becomes a means of illustrating a number of general propositions, instead of being explored for its own sake. In order to grasp how religion was experienced through domesticity, and how domesticity was understood in religious terms, we need to see the family in something like its actual complexity and integrity, even if this means looking at rather few of them.

In this chapter, my point of departure is the domestic experience of three nineteenth-century middle-class men: Joshua Pritchard, a Manchester exciseman; Isaac Holden, a West Riding mill-owner; and Cornelius Stovin, a Lincolnshire farmer. Each shows the ways in which religion permeated family life and family decisions. Each man was a Methodist, thus allowing the varieties of family experience within a particular tradition to come into focus. And each case study concerns primarily the husband or father, because it is still true that men are under-represented in family studies. The challenge of gender is to study the history of men, not on terms which reinforce their privileged access to the historical record, but from a truly relational perspective. 'Masculinity', so often loosely employed in common speech to indicate a men-only world premised on the exclusion of women, needs to be reclaimed as a historical identity constructed in relation to femininity. There is no better place to start than the domestic sphere, where masculinity is formed through early relations of nurture and discipline, and later articulated every day through identity and conflict with the opposite sex.[7]

II

Joshua Pritchard worked for the excise authorities, based in Manchester. He was a man of strong domestic affections towards his wife Mary, whom he married in 1818 when he was twenty-eight, and towards his four children. And, like his wife, he was a devout Methodist, apparently a Wesleyan. Occupation, family and religion were the elements from which a new middle-class identity was forged in the early nineteenth century. Pride of place is often given to the first. Such was the power of the work ethic and of 'calling' in a secular sense, that we might assume that Pritchard was an exciseman first, preoccupied with his reputation as a public servant, and only secondly a husband and a Methodist. Nothing could be further from the truth. His letters and diaries contain almost no reference to his work experience. What they reflect very directly is a painful conflict between work and the rest of his life. Being an exciseman meant being available for sudden postings of several months at a time to other towns, depending on the pattern of illegal distilling.

For Joshua these periods were a desolate exile from all he held dear. 'I can assure you', he wrote to Mary from Nottingham in 1835, 'that my mind is continually hankering after you and the children.' The lodgings were comfortable, and they belonged to 'one of John Wesley's hearers . . . a tried stone'. 'But yet I want you to talk with, and the children to play with a bit, to drive dull care away.' He had to content himself instead with buying expensive presents for all the children – including a watch for his eldest boy.[8] After eighteen years of marriage Joshua still found these separations almost insupportable. From London he wrote: 'Bless you Mary, I love to be at home, I now wish you were with me, I am sitting by the fire alone. O bless you my Love, my Dove, my Dear one, my best, my sweetest.' As a saved believer he was confident that he would never be parted in spirit from his wife, but this made the physical separation no easier to bear. From one posting, with leisure on his hands, he wrote in 1836, 'I have now time to talk to my Mary, but no *my Mary* to talk to me. There are 3 Marys in the house but not *my* Mary.' Self-pity sometimes got the better of him. On one occasion he complained, 'O yes, to be sure, Joshua must write long letters, but I wonder who writes long letters to him.' In 1837 he told Mary that, though he no longer had the same 'bloom of youth' as when she had first fallen in love with him, 'thank God our Love is not abated'. That seems to have been the truth. It brought Joshua intense happiness, but their repeated separations were less than manfully endured.[9]

In Joshua's mind there was at times an even stronger tension between family and religion. This was not because the family was at odds with his religion. Mary Pritchard was a Methodist too, and great care was given to the spiritual upbringing of the children. Joshua could sign off his letters home by sending his love to 'all the Class', knowing the message would be passed on. But there was a conflict in his mind about purity. As the rhapsodizing of 'My Dove, my Dear one' suggests, Joshua was a man of strong sexual need. His conscience was not to be satisfied with the comforting notion that marital sex was divinely sanctioned (in the way that, say, Charles Kingsley argued). He believed his passionate nature was a spiritual diversion for his wife. 'I can assure you', he wrote from London in 1835, 'that I very frequently thought, when I was at home, and have also thought so since, that I was a hindrance both to you and the children, and that in consequence of my passionate Spirit, you will be enabled to serve God better in my absence than when at home with you.'[10]

Joshua also questioned whether he should be so attached to *any* human being – lest she become 'in the place of Christ' to him.[11] Fourteen years previously, as a newly married man, he had been tormented by an even more disturbing thought: that he had a calling to the ministry which could not be obeyed so long as he had responsibility for his wife and baby daughter. He wrote in his diary:

Oh that I could for faith incessant cry to the great, the holy, the high! I have almost been ready to beseech the God of love to take my Wife and child to himself and then I would labour for him by his grace and assistance in this world below – and then again when I looked on my child and she of my bosom with whom I had took sweet counsel, I did not like to part with either of them. It is a struggle to me which way the contest will turn.[12]

In the event, Joshua's conscience allowed him to resist the call and remain in secular employment. But he remained a Methodist before anything else – certainly before occupation and sometimes before family.

For Joshua domesticity meant not only the bliss of a happy marriage but also the loving duty due to his children. The standards he set himself were exacting, especially for his first child, Mary Ann, born in 1819. He recorded his successes and failures in a special section of his diary which he addressed to her in the second person, intending her to read it when she was older. For Joshua the most important pointer to his daughter's spiritual state was her attitude to prayer. 'Prayer is a solemn thing which your Father is often obligated to tell you,' he wrote. At eighteen months Mary Ann was joining her hands before meals. Her parents tried to get her to kneel down with them at afternoon prayer, and her backsliding was variously attributed to bad influences, playfulness and the machinations of the devil. Blackmail was also attempted: when she was five Joshua told her that, if she was unwilling to pray with him, God 'could affect you and make you unwell'. Shortly before, she had had a dream that God wanted to take her – Joshua told her to keep this in her memory for the rest of her life, just as he surely never forgot his own wish that God would take both wife and daughter in the cause of the Gospel. Mary Ann's life proved short enough. She died before reaching her teens, probably never having read the diary her father had written for her edification. Unfortunately there are no records of that time which might tell us whether she died in morbid repentance of her earlier failures in prayer, or whether she had attained her own assurance of God's grace. Joshua did not believe she was perfect – 'she had her little ways' he later conceded – but he was confident that she was with her Father in heaven.[13]

As often happens when parenting is undertaken too zealously, Joshua was less demanding of his three subsequent children.[14] He allowed himself to take more pleasure in their company, to play with them and to lavish presents on them. But they could have been in no doubt that life was to be lived in godly earnest. 'Tell the children that their Father had them all up before the throne of Grace,' Pritchard told his wife in 1835 when he was away on business. He urged them to pray themselves, holding up the example of Mary Ann as someone who had attended to prayer and had properly regretted her lapses. He drew particularly pointed lessons for his one remaining daughter, Emma: Mary Ann was interceding for her, and she must emulate her qualities of meekness and modesty.[15] The spiritual destiny of his children, his wife and himself weighed on his mind as ultimately the only real foundation of life.

III

With Isaac Holden, my second case study, the claims of work were much more to the fore. He was not, like Pritchard, at the beck and call of his superiors, but a self-made entrepreneur whose career is a vivid illustration of the new industrial class. Born in Scotland, the son of impecunious English immigrants, Isaac Holden began his working life as a child labourer in a Paisley cotton mill. But he came of strongly Methodist stock – his paternal grandparents had been converted by John Wesley himself – and this gave him access to a closely knit, dispersed community, for whom helping one another in business had been explicitly prescribed by the founder.[16] Having briefly considered the Methodist ministry, in 1830 Isaac secured the post of book-keeper in a firm of Wesleyan worsted manufacturers at Cullingworth, near Keighley in the West Riding. This gave him the means to marry Marion Love, who came from a very similar Methodist background in Scotland. Fourteen years of stability followed. The Holdens had four children without mishap, and Isaac became more and more indispensable to the Cullingworth mill. In 1846, however, he left his employment to set up on his own, and Marion died of tuberculosis. At just the time when Isaac's hands were full with what turned out to be a failing business (a mill he had leased in Bradford), his home was without a head and he was deprived of his domestic support. His solution was to marry again, but this time to marry money. Sarah Sugden was a spinster as old as he was, from another Methodist mill-owning family. They were married in 1850, and they set up home near the factory where Isaac could now make an entirely fresh start.[17]

But this was not quite the whole picture. The new start was made not in Yorkshire, but in France – at St-Denis near Paris. If this seems a move of breathtaking boldness, it is not surprising that Sarah Sugden was not ready for it either. She complained (probably with some justice) that amid all the preparations for marriage Isaac had not dealt plainly with her in this matter. Isaac intended to stay in France for some years in order to give his factories there his full personal supervision. Sarah wanted him to settle in Yorkshire again, and ideally to abandon business altogether for the ministry. Seven months after the wedding she left St-Denis for her family home in Oakworth, with no date fixed for her return. She stayed with her brothers, for whom she had kept house for so many years, until the disagreement could be resolved. There followed a period of intense correspondence, at the end of which it was agreed that the family home would be at St-Denis, but that Sarah would live in Oakworth for two extended visits amounting to three or four months each year. In effect she had two homes, with a managerial role in each of them. This compromise brought to an end the acute phase of their quarrel, but the old tensions regularly resurfaced whenever the couple were separated, up to Isaac's return to Yorkshire in 1860.[18]

The correspondence was not entirely acrimonious. As a couple the Holdens were united by their unquestioning loyalty to the Methodist way of life – the class, the chapel, the preaching, the hymn-singing. Both had been formed in this tradition from birth. In Sarah's family that tradition was reaffirmed by the duly recorded last words of her parents, both youthful converts to Methodism: 'Heaven! Glory! Come!' (her father), and 'I am on the Rock and have firm footing' (her mother).[19] Isaac and Sarah had each won recognition for their leadership qualities – he as a possible candidate for the ministry, she as a class leader. Both took an Evangelical view of the world absolutely for granted. They conducted their social life entirely within the fold of the Methodist community, which was not difficult to do in the West Riding. There Methodists were very thick on the ground: in Bradford the Wesleyans alone amounted to 17.4 per cent of Sunday worshippers in 1851, the second largest group after Anglicans at 23.1 per cent.[20] The devotion of the Holdens to Methodism was a lifelong commitment: in his seventies Isaac was to become a leading lay spokesman for the movement in the House of Commons; Sarah performed a ceaseless round of local engagements which only ended when, aged eighty-six, she caught a fatal chill after opening a bazaar at Haworth.[21]

Furthermore, the nature of Isaac's work – 'masculine' and instrumental though it might seem – was in some ways common ground between them.

Their marriage was one of occupational endogamy, like so many in the business classes of early industrial England. Sarah's brother, Jonas Sugden, headed the family worsted business in Oakworth; the house was close to the mill, and in her forty-odd years of living there Sarah had acquired much knowledge of the business. Indeed, she would have been failing in her duties as a class leader had she not done so. The Wesleyan leadership paid particular attention to the needs of businessmen, and class leaders whose flocks included businessmen were urged to acquaint themselves with their concerns. By the time she married Isaac, Sarah was well versed in the intricacies of worsted manufacture.[22]

The correspondence also reveals not only shared interests in religion and work, but a mutual physical attraction. This would certainly not have been taken for granted in a marriage between two people in their forties – one of them a virgin – with more than a suspicion of business convenience about it. Yet the letters allow no other conclusion. Isaac was the less inhibited of the two. To 'taste in imagination the sweet conjugal feeling' was not enough, he wrote from St-Denis in December 1850; the memory of her 'spirited and affectionate embrace' made him 'long to squeeze you well'. Eighteen months later he wrote, 'I had to go to my solitary couch thinking of you with heart warm and something else as warm. I feel the want of you more than on any former occasion.'[23]

On her side Sarah was not offended by this overtly sexual language. In the privacy of her bedroom at Oakworth, she imagined herself in Isaac's arms, 'entwined in each other's embrace', and she longed for the warmth of his flesh. The marriage carried an erotic charge from the beginning – perhaps even earlier (though hardly any courtship letters survive). There is no sign of sexual guilt in either of them, which is interesting in view of John Wesley's profound discomfort with carnal desire.[24]

At the heart of this correspondence, however, was a disagreement about the nature of home and its claims on husband and wife. Sarah took her stand on two principles. First, she was alarmed at Isaac's devotion to material concerns. One of the issues which Methodist class leaders were expected to address with 'godly jealousy' was the conflict between business and spirit. With that experience behind her, Sarah did not hesitate to remind Isaac of 'the awful danger there is of being too much entangled with the world'. Any man who was prepared to immerse himself in work in a Catholic country was, in her view, far gone in this direction. 'You may think yourself different from other men and feel yourself adequate for what you engage in,' she warned him in 1858, 'but I trust you do not forget that the hand that strikes others is the same that may smite you.' This is surely the tone of the class leader rather than the wife.

In the second place, for Sarah the countervailing influence of home depended not merely on the immediate domestic circle, but on the community of which it formed a part. Sarah felt herself bound to this wider circle by ties of kinship as well as spiritual fellowship. She could not contemplate living without daily access to her brothers and sisters and chapel associates, from whom she derived her 'spiritual enjoyment'. Sarah Holden comes over in this correspondence as self-willed and outspoken, but it would be wrong to interpret her firmness as a bid for independence. Her view of marriage was entirely conventional. When engaged to Isaac, she had looked forward to 'a proper yoke to bear' and disclaimed any wish to be 'a lawless subject'. Her aim in this dispute was not autonomy for herself, but the restoration of the sacred proprieties of life by which they would both benefit. Her sense that his salvation and her own were at stake gave her the power to speak out.[25]

Isaac, on the other hand, was a workaholic in love with his factory. He had only to 'come within the sound of the dear old combing machines' and 'the old passion' came over him, and all other concerns (including his wife waiting for a letter) were forgotten in a moment. The pressing need to 'keep close to the Business' meant that he would not spin out his leisure time at home, or go on holiday, much less visit Sarah at Oakworth or Blackpool. How he ran his business, and where he located it, were matters between him and Divine Providence. 'As a Man of Business,' he told her, 'I enter into the most inviting openings that Providence places before me and remain, with contented mind, till Providence directs my path into a course more desirable' – as comforting a gloss on entrepreneurial ambition as one is likely to find. (In later life Isaac claimed to have been guided to the site of his first French factory by a dream.[26]) Sarah's views were therefore beside the point, however knowledgeable about business she might be. And, while Isaac invoked divine authority for his own preferences, he represented Sarah's attachment to Yorkshire as no more than a selfish desire to have her own way. Providence, it seemed, was profoundly gendered.

But on the question of where Sarah should live, Isaac was more conciliatory. He certainly did not discount the importance of home. His invocation of 'its sweet social intercourse and its reciprocal duties of affection and fidelity' was an impeccably Evangelical sentiment. He knew that he needed a serious Methodist as partner to provide moral ballast to his home, while he got his hands dirty in the business; he needed this both for himself and for his two school-age daughters. As far as Isaac was concerned, all this could be as readily created in France as in England. The fact that in France he must do without the wider local community of the godly counted for little in his mind, since the hectic pace of his life at St-Denis left him no time to enjoy it. Isaac also knew that to live in or near Oakworth, as Sarah demanded, would involve more intercourse than he could tolerate with his in-laws, and especially with the head of the family, Jonas Sugden, whom he disliked intensely. But he refrained from ordering Sarah back to France, as was certainly his marital right. He knew that if she returned to St-Denis, they would probably both be made miserable; whereas if she remained in Yorkshire one at least of them would be content.[27] 'I feel willing to allow *you* to decide when you can *willingly* and cheerfully come to me. . . . Therefore my dear Sarah enjoy yourself so long as you can be happier without me, and do not decide on coming till you can be happy with me.'[28] It was a generous gesture and it worked. Within two weeks Sarah was on her way to France, with the bones of a working compromise agreed. Isaac was temperamentally drawn to a companionate marriage rather than a patriarchal one. He believed instinctively that his wife's autonomy should be respected, and he quickly learned that this was also the path to securing her compliance.

We see here two contrasting views of domesticity grounded in the same quite narrow Evangelical tradition. Methodism furnished the materials for a feminine, as well as a masculine view of the world, and even for a measure of challenge to patriarchal authority. Isaac justified his scale of priorities by citing the guidance of Divine Providence which worked through the actions of *men*. In his eyes this justified a devotion to work and a somewhat narrow conception of domesticity, typical of the self-denying work ethic of first-generation entrepreneurs.[29] Sarah took her stand on what she thought were the higher claims of home, founded on divine prescription and example. In this she echoed a generation of women's Evangelical writing, which asserted the moral prestige of women as guardians of the home, and the moral obligation on men to play their part in home life. The uneasy compromise between these two positions lasted for ten years. The tensions were only resolved when the couple moved back to Yorkshire in 1860. By then Jonas Sugden had died. Isaac and Sarah moved into his house, which Isaac drastically remodelled so that its earlier associations were almost completely erased. The Holdens lived together as an exemplary Methodist couple for another thirty years.

IV

Cornelius Stovin, my third example of Methodist domesticity, was also much preoccupied with the workings of Divine Providence. He could hardly fail to be, given that the prospects of his 600-acre farm at Binbrook in north Lincolnshire depended so much on the vagaries of the weather. Judging by his diary for the 1870s, hardly a day went by without uplifting reflections on the operation of Providence in the world. When his barley crop was drenched for the third time, he speculated that Divine Providence intended to drive him through prayer to more humble dependence on God. When the invention of new machinery undercut the bargaining power of his farm labourers, he exclaimed 'What a kind Providence!' His metaphorical view of the natural world tended in the same direction. Every cornfield, with its cycle of germination, growth and maturity, seemed to him an expression of the Divine plan, and a vivid refutation of the Darwinist heresy.[30]

Unlike Isaac Holden, however, Cornelius Stovin did not need to invoke Providence in order to justify his choice of occupation or his commercial decisions. He was a farmer like his father before him, and his wife, Elizabeth Riggall, was also the daughter of a local farmer. There were no clashes over calling or place of residence. But other causes of friction took their toll. Of the three marriages considered here, this was almost certainly the weakest. Elizabeth came from a wealthier family with expectations which Cornelius could not match. She objected to the poor amenities of Binbrook farm and nagged her husband to demand improvements from the landlord, whereas he would have been content with something 'chastely comfortable'. She complained, as did he, about the poor quality of domestic servants to be found 3 miles from the nearest village. Elizabeth's health was also poor. She was often not strong enough to nurse her growing family herself and frequently retired to her parents' house 20 miles away for extended periods of rest. Cornelius seems not to have anticipated how much he would miss her – perhaps because he had remained a bachelor until the age of thirty-one. He noted in 1875 that he seemed 'to have become so thoroughly domesticated that my happiness is diminished by their absence'. He found it hard to conceal his frustration. He wrote to her during one bitter November: 'You must not forget that your absence detracts from the sweetness and joy of my life. . . . It is cool work entering my empty bedroom at night. You may be sure I wrap round me the bedclothes pretty close. . . . It has been comfortless for me through the night by reason of the cold.'[31]

There was also a significant difference between them in religious loyalties. Like the Holdens, the Stovins had the satisfaction of living in a region which was strongly committed to Methodism: according to Alan Everitt, some 40 per cent of the population of Lincolnshire were connected with it.[32] But whereas Elizabeth belonged to the official Wesleyan church, Cornelius subscribed to the breakaway Free Methodists, who (in rural Lincolnshire at least) tended to be poorer and less worldly. She firmly believed that he could have made more of the farm, had he not given beyond his means to the circuit, and spent so much time as preacher and chapel official. In fact the way in which Cornelius interpreted the call of public duty meant that he was away from home much more than might be expected of a farmer. Apart from preaching engagements and circuit meetings, he was also a Poor Law guardian. These commitments kept him on the road a good deal. He relished the switchback character of his life: 'My career as an agricultural-ist is wildly eccentric. One day I mount the pulpit and platform and pour forth a torrent of rude, sometimes incoherent eloquence. Another day I plunge heart and soul into my dear children's amusements.' In 1875 he summed up his objectives in life as '20 more years of hearty service in the cause of Christ . . . while improving my business, making it more profitable, and my house . . . so that my family may have a good start in life both physically, mentally and spiritually'. What made sense to him as an attempt to lead a godly life in all its manifestations caused friction with his wife.[33] Cornelius was mortified by the lack of real communion between them, for he had elevated ideas about marriage. Years later, when giving a speech to mark the golden wedding of his parents-in-law, he observed that the unity of man and woman was like the fingers of a single hand, rather than two railway carriages coupled together.[34]

The vicissitudes of the Stovin marriage were common enough. More difficult to evaluate is how typical Cornelius's behaviour as a parent was. This was not what we might expect of a Victorian father, much less a devout Methodist. Cornelius conducted family prayers each morning. Like so many fathers, he looked somewhat apprehensively to the future, and he prayed for his children's spiritual as well as their mental advancement. He also looked to their early training in 'self-government', proudly recording how his eldest son Denison began his business career at the age of seven with a commission to spend 4s 6d on groceries in Louth Market.[35] Yet Cornelius's attitude towards his children was anything but joyless and deny-ing. He took an unequivocally Romantic position on the true value of the child. Of his second son Frank, aged two, he wrote in words that might have been inspired by the Lakeland poets: 'He is a splendid divinely con-stituted ray of sunshine to brighten my lonely hours. He laughs and sings and chatters and enjoys life as if he were on the borders of Paradise.' Cornelius was unperturbed by the demands that babies placed on everyone around them. When Frank was a few weeks old, his father remarked in appreciative wonder, 'He seems to have revolutionised the whole household. Every other interest has more or less to bend to his. At present his sway is almost royal.'[36]

Cornelius regularly stepped into the breach to make life easier for his invalid wife. On one occasion in 1874 when Elizabeth was well enough to go to chapel, he stayed at home with the baby. 'While the saints are honouring God in the chapel I will praise him at home,' he wrote. He bottle-fed babies without demur and saw them though the dark watches of the night when they were ill, recreating the model of the 'nursing father' which had been much more common early in the nineteenth century. He was undismayed by displays of temper in his children, knowing that they would soon be succeeded by laughter and joy. There were punishments (unspecified), but the emphasis was on affection: 'Parental discipline does not in the least interfere with or check their buoyancy.' Cornelius believed in self-expression. 'Every kind of innocent playfulness is encouraged,' he wrote, perhaps oblivious that this was in direct contravention of Wesley's killjoy teaching on the subject. Cornelius looked on with pleasure as Frank played with marbles, made 'original and spontaneous remarks' and clambered over the dining-room furniture. Cornelius was what Americans at that time referred to as a 'frolicking father'. He enjoyed a good romp and was to be seen chasing Frank around the kitchen. He took seriously his children's spiritual and moral development, but 'childlike joyousness' remained at the centre of his vision. Nothing could have been more different from Joshua Pritchard's preoccupation with every detail of his daughter's spiritual training.[37]

Some of this fatherly involvement arose from the pressing circumstances of the Stovin household. Because of the servant problem, there was limited scope for delegating childcare. As a result the little ones were not 'imprisoned in the nursery', and they received much more attention from their parents. But there was nothing forced or reluctant about Stovin's performance as an engaged father. It provided the sparks of joy and vitality in what was all too often a life of toil and anxiety. The emotional costs were high as well. When Denison caught scarlet fever at school in 1874, Cornelius feared the worst (as well he might): 'To see him thrown so far out of my own and his dear mother's reach and to have become so complete a burden to his friends shook my manhood. Tears would rush up from the fountain of grief within me. I still feel myself in a fix.' For good or ill, fatherhood was integral to Cornelius's sense of his divinely ordered place in the world, and inseparable from his masculine self.[38]

V

It is sometimes tempting to think of Methodism, like Evangelical Anglicanism, as a 'badge' of class identity. Joshua Pritchard should give us pause. For him the raising of children had little to do with social status and everything to do with his account with God. Domestic life was not a subsidiary interest; it was the very centre of Joshua's emotional and spiritual existence. It was a vital part of that 'recognizable spirituality . . . refined into a recognized culture' which Clyde Binfield has identified as the hallmark of the Wesleyan middle class in Leeds at this time.[39] Of course the cult of the home in Victorian England was a consequence of work being removed from the domestic environment, and of a profound sense of alienation from the city. But in the long run the convergence between the spiritual and the social was crucial. Evangelicalism ennobled work as a struggle carried on in an ungodly world, while at the same time showing how domestic life could comfort and elevate the worker. The home might no longer be the site of production, but its deeper, more moral purpose now became clear.

In drawing religion into the home at the same time as work was being taken out of it, the Methodists greatly intensified the hold of domesticity over the middle class and produced much of its characteristic tone and atmosphere. Methodism, like other forms of Evangelicalism, had its own theological rationale for locating so much religious observance in the home. It was a 'religion of the heart' which valued the spiritual feelings of the individual. The relative intimacy of the small domestic gathering made space for an atmosphere of spiritual fellowship, in which the soul was bared, guidance sought and reproof administered. This new dispensation, it has often been pointed out, enhanced the status of women, since it implied a new spiritual dimension to their traditional role as guardians of the hearth.[40] But there were vital implications for men as well. What bound men to the home, in the early Victorian period especially, was not just the popular ethic of companionate marriage, or the emotional and material needs of the breadwinner, but the conviction that home was the proper place to cultivate one's spiritual well-being. The godly household was a corner of heaven on earth.

When Methodism became more routinized, it retained its domestic bent by making the class the focus of pastoral care and discipline. The class habitually met in private households for the practical reason that, in the early days, there had been nowhere else for it to convene. But the special spiritual intimacy which was possible in a domestic setting soon became its hallmark. In the homely metaphor of one of Wesley's preachers, 'when live coals are put together, the fire burns vehemently; but, when the coals are scattered, the fire dies away'.[41] Even in the Victorian period the leader of the class was often the master or mistress of the house, with the rest of the family (including servants) furnishing the core of the membership. The class which Sarah Sugden had led before her marriage was of this type. In the mid-nineteenth century the chapel tended to become more important than the class – indeed the distinction between them became blurred as class meetings were increasingly held in chapel (as in Stovin's case).[42] But Methodism continued to be, in part at least, a 'felt' religion, with a pronounced emphasis on domestic religious disciplines.[43]

The implications for marriage were far from straightforward. A shared religion was no guarantee of marital harmony. Church teaching on marriage was shot through with contradictions. It could of course be read as a charter for sexual inequality. The Methodists looked back to the unyielding prescription of John Wesley: 'Whoever, therefore, would be a good wife, let this sink into her inmost soul, "My husband is my superior, my better: he has the right to rule over me. God has given it him, and I will not strive against God".'[44] In the theology of most Evangelicals, the ideal was an earthly father who revealed to his children something of the love and mercy of the Almighty himself. But against this old-style patriarchy must be set the commitment of all the Evangelical churches to the power of the moral mother as the foundation of family life. Once home was recognized as the prime site of 'the religion of the heart', the religious standing of the wife was bound to rise. If the husband reflected the authority of the Father in Heaven (often unseen but ever present), the wife stood for Christian love and spiritual intuition. It was an open question, for example, whether the bed-time prayer of mother and child was not more efficacious than the daily family prayers led by the father.[45]

Religion might therefore inform and justify sharply differing interpretations of the marital relationship, even within the same denomination. The enhanced prestige of women, and above all of mothers, gave them potentially great leverage within the home. But, in what seems a strange paradox, even Nonconformists, who took a rigorously non-sacerdotal interpretation of the ministry, referred to the household head as 'priest'.[46] Patriarchal values certainly seem to have had some bearing on the cases discussed here. Each of the husbands possessed acknowledged spiritual authority – Isaac Holden as a possible candidate for the ministry, Cornelius Stovin as a local preacher and Joshua Pritchard as a man who wore his intense spirituality on his sleeve. Consequently the balance of domestic authority was uncertain. Sarah Holden lacked the status of mother, but she had formal religious standing as an experienced class leader. She was also forty-five when she married Isaac. For all these reasons she was able to act independently and force a compromise over where and how they should live. Elizabeth Stovin, on the other hand, received from her husband all the praise and respect due to the mother of seven healthy children. She was less devout than he and had no formal position in chapel, but her views on domestic matters carried weight. Her ill-health and depression were real enough, but they also served to reinforce her case for the radical improvements to the farmhouse which she had set her heart on. Mary Pritchard is an altogether more shadowy figure. Her few surviving letters are short, devout and practical. She appears to have identified completely with Joshua's spiritual regime for the children, borne along by his passionate enthusiasm. In none of these cases do we find that rivalry and tension between mother and father which was so characteristic of Victorian parenting.[47] The essential precondition was a deeply shared religious outlook, which left something to be desired only in the case of the Stovins.

That same religious understanding should have led to a deep disquiet on the subject of sex. John Wesley had rated purity so highly that he never fully endorsed sex within marriage and was very reluctant to perform marriage ceremonies. Something of the founder's doubts is to be seen in Joshua Pritchard's agonizing about the spiritual threat which his exuberance posed to his wife. But there is no trace of this ambivalence in the other two cases. Cornelius Stovin made no bones about hating his empty bed when Elizabeth was away. Isaac and Sarah Holden both employed relatively explicit language to keep their connection alive through repeated separations. There was no sign of sexual guilt. Peter Gay does not make the point in his two-volume study of bourgeois sexuality, but it is worth bearing in mind that a belief in the sacred nature of marriage was not inherently hostile to the enjoyment of sex.[48]

VI

The differences to be found in the three families examined here with regard to child-rearing were even more marked. The nineteenth century is associated primarily with the Romantic idea that childhood is a state which should be enjoyed for itself, and with which adults need to remain in touch if they are to realize their full humanity. From this perspective the Evangelicals have usually had a bad press. They were above all concerned to bring up children to lead disciplined lives and be receptive to God's grace. Unlike the Romantics they attended to the adult in the making, rather than the child in the present. So far from possessing celestial natures, children were born in original sin. The parent's task, as Wesley and countless others asserted, was to break the child's will by enforcing absolute obedience. Moderate Evangelicals emphasized instead the need for nurture based on gradual principles, rather than conversion with its implied damning of all that went before. They preferred the image of bending and shaping, rather than breaking the child's will, and this perspective led them to attend more carefully to the child's feelings. But each strategy exposed the child to intrusive control, of the kind practised by Joshua and Mary Pritchard.[49] Isaac Holden, like many a Methodist father, anxiously awaited news that each child had given his or her heart to God, thus signalling that his main spiritual duty as a parent had been accomplished.[50]

The contrast with the teaching of Rousseau or Wordsworth is obvious enough. But the two systems had something in common all the same. Protective seclusion was vital to both: to the Romantics because children needed a playground beyond the reach of the adult world; to the Evangelicals because children's delicate spiritual state was so vulnerable to corruption. The Congregationalist minister John Angell James captured this dual tradition when he included among the 'blissful associations of home' both 'the nursery of virtue' and 'the playground of childhood'. The logic of Evangelical doctrines about man and salvation was to place children near the centre of domestic attention, just as the Romantic sensibility did for quite different reasons. Infant wills could be neither broken nor shaped without a great deal of time and patience. The child in an Evangelical household faced a constant stream of prayers, readings, catechisms and homilies.[51]

But parent–child interaction was never confined to these serious matters. The reputation for joyless and repressive family life is partly due to the subsequent spread of the externals of Evangelical observance, like family prayers and 'the English Sunday', which could weigh very heavily on the young. At the beginning of the century the Romantic view was still fresh and attractive enough to impinge on the practice of Evangelicals like everyone else. Reminiscences of Evangelical childhood in the heyday of the movement strike a comparatively light note. There was no ban on pleasure for its own sake, only on morally dubious diversions. Parents balanced their inflexible religious routines with playfulness; parties were given and holiday trips undertaken. Evangelicalism was serious-minded but not necessarily killjoy. The eminent Methodist minister Adam Clarke frolicked with his children and wrote them long chatty letters. He was 'both paterfamilias and playmate', as Doreen Rosman has aptly put it. This tradition was still alive fifty years later. G.E. Sargent wrote in 1854 that children's wills needed to be broken, but they should nevertheless be able to invite their father to play with some confidence that he would. Plenty of fathers were happy to follow this advice, though with an ever-decreasing resolve to break wills. Cornelius Stovin's relaxed blend of fatherly guidance and participation in play probably represented the outer limit of what was acceptable. Most Methodists could only have followed his example with considerable strain.[52]

That strain was above all to do with gender, since proper paternal behaviour was an important constituent of manliness. As the ascribed characters of men and women became more polarized in the early nineteenth century, there was less tolerance for paternal behaviour which seemed to encroach on the mother's sphere. The mother's special qualities – her quickness of sympathy, her emotional insight and her moral purity – were defined in ways which tended to disqualify men. This increasingly sharp distinction in parental roles was reflected in a revealing change in vocabulary. There was less talk of 'authority' and much greater emphasis on 'influence' – particularly among moderate Evangelicals, who stressed nurture over time rather than the transformative quality of conversion. Because the child's individuality was now more readily recognized, its upbringing had to be carefully adapted to its particular temperament, requiring observation and flexibility from day to day. Once parenting was seen in these processual, developmental terms, fathers were inevitably sidelined. It followed that the father who trespassed in these domains was abandoning masculine for feminine traits. The home was suspect as a feminine sphere – the softening power of children its most beguiling threat to manhood. Cornelius Stovin, as we have seen, does not appear to have been troubled by such doubts, partly because of his spiritual certainty, and partly because of his grounding in Romantic ways of thought – not to mention his relative isolation. The redeeming power of childhood was to him an article of faith, fully borne out by his daily experiences.[53]

Lastly, mention of an unstable or vulnerable masculinity prompts the question of whether this period saw the appearance of a 'new man'. The phrase was used at the time in two distinct senses. It could mean a man newly risen in the social scale, as when Elizabeth Gaskell described the Congregationalist James Watts in 1855 as 'a new man and a new Mayor' of Manchester.[54] Alternatively the term was applied to someone who had undergone an Evangelical conversion, and whose life showed the fruits thereof in piety, domesticity and a sense of social responsibility. To be a new man in both senses was a passport to respectability and reputation. Leonore

Davidoff and Catherine Hall, who use the term without quotation marks, suggest that middle-class masculinity in this period rested on a new conception of 'calling' and a new relationship with the home.[55] At a broad level this was true. But the three case studies examined here suggest that the relation between these elements was a good deal more unstable than is sometimes assumed. For Isaac Holden, the exigencies of his 'calling' confined the claims of home to a vestigial portion of his life. Cornelius Stovin too was constantly drawn away from wife and family by the self-imposed demands of public life. For Joshua Pritchard, on the other hand, work was an undignified burden, while almost everything of significance in his life took place at home. What seems true in all three cases is that the appeal of home was not just *mediated* through religious idiom; it derived its emotional and spiritual hold from the very distinctive role which Evangelical Christianity accorded to a sanctified domestic sphere. The potential for gender conflict was present here, as it is in any family system. The domesticated religious life both fuelled such conflict and suggested ways in which it might be transcended or repressed.

Notes and references

1 See for example John Gillis, *For Better, For Worse: British Marriages since 1600* (New York, 1985), and Rosemary O'Day, *The Family and Family Relationships, 1500–1900* (London, 1994).

2 M. Jeanne Peterson, *Family, Love and Work in the Lives of Victorian Gentlewomen* (Bloomington, 1989).

3 Leonore Davidoff and Catherine Hall, *Family Fortunes: Men and Women of the English Middle Class, 1780–1850* (London, 1987).

4 A. James Hammerton, *Cruelty and Companionship: Conflict in Nineteenth-Century Married Life* (London, 1992).

5 Davidoff and Hall, *Family Fortunes*, pp. 126–34.

6 Ibid., pp. 180–5, 340–2; Hammerton, *Cruelty and Companionship*, pp. 75–8, 88–90.

7 John Tosh, 'What should historians do with masculinity? Reflections on nineteenth-century Britain', *History Workshop Journal* 38 (1994), pp. 179–202 (see above, Chapter 2); Michael Roper and John Tosh, 'Historians and the politics of masculinity', in Michael Roper and John Tosh (eds), *Manful Assertions: Masculinities in Britain since 1800* (London, 1991), pp. 1–24.

8 Manchester Central Reference Library (hereafter MCRL), Pritchard papers, M375/I/4: Joshua Pritchard to Mary Pritchard, 31 Aug. 1835.

9 MCRL, M375/I/4: Joshua Pritchard to Mary Pritchard, various letters 1835–7, *passim.*

10 MCRL, M375/I/4: Joshua Pritchard to Mary Pritchard, 15 Aug. 1835.

11 MCRL, M375/1/4: Joshua Pritchard to Mary Pritchard, 26 June 1836.

12 MCRL, M375/I/3: Joshua Pritchard, diary for 10 May 1821.

13 MCRL, M375/I/3: Joshua Pritchard, 'Observations on the deportment of Mary Ann' (1820–4).

14 A moving Victorian example is the family of Edward and Mary Benson. See David Newsome, *Godliness and Good Learning: Four Studies on a Victorian Ideal* (London, 1961), ch. 3.

15 MCRL, M375/I/4: Joshua Pritchard to Mary Pritchard, 15 Aug. 1835, 18 Sept. 1836.

16 Henry Abelove, *The Evangelist of Desire: John Wesley and the Methodists* (Stanford, 1990), pp. 99, 108.

17 Elizabeth Jennings, 'Sir Isaac Holden (1807–1897)' (PhD thesis, Bradford University, 1982); John Tosh, 'From Keighley to St-Denis: separation and intimacy in Victorian bourgeois marriage', *History Workshop Journal* 40 (1995), pp. 193–206.

18 Tosh, 'From Keighley to St-Denis'.

19 R.S. Hardy, *Commerce and Christianity: Memorials of Jonas Sugden of Oakworth House* (London, 1857), pp. 15, 20.

20 Theodore Koditschek, *Class Formation and Urban Industrial Society: Bradford 1750–1850* (Cambridge, 1990), pp. 253, 255.

21 Elizabeth Jennings, 'Sir Isaac Holden, Bart (1807–97); his place in the Wesleyan Connexion', *Proceedings of the Wesley Historical Society* 43 (1982), pp. 117–26, 150–9.

22 Wesleyan Conference Office, *A Class Book* (London, n.d.), p. 5.

23 Bradford University Library [hereafter BUL], Holden/21: Isaac Holden to Sarah Holden, 20 Dec. 1850; BUL, Holden/23: same to same, 13 June 1852.

24 BUL, Holden/21: Isaac Holden to Sarah Holden, 20 Dec. 1850; BUL, Holden/23: same to same, 13 June 1852; BUL, Holden/44: Sarah Holden to Isaac Holden, undated (early Nov. 1851); Tosh, 'From Keighley to St-Denis'; Abelove, *Evangelist of Desire*, pp. 49–58.

25 *A Class-Book Containing Directions for Class-Leaders* (London, n.d.); BUL, Holden/21: Sarah Holden to Isaac Holden, 4 Dec. 1850; BUL, Holden/52: Sarah Sugden to Isaac Holden, 6 Oct. 1849.

26 John Hodgson, *Textile Manufacture and Other Industries in Keighley* (Keighley, 1879), p. 116.

27 BUL, Holden/32: Isaac Holden to Sarah Holden, 23 April 1861; BUL, Holden/22: same to same, 10 Jan. 1851; BUL, Holden/21: Isaac Holden to Sarah Holden, 20 Dec. 1850.

28 BUL, Holden/22: Isaac Holden to Sarah Holden, 10 Jan. 1851.

29 Theodore Koditschek, 'The triumph of domesticity and the making of middle-class culture', *Contemporary Sociology* 18 (1989), pp. 178–81.

30 Cornelius Stovin, journal entries for 9 Sept. 1871, 12 July 1872, 22 Aug. 1871, in Jean Stovin (ed.), *Journals of a Methodist Farmer 1871–1875* (London, 1982), pp. 33, 73–4, 26.

31 Cornelius Stovin, journal, 27 Nov. 1874 and 28 April 1875, ibid., pp. 159, 219; Stovin Papers (private collection): Cornelius Stovin to Elizabeth Stovin, 7 and 9 Nov. 1876 (transcripts).

32 Alan Everitt, *The Pattern of Rural Dissent: the Nineteenth Century* (Leicester, 1972), p. 48.

33 Journal for 5 Sept. 1872 and 12 Jan. 1875, in Stovin, *Journals*, pp. 96, 178.

34 Stovin Papers: Journal, 18 March 1890.

35 Journal, 13 Sept. 1871, in Stovin, *Journals*, p. 36.

36 Journal, 22 Jan. 1875 and 1 Oct. 1872, in Stovin, *Journals*, pp. 181, 104.

37 Cornelius Stovin, journal entries for 20 Dec. 1874 (Stovin Papers), 12 Jan. 1875, 11 Feb. 1875, 14 Nov. 1874, 12 Jan. 1875 (Stovin, *Journals*, pp. 178, 190, 152, 177). Abelove, *Evangelist of Desire*, pp. 97–8, 101–2; Doreen Rosman, *The Evangelicals and Culture* (London, 1984), p. 107; Stephen M. Frank, *Life with Father: Parenthood and Masculinity in the Nineteenth-Century American North* (Baltimore, 1998).

38 Cornelius Stovin to Elizabeth Stovin, 14 Nov. 1874, in Stovin, *Journals*, p. 152; Cornelius Stovin, diary, 19 Nov. 1874, ibid., p. 155.

39 Clyde Binfield, '"An optimism of grace": the spirituality of some Wesleyan kinswomen', in Clyde Binfield (ed.), *Saints Revisioned* (Sheffield, 1995), p. 68.

40 Jane Rendall, *The Origins of Modern Feminism: Women in Britain, France and the US, 1780–1860* (London, 1985), ch. 3; Davidoff and Hall, *Family Fortunes*, pp. 155–92; Gail Malmgreen, 'Domestic discords: women and the family in East Cheshire Methodism, 1750–1830', in J. Obelkevich, L. Roper and R. Samuel (eds), *Disciplines of Faith: Studies in Religion, Politics and Patriarchy* (London, 1987).

41 William W. Dean, 'The Methodist class meeting: the significance of its decline', *Proceedings of the Wesley Historical Society* 43 (1981), p. 43.

42 See, for example, Stovin, *Journals*, pp. 28, 119.

43 Leslie F. Church, *The Early Methodist People*, 2nd edn (London, 1949), pp. 153–81; Thomas Shaw, *A History of Cornish Methodism* (Truro, 1967), pp. 21–4; David L. Watson, *The Early Methodist Class Meeting* (Nashville, 1985), chs 4–5.

For an instructive American parallel, see Gregory A. Schneider, *The Way of the Cross Leads Home: the Domestication of American Methodism* (Bloomington, 1993).

44 John Wesley, quoted in Philip J. Greven, *The Protestant Temperament* (New York, 1977), p. 127.

45 Cf. Colleen McDannell, *The Christian Home in Victorian America, 1840–1900* (Bloomington, 1986), pp. 109, 127, 130–5.

46 John Angell James, *The Family Monitor, Or a Help to Domestic Happiness* (Birmingham, 1828), p. 17; Brewin Grant, *The Dissenting World: an Autobiography*, 2nd edn (London, 1869), p. 12.

47 Claudia Nelson, *Invisible Men: Fatherhood in Victorian Periodicals, 1850–1910* (Athens, 1995); John Tosh, 'Authority and nurture in middle-class fatherhood', *Gender & History* 8 (1996), pp. 48–64 (see above, Chapter 6).

48 Abelove, *Evangelist of Desire*, pp. 49–58; Peter Gay, *The Bourgeois Experience, Victoria to Freud*, vols 1–2 (New York, 1984–6).

49 Paul Sangster, *Pity My Simplicity: the Evangelical Revival and the Religious Education of Children, 1738–1800* (London, 1963); Greven, *Protestant Temperament*, pp. 32–43, 156–7; Kathryn Kish Sklar, *Catharine Beacher: a Study in American Domesticity* (New York, 1976), pp. 153, 260.

50 Isaac Holden to Margaret Holden, 26 Nov. 1856, 10 June 1858 and 14 April 1859, in E.H. Illingworth (ed.), *The Holden–Illingworth Letters* (Bradford, 1927).

51 John Angell James, *Female Piety* (1856), quoted in Davidoff and Hall, *Family Fortunes*, p. 115.

52 David Newsome, *The Parting of Friends* (London, 1966), pp. 32–6; Standish Meacham, *Henry Thornton of Clapham* (Cambridge, 1964), pp. 49–53; J.B.B. Clarke (ed.), *An Account of the Infancy, Religious and Literary Life of Adam Clarke*, 3 vols (London, 1833) 2, p. 38; Rosman, *The Evangelicals and Culture*, p. 107; G.E. Sargent, *Home Education* (London, 1854), pp. 16, 26.

53 Sarah Ellis, *The Mothers of England* (London, 1843), pp. 27, 160, 366. See also Nelson, *Invisible Men*, pp. 14–16; Steven Mintz, *A Prison of Expectations: the Family in Victorian Culture* (New York, 1983), pp. 27–39.

54 Quoted in V.A.C. Gatrell, 'The commercial middle class in Manchester, c. 1820–1857' (PhD thesis, Cambridge University, 1971), pp. 44–5.

55 Davidoff and Hall, *Family Fortunes*, p. 113.

PART FOUR

Empire

CHAPTER 8

'All the masculine virtues': English emigration to the colonies, 1815–1852

I

Another letter, and another, and perhaps another, and then my next letter will be dated on the blue, wide ocean, where I can have no answer – and then more than a long weary year must pass away before I can hear from you again.

So wrote Henry Parkes to his sister in Birmingham in February 1839, as he waited in London to embark for Australia. His sister apart, Birmingham held bitter memories. The first two children of Henry and Clarinda Parkes had died in infancy; Henry's parents were old and ill; his own life as a turner had been one of grinding poverty, and he was in debt. Now, at the age of twenty-three, Parkes was resolved to sail with his wife to seek land in New South Wales. The forthcoming voyage, which might last anything from three to five months, loomed large in his thoughts. As he wrote in 'The Emigrant's Farewell to His Country':

I go, my native land, far o'er
The solitary sea,
To regions, where the very stars
Of Heaven will strangers be,

Published here for the first time.

To some untrodden wilderness
Of Australasia's land –
A home, which man has here denied,
I seek at God's own hand.

Solitary the voyage proved to be – 'more solitary and companionless than I ever was in all my life in this stagnant crowd of human beings', as he reflected on board ship.[1]

The evidence for Parkes's emigration may be unusually vivid, its survival owing not a little to his later distinction as a politician in New South Wales. But it reflects experiences which were very widely shared. Between 1815 and 1852 something in the region of half a million people emigrated from England.[2] The majority were drawn from the labouring classes. Tragedy, failure and the pain of parting were the lot of countless emigrants. Their experience belongs to at least three histories. The United States took by far the largest share of emigrants from England, and their contribution to the development of American society has been the subject of some distinguished historical work.[3] The British Empire took a smaller share, perhaps 100,000, but these people had a disproportionate impact on their countries of settlement: emigrants from Britain were the raw material out of which white colonies were constructed in Canada, Australasia and South Africa, and these new societies were indelibly stamped by the experiences of emigration which the settlers brought with them. Lastly – and least considered – emigration was a hugely significant fact in English society – demographically in terms of lost population, and socially in terms of the drastic realignments of family and community. It is true that the English experience of emigration was not as traumatic as that of Ireland or the Scottish Highlands during the same period.[4] But both the numbers of English emigrants and the subsequent strength of the continuing sentimental ties between England and the colonies suggest that emigration was a significant aspect of the English social experience.

Yet, unlike Ireland and Scotland, England's experience of emigration has received only cursory attention from historians. As James Hammerton has put it, emigration has been the 'poor relation' of imperial history.[5] Overseas historians were more concerned with the recruitment of emigrants than with the experiences of the emigrants themselves.[6] Only recently has the link between social conditions in England and the shape of the new societies overseas been closely examined, notably in the work of Robin Haines.[7] Within a metropolitan frame emigration is most often seen as a problem for government policy, and one particularly subject to the influence of economic theory.[8] The standard modern works on nineteenth-century

British history do not dwell on the experience of emigration: some do not mention it at all.[9] Yet the implications of large-scale emigration for our understanding of the mother country are considerable. Empire represented a range of possibilities which emigrants sought to realize; but it is highly unlikely that these aspirations were *confined* to emigrants: they were rather embedded in the social situation which the emigrants were leaving. Emigration concentrated the mind on one's most important priorities and values, throwing into relief what really counted and what could be dispensed with. Hence the decision to emigrate sheds light, not only on the expectations which helped to mould the new societies overseas, but on a range of social attitudes which characterized the old society – attitudes to class, gender, community and empire itself.

To the extent that emigration features in British historiography, it serves as a crude but compelling indicator of economic malfunction and social distress. Consider one of the fullest surviving personal narratives from this period. It was written in the Cape Colony in the 1850s by Jeremiah Goldswain, drawing on the diary he had kept since his teens. In the autumn of 1819 Goldswain, then a seventeen-year-old sawyer, attended a public meeting in Great Marlow about a scheme of assisted emigration to the Cape Colony. The speaker was William Wait, a Middlesex wine-merchant, who had been designated by the Colonial Office as leader of a party of indentured servants. Flanked by the parish overseers of the poor, Wait outlined the conditions that emigrants could expect during their service: a free outward passage, eight hours' work a day and half an acre for cultivation; at the end of six years they would be free, with every prospect of making good. Goldswain had no work and little prospect of any. He decided then and there to emigrate – a bold decision for someone to whom 'nothing purticler' had occurred in his life until then. He would have signed up immediately but for his mother's vociferous opposition. A domestic argument ensued, resolved by a compromise that Goldswain would return home at the end of his indentures. On 26 December the emigrants left Great Marlow, breaking their journey at Hounslow, where Goldswain passed a sleepless night, his mind 'ocupied on former things and thoues that I had left behind'. Next day they boarded the *Zoroaster* at Deptford. South Africa fully came up to expectations. After being released early from his indentures, Goldswain resumed his trade as a sawyer and later went into farming and trading in the Eastern Cape. He married the daughter of another emigrant in 1822. By the time Goldswain died in 1871 he had nine grown-up children and was well respected in settler circles (with a street in Grahamstown named after him).[10]

Stories such as Goldswain's are generally subsumed in a strictly economic interpretation of emigration. His plight mirrored that of countless young men during the recession after the Napoleonic Wars. Many single men took a bleak view of their prospects in England and enlisted in parties like William Wait's. In the Cape Colony they greatly outnumbered young single women.[11] The economic pressure bore even more heavily on young men with families. Many grasped at the opportunity which the Cape of Good Hope seemed to hold out of leaving what one applicant called 'the Cape of Despair in this our Native Land'.[12] When aspiring emigrants petitioned for support from public or charitable bodies, they nearly always stated their case in narrowly material terms, citing 'distress', or the downturn in trade, or rack-renting or unemployment, since this was the surest route to receiving support.[13] But economic betterment is a very blunt instrument with which to capture the motivation of nineteenth-century emigrants. Without it, there would indeed have been little or no emigration. On the other hand, the desire for material improvement was expressed in terms which were permeated by other values and aspirations. In this respect, gender has been almost totally neglected. Yet just as we have come to see the success stories of middle-class men and skilled artisans in gendered terms,[14] so we need to reassess the motivation and mentality of those who cut their losses and opted for the draconian course of emigrating.

The critical questions concern masculinity. Governments and emigration agencies were well aware that a balanced sex ratio was the best foundation for the development of the colonies, and in the case of assisted emigration to Australia between 1831 and 1860 this was actually achieved.[15] But elsewhere there was a marked preponderance of males. Between 1833 and 1837 just under 55,000 adult men disembarked in the Canadian ports of arrival, compared with 34,000 women.[16] Over the century as a whole men comprised around 60 per cent of all emigrants from Britain.[17] In recent years a great deal of scholarship has been devoted to emigrant single women; in the Australian case the point has been reached where we know more about the circumstances of female than male migration.[18] It is also clear that many single women subscribed to an ethic of self-improvement which was little different from that of the men; indeed their success overseas positively depended on developing qualities traditionally thought of as 'masculine'.[19] It is sometimes forgotten, however, that single women were a minority of female emigrants. Most women travelled in family groups, subject to the institutionalized power of husbands, fathers and brothers. William Cobbett may or may not have been correct in saying that emigrant women valued the ties of family and neighbourhood more highly than their menfolk did.[20]

But in the last resort they were not in a position to make the decision or to carry it through. That responsibility usually lay with the head of the household.

In this chapter I aim to explore two dimensions of the relationship between emigration and plebeian masculinity. First, the act of emigration itself required a convincing display of masculine attributes – the qualities of self-reliance and perseverance which were integral to popular under-standings of 'manliness'. Though often written off as failures or misfits, emigrants can with more justice be regarded as among the most energetic and determined of the population. Their momentous and testing decision to quit their native shore was a test of manly character. Secondly, settlement overseas was embraced as a means of achieving the material and social prerequisites of a secure adult masculine status. For the agricultural labourer denied his own land, or the artisan faced with indefinite unem-ployment, the colonies held out economic opportunities which were not only attractive in a material sense, but also carried the prospect of 'inde-pendence'. Jeremiah Goldswain's story illustrates both these dimensions. In running the gauntlet of family opposition, and in braving the ocean for the first time in his life, he showed considerable courage and resolve. And it is a reasonable inference from his account that the economic self-reliance and early marriage which he achieved at the Cape corresponded to his hopes for independence. Emigration both demonstrated masculine potential and was expected to make possible its full realization.

In exploring the emigrant experience, there is no substitute for the writ-ings of the emigrants themselves. Literacy rates were higher among emig-rants than the average in Britain,[21] and archival reclamation has been taken extremely seriously in all of the receiving countries. But in turning to con-sider these materials, it quickly becomes clear that the silence of historians on this topic is, in part at least, due to the reticence of the emigrants them-selves. By the time the youthful emigrant achieved seniority and position overseas, his memories had become part of the collective self-image of the new colonial society. But it was the pioneering days in the colony itself that counted, not life before the voyage out. Settler reminiscences usually make only brief and stereotypic reference to circumstances in the old country. Very few give the kind of detail which might explain the reasons for emig-rating, as Goldswain does. Many begin their account with the voyage itself. It seems that a confident colonial image was incompatible with an honest account of the often painful decision which had changed their life course.[22]

Fortunately settler reminiscences can be supplemented by other sources. The material is uneven and highly dispersed. Three categories have been drawn on in the present study. First, there are the requests made by intending settlers for admission to assisted-emigration schemes. By far the largest surviving body of material dates from 1819, when the Cape scheme attracted widespread interest.[23] These petitions have the merit of having been composed at the moment of decision, but with the drawback of a somewhat formulaic and impersonal approach. Secondly, there are the letters and diaries written by emigrants on board ship or soon after their arrival overseas. These are a wonderfully vivid source, but like the reminiscences composed at a later date, they do not tend to dwell on the pre-emigration past. Emigrants preferred to write about the challenge and promise of the future rather than look back to what they had bidden farewell to.[24] Lastly, a surprising number of emigrants' letters appeared in print soon after being written; they were published in pamphlets or in newspapers by emigration promoters.[25] Historians of the receiving countries have been rightly sceptical about these letters, since they may well have been doctored to give a glowing account of the new life awaiting the emigrant.[26] But their effectiveness as propaganda depended on some correspondence with emigrant aspirations, so they are rather more useful for a study of outward impulses from Britain.

II

Nineteenth-century free emigration has sometimes been characterized as barely one step removed from transportation: the emigrants appear as utterly impoverished people whose destiny was in the hands of the Poor Law authorities concerned to reduce the burden on rate-payers, or landlords who wished to rid their estates of paupers. In fact only a handful of English landlords sponsored emigration schemes, and the best documented, that of Lord Egremont at Petworth, relied on applications rather than direction.[27] As for the parish overseers (and later Poor Law guardians), they certainly had an interest in off-loading paupers overseas, and after 1834 they were permitted to fund emigration from the rates: the outlay on a passage to Canada, for example, was recouped by the saving on outdoor relief in two years. But between 1834 and 1852 the total number of emigrants funded under the New Poor Law was fewer than 25,000.[28] In most years workhouse inmates were not eligible at all.[29]

In fact the authorization for Poor Law guardians to fund emigration was soon followed by the entry of central government into this field, through the Colonial Land and Emigration Commission, set up in 1840. Rather than pay directly for emigrant passages, it suited the Poor Law authorities to put up applicants for the state scheme, but this was at the cost of largely excluding the destitute; since the Commission was funded by the colonial governments, its brief was to send overseas potentially useful colonists rather than unwanted inadequates. The Poor Law authorities did not compel paupers to emigrate; they advertised and then selected from the applicants. The agency of emigrants was thus a crucial dimension. Whether addressed to the squire, or the parish authorities, or the government itself, the letter of application was the essential first step. It might give a full account of the applicant's circumstances; it might seek to persuade by rhetoric – like the joiner who lamented 'drawing an excessive number of blanks' from 'life's uncertain lottery';[30] or it might merely state (as a London cabinet maker did in 1819), 'I live with my Father and Mother there are reduced circumstances and I have a great desire to go.'[31]

No doubt many were placed under informal pressure to emigrate, but their indication of intent was real. It could also be rescinded: emigrants continued to weigh up the odds after their initial application, and they sometimes changed their mind at the last minute.[32] Robin Haines has shown that government-assisted emigrants to Australia between 1831 and 1860 were not 'mere ciphers', but 'well-informed, self-selecting, literate individuals'.[33] Similar conclusions have been reached by Gary Howells in his study of pauper emigrants.[34] Referring to Norfolk, Anne Digby comments that emigrants subsidized by the parish were 'generally enterprising people who disliked being forced to seek poor relief occasionally, rather than inadequate individuals habitually dependent on the Poor Law'.[35] Jeremiah Goldswain was in fact typical. He was under no compulsion to emigrate, nor was he a pauper. His acceptance of indentures had more the character of a stratagem for self-improvement than a surrender to servitude.

Voluntary recourse to emigration implied a plentiful endowment of the sterling virtues. A central aspect of manliness was the core moral values required to make an impression on the world – resolution, courage, perseverance and self-reliance. It would be hard to imagine an enterprise in which these qualities would be at a higher premium than in emigration. As Geoffrey Best has observed, emigration required 'positive moral strength' and a readiness to flout traditional affections, loyalties and attachments.[36] In terms of social status, emigration might be construed as failure – an act of renunciation and withdrawal – and emigration promoters believed that the stigma of defeat deterred some.[37] But in personal terms emigration was an extended test of character. The severance of family ties was particularly demanding. In the second half of the century many emigrants would go to join family members already overseas, but that only became a common experience once a critical mass of emigrants had been reached. Before the 1850s few emigrants could call on existing ties in their country of settlement. The farewell to family and friends was also likely to be permanent, given the cost of unassisted sea passages back home. As we have seen, Jeremiah Goldswain took the decision to emigrate as a gesture of independence *vis-à-vis* his parents, but he was still weighed down by thoughts of 'thoues that I had left behind'. Both he and his mother probably knew that assurances of return were empty. Others were almost overwhelmed by the pain of separation, like Henry Parkes, with whom this essay began. Then came the voyage itself. Many emigrants had never seen the sea before they arrived at port to embark, and hardly any had been on a sea voyage. Yet now they had to come to terms with a steerage berth for voyages of five or six weeks in the case of Canada, and three to five months in the case of Australia.

And what of the countries of destination? Casting a shadow over the whole venture was ignorance about the alien lands that emigrants were destined for. Later in the century, the typical emigrant would leave to take his place in an established British community overseas. But during the first half of the century such communities were in the making, and the imprint of metropolitan culture was thin. What the aspiring settler could anticipate was much less reassuring. The promoters of emigration sought to raise expectations by sponsoring official guide books and by publishing letters from previous emigrants. As noted already, literacy rates among emigrants were higher than the average, and these publications were certainly read.[38] But it is unlikely that they assuaged the multiplicity of fears which emigration aroused, and there was competition from more critical accounts.[39] Climate and health were a major concern. Disturbing fantasies of the colonial 'other' readily came into play, and were projected onto the indigenous population ('the ungrateful savage') as well as the world of nature ('red in tooth and claw'). Above all, there were deep anxieties about gaining acceptance in colonial society and replacing the bonds of community which had been severed back home. Henry Parkes had heard that Sydney was a town where 'everyone is taught only to take care of himself', and on arrival he was to find himself entirely friendless.[40] That theme of sturdy individualists who had learned to shift for themselves would become one of the founding myths of the emerging white settler communities overseas. The emigration propagandist Christopher Hursthouse was hardly stretching the point when he wrote in 1857, 'emigration is a career which calls for pluck, bottom, energy, enterprise, all the masculine virtues'.[41]

III

If the decision to emigrate was proof of manly fortitude, the benefits of settlement overseas were most often summed up in terms of another cardinal feature of masculinity – 'independence'. Charlotte Erickson has made a similar point in relation to British emigration to the USA during the same period,[42] but she has not explored its implications for masculine identity. At root independence meant the ability to live by an honest occupation, and by one's own energy (and the labour of one's family). Hence men were vitally concerned not only with how much they could earn, but *how* it would be earned: one should aim to be architect of one's own fortunes, or, as one Natal emigrant put it, 'captain on my own quarter deck'.[43] The working-class man sought to maintain his dependants without assistance, and to keep the Poor Law at bay in his old age. Heading a household and providing fully for its material needs were the nub of independence. Sarah Greenwood confided her anxieties on this score to her grandmother on the eve of her departure for New Zealand in 1841: 'after a struggle of five years during which my poor Husband has *never* felt the satisfaction of saying "I am supporting my family", you may well suppose that our labours would be sweet indeed if attended by any success'.[44] Such aspirations were in tune with the emigration schemes of the day. As Dudley Baines has pointed out, the first half of the century was *par excellence* the era of 'folk' or family migration,[45] when men sought to create overseas the independent household which appeared beyond their grasp at home.

The colonial governments who funded assisted passages from the 1830s onwards preferred young married couples to all other applicants. The next best candidate was the healthy, young, single man whose ambitions were directed towards achieving independence in the conventional sense of acquiring land and reproducing domestic patriarchy. Unassisted emigration showed a comparable bias in favour of family groups. According to Charlotte Erickson's work on shipping lists, the percentage of English and Welsh migrants to the USA travelling in family groups was 76.6 in 1831 and 71.9 in 1841.[46] The evidence for colonial destinations is less comprehensive, but it points the same way. Of the 1,012 passengers who sailed from Plymouth under the auspices of the New Zealand Company between 1840 and 1842, only 4 per cent travelled without kin.[47] In the case of government-assisted arrivals from England in New South Wales between 1848 and 1860, 81 per cent travelled in family groups.[48] There was a strong link between emigration and marriage prospects which accorded with working-class notions of manliness. Of course emigration did not exclude 'persons who had hung loose on society', as the Cape settler Thomas Pringle put it.[49] But men who were committed to the single life, or who lacked the energy to establish an independent household, were not encouraged. As Edward Gibbon Wakefield said of New Zealand, 'a new colony is a bad place for a young *single* man. To be single is contrary to the nature of a new colony, where the laws of society are labour, peace, domestic life, increase and multiply.'[50]

Traditionally the surest foundation of independence was land. During the first half of the century, before the gold rushes and the rise of the colonial city, the promise of a small-holding was by far the most significant material inducement to emigrate. Most emigrants were landless. Some were alienated townsmen, like those who were attracted to the ill-fated Chartist Land Plan in the 1840s.[51] Some were tenant farmers at the mercy of variable rents and insecurity of tenure. The majority were landless labourers in rural areas. Hence the language of emigration promoters is heavily laced with the image of the yeoman farmer. James Methley was both an emigrant to Natal and an influential propagandist:

Your bread tastes doubly sweet when you think that you first turned over the virgin soil, put in the seed, and reaped the first crops from the land which is to support future generations. When you pluck the first ripe fruit from the trees you planted, and see comfort and plenty springing up around, you feel a fresh accession of dignity, as you consider that it was by your unaided effort that all this was accomplished.[52]

J.S. Christopher extolled the virtues of South Africa in similar terms:

There is a land with sunny skies,
Where gold for toil is giving,
Where every brawny arm that tries
Its strength, can grasp a living . . .
Where every arm that clears a bough
Finds plenty in attendance;
And every furrow of the plough
A step to independence.[53]

Many emigration schemes, like the Cape in 1819, promised an outright grant of land. One navvy who sailed for Natal in 1849 was reported as saying that, being 'a tolerable fist at the spade', his 20-acre holding would enable him to 'live the life of an independent person'.[54] More established colonies like those in Canada and Australia did not have land to give away; instead they emphasized how cheap land was, and how quickly it could be

purchased by an industrious immigrant. Australia in particular was represented in the 1830s and 1840s as an agrarian Arcadia where traditional standards of masculine independence lay within the settler's grasp.[55] Nature was
thought to be bountiful, land free of tenurial restrictions, and labour fairly
rewarded. The most common image was of virgin bush, to be cleared by the
settler's own exertion, which set the seal on his entitlement.[56] Prospective
settlers were not told whether the land was also 'free' in the sense of being
uncontested, or what had happened to its previous occupiers. Emigrants were
in some cases attracted to South Africa on account of its cheap indigenous
labour, but they knew nothing of how those workers had been dispossessed.
In 1852 the *Bedfordshire Times* published a letter from a Natal settler which
expressed his grief at the thought of 'the poor starving people in England
while this beautiful land is laying [sic] waste'.[57] To prospective emigrants
in Britain the process of white conquest was rendered invisible.

This promise of freely available land was highly seductive, both to the
oppressed agricultural labourer and the alienated townsman. For young
men especially, a productive freehold farm was the surest sign of full adult
status. Joseph Silcox reported in 1831 that the young men of his settlement
would not return to England even if they were offered a 200-acre farm rent-
free; they preferred to stay in Canada, working their own land.[58] Some
emigrants went ahead of their families to determine whether the idyll was
grounded in reality, and then urged their dependants to follow them. Robert
Slade wrote to his wife from Canada in 1834: 'We have no landlord to come
at Michaelmas, to say I want my rent; no poor-rates to pay; we are in a free
country. It is a pretty thing to stand at one's own door and see a hundred
acres of land of his own.'[59] Others went single and then married as soon
as they had come by the means to support a wife. George Menzies, writing
from Canada in 1834, offered this advice to those back home: 'Go to *the
Bush*, with a strong arm, a light heart, and, if possible, a few sovereigns in
your pocket – and there with your axe . . . Clear away for yourself a site for
an "abiding place", where, in a few years, you may, if you will, be independent.'[60] Letters like this from Canada were all reproduced in promotional
literature, and they doubtless presented a somewhat one-dimensional
picture of settler life. But they indicate clearly one of the main attractions
of emigration.

Even in the heyday of cheap colonial land, not all emigrants were looking for a farm of their own. Many working men wanted to reverse the decline
in their conditions of employment and their status as artisans. As one
emigrant bound for Australia remarked in 1849, 'in England masters were
a deal too saucy, and did not know how to treat the working man'.[61]

Many were looking to realize the ideal of the independent working man – respected by his peers, treated with due consideration by his master, and paid a fair wage with which to support a family in dignified domesticity.[62] In the colonies labour of all kinds was in short supply, from the skilled crafts-man to the day-labourer, and wages were high. Moreover, the invidious social distinctions of the home country were far less in evidence. The result was a rough-and-ready equality. 'Jack is as good as his master here. I tell you the truth as I find it. We are all as one here,' wrote an emigrant labourer in Canada.[63] But it was Australia which enjoyed the highest reputation as a haven for the independent working man from the 1840s onwards. The eight-hour day, first introduced in the Melbourne building trades in 1856, symbolized Australia's reputation in this respect – as did the coming of man-hood suffrage in South Australia the same year. Among Chartist émigrés Australia was the only destination that could vie with the United States. 'Here the master and man turn out together, and go to their day's work and do it cheerfully,' wrote one migrant from Adelaide in 1847.[64] 'I can say I am independent of the world for I work when I like and I play if I like,' said another.[65] This was the moral economy which approximated most closely to the aspirations of the skilled artisan in Britain.

For many youngsters independence in this material sense was almost indistinguishable from independence in the familial sense. Unemployment or lack of access to apprenticeship not only pointed to a life of poverty; it also held out the humiliating prospect of continuing dependence on the older generation. Jeremiah Goldswain's most telling language was devoted to his struggle to free himself of parents, fired by the conviction that 'at my age I could do sumthing for myself'. On the night of the public meet-ing at which he heard about the Cape emigration scheme, he threatened to leave his parents for ever if they did not stop weeping. As an only child, Goldswain was open to the charge of ingratitude and lack of filial duty. The full resources of the family were mobilized against him by his mother. He might have given in, but for the unexpected support of an uncle who urged him to 'tuck care of number one as he had don' and gave him some money. Goldswain's early marriage in the Cape suggests an ambition to achieve full adult manhood as soon as possible.[66] Older emigrants still living under the parental roof must have experienced an even greater sense of urgency. William Pilkington, a farmer and butcher, was twenty-nine and still living under the paternal roof when he wrote to the organizer of the Nottinghamshire emigrants to the Cape complaining of the treatment he received from his father.[67] Whatever else it offered, emigration could be a dramatic way for sons to signal their autonomy from paternal authority.

IV

The notion that emigration to the colonies might be the making of manhood could be understood in different ways, but physical strength was fundamental. It is often forgotten that the primary, traditional meaning of 'manliness' was strength and vigour of body. Whatever moral gloss churchmen tried to impose on it, manliness retained its physical associations in nineteenth-century common culture.[68] The body was the seat of force and energy, the prerequisite for action and impact on the world. A 'manly figure' was athletic and robust; 'manly exercises' were the most commendable leisure pursuit; to be weak or sickly or impotent was to be less than a man. In many walks of life in early industrial Britain men were acutely aware of this danger. A feared loss of manhood was one expression of the alienation of labour, be it in the factory, the field or the office. As one advice manual put it in 1838, competition between one man and another was leading Englishmen to 'seriously hurt their constitutions by working beyond their strength'.[69] The colonies were constructed as a place where men would be liberated from these debilitating circumstances. Empire was quintessentially the sphere of physical manliness. It was widely depicted as a strenuous open-air life, requiring energy, resilience and physical adaptability.

To some commentators in the early Victorian period, the promise of vigour was reason enough to encourage emigration. Thomas Carlyle looked forward to a time when sons would be hardened into men 'by the sun of Australia or the frosts of Canada'.[70] But what mattered to the mass of poor emigrants was not climate but diet. Almost all the published letters home from newly arrived settlers speak of high wages and cheap food, especially meat, and this prospect clearly framed the expectations of emigrants. As one agricultural labourer from Wiltshire put it in 1851, 'Off we go to Adelaide, as fast as we are able. / Beef and mutton we expect to see upon the table'.[71]

Meat consumption was also enhanced by the freedom to hunt. Most emigrant destinations were rich in game. It is worth remembering that, beneath the level of the landed class, Englishmen were a nation of frustrated hunters. For countrymen the game laws defined most kinds of hunting as poaching, with heavy penalties. For first-generation townsmen hunting was often the country pursuit most missed. Newly arrived settlers in Canada could not quite believe their luck. 'I am at liberty to shoot turkeys, quail, pigeon, and all kinds of game which I have in my backwood', wrote a day-labourer from Wiltshire.[72] 'I can take my gun and go a-shooting, as well as any of the farmer's sons; and we can go a-fishing when we please, and when we are hunting we don't have no need to be afraid of the gamekeeper,' wrote another Canadian settler to his son in England in 1850.[73] Hunting was emphasized in colonial prospectuses. The intending emigrant to South Africa was told by *Sidney's Emigrant's Journal* in 1848 that 'No officious gamekeeper calls upon him to surrender his gun, partridge or hare, every wild animal being considered the property of all'.[74] Emigrants keenly anticipated a hunting free-for-all, and those who could afford to purchased guns before leaving home.[75] The rapid depletion of game in the Eastern Cape during the 1820s is a measure of the settlers' enthusiasm for hunting.[76] Plentiful game and cheap joints of meat held out the prospect of better health and enhanced masculine vigour.

V

After 1852 the character of colonial emigration changed. The discovery of gold in Australia, and the ensuing gold rushes elsewhere in the empire, not only swelled the number of emigrants, but raised the proportion of single men at the expense of married couples. The proportion of emigrants receiving assisted passages rapidly dwindled. Improved sea communications (especially the rapid expansion of steam) made return emigration much more feasible. The growth of juvenile adventure literature in Britain endowed emigration with a much more romantic glow. All these factors made for a more mobile and restless emigrant population.[77] Between 1815 and 1852, however, colonial emigration attracted a steadier type. Its appeal lay in the opportunity it seemed to offer, to young men overwhelmingly, of achieving a fully adult masculinity which was recognized as such both at home and in the new social environment. For some, the colonies offered the prospect of full health and vigour; for others, the material means of independence, whether through land-holding or properly rewarded labour. For single males the colonies meant emancipation from the constraints of a cadet status back home; for those with children the colonies were more likely to provide the conditions in which their own manhood might be reproduced in their sons. Colonial emigration was seldom embraced with unqualified enthusiasm: too little was known about the destination in most cases, and too much had to be surrendered at home. But both the aspiration to emigrate and the experience of emigration were constructed in essentially masculine terms. Empire-building was man's work; the colonies were a man's world; and manhood might be secured or enhanced by becoming a colonist.

Emigration was an inescapable social fact in nineteenth-century Britain. Most people either had the experience of saying farewell to family members, or knew others who had done so. As Andrew Hassam points out, groups of emigrants with all their luggage must have been a familiar sight on trains, in railways stations and at ports.[78] Yet this upheaval left only a small cultural residue, and particularly among the labouring classes who supplied the bulk of the emigrants. Both the soldier and the missionary were culturally visible because each was dignified as part of a national epic. Emigration did not have that public resonance: its connection with a national project was more tenuous; it exemplified the individual virtues of self-help and improvement rather than the preferred heroic attributes. Public culture gave scant recognition. Emigration by the labouring classes featured in the work of some novelists, for example Kingsley and Dickens, but it was marginal to working-class cultural forms.[79]

This cultural lacuna did not, however, mean that emigration was lost from view. The social memory of emigration survived not so much in public culture as in the atomized form of personal correspondence. By the 1880s few families in Britain did not have relatives living in the colonies, and the rapid improvement in postal communications in the same period meant that they were in closer contact with them than ever before. The colonies were associated in the popular mind with a resilient masculinity, on which the destiny of departing sons or brothers depended; and the association grew stronger over time as their kinsmen overseas made a success of their lives. The significance of that link in forming popular attitudes towards the empire should not be underestimated. Imperial sentiment in Britain was founded not only on jingo notions of military superiority but on the global spread of the British people. The figure of the departed emigrant cast a long shadow.

Notes and references

1 Henry Parkes, *An Emigrant's Home Letters* (Sydney, 1897), pp. 58, 83, 150.

2 Before 1853 all British emigration statistics are flawed. So far as English emigration is concerned, estimates range from 430,000 for the years 1815–50 in Imre Ferenczi, *International Migrations* (New York, 1929), vol. II, p. 99, to 662,143 for the years 1811–51 in E.A. Wrigley and R.S. Scofield, *The Population History of England, 1541–1871* (London, 1981), pp. 219–23. See also Dudley Baines, *Migration in a Mature Economy: Emigration and Internal Migration in England and Wales, 1861–1900* (Cambridge, 1985), pp. 58, 299–300.

3 Notably by Charlotte Erickson; see her *Invisible Immigrants: the Adaptation of English and Scottish Immigrants in Nineteenth-Century America* (London, 1972),

and *Leaving England: Essays on British Emigration in the Nineteenth Century* (Ithaca, 1994).

4 On Ireland, David Fitzpatrick, *Oceans of Consolation: Personal Accounts of Irish Migration to Australia* (Cork, 1994) is a superb work of historical recovery. On Scotland, see Eric Richards, *A History of the Highland Clearances*, 2 vols (Beckenham, 1985) and Marjory Harper, *Adventurers and Exiles: the Great Scottish Exodus* (London, 2003).

5 A. James Hammerton, 'Gender and migration', in Philippa Levine (ed.), *Gender and Empire*, Oxford History of the British Empire: Companion Series (Oxford, 2004), pp. 247–81.

6 Thus Helen Woolcock, *Rights of Passage: Emigration to Australia in the Nineteenth Century* (London, 1986) displays almost no curiosity about the motives and mentality of the emigrants.

7 Robin Haines, *Emigration and the Labouring Poor: Australian Recruitment in Britain and Ireland, 1831–60* (Basingstoke, 1997). For the later period, Rollo Arnold, *The Farthest Promised Land: English Villagers, New Zealand Immigrants of the 1870s* (Wellington, 1981), is a fine study.

8 For example, H.J.M. Johnston, *British Emigration Policy, 1815–1830* (Oxford, 1972).

9 For example, J.V. Beckett, *The Agricultural Revolution* (Oxford, 1990); John Belchem, *Industrialization and the Working Class: the English Experience, 1750–1900* (Aldershot, 1991).

10 Una Long (ed.), *The Chronicle of Jeremiah Goldswain* (Cape Town, 1946), vol. I, pp. 1–6.

11 Winifred Maxwell, *Reconsiderations* (Grahamstown, 1970), p. 13. Cf. Wendy Cameron *et al.*, *Assisting Emigration to Upper Canada: the Petworth Project, 1832–37* (Montreal, 2000), pp. 87–9, 92, 94; John Clark, *Natal Settler-Agent: the Career of John Moreland, Agent for the Byrne Emigration Scheme of 1849–51* (Cape Town, 1972), app. I.

12 Henry Holland to E.S. Godfrey, 18 Oct. 1819, Nottingham Record Office, QACP/5/1/4.

13 See for example the hundreds of petitions to the Colonial Office in 1819. PRO CO 48/41–46.

14 Leonore Davidoff and Catherine Hall, *Family Fortunes: Men and Women of the English Middle Class, 1780–1850* (London, 1987); Sonya O. Rose, *Limited Livelihoods: Gender and Class in Nineteenth-Century England* (London, 1992).

15 Haines, *Emigration and the Labouring Poor*, pp. 31–3.

16 Cameron, *Assisting Emigration*, p. 90.

17 Baines, *Migration in a Mature Economy*, pp. 163, 184. In Irish emigration, on the other hand, the sexes were much more evenly balanced.

18 A. James Hammerton, *Emigrant Gentlewomen: Genteel Poverty and Female Emigration, 1830–1914* (London, 1979); Rita S. Kranidis, *The Victorian Spinster and Colonial Emigration* (Basingstoke, 1999); Janine Gothard, *Blue China: Single Female Migration to Colonial Australia* (Melbourne, 2001).

19 Gothard, *Blue China*, p. 21.

20 William Cobbett, *The Emigrant's Guide* (London, 1829), pp. 33–6. Robin Haines has tentatively suggested that women may have been the prime movers in the drive to improve their families' prospects overseas, but she does not address the structure of relations between spouses. Haines, *Emigration and the Labouring Poor*, pp. 256–7.

21 Haines, *Emigration and the Labouring Poor*, pp. 70, 254–5.

22 This point is most clearly borne out in the individual settler histories requested in 1893 by the government of Natal from all survivors of the 1849–51 migration. Bird Papers A79, Natal Archives, Pietermaritzburg.

23 PRO CO 48/41–46. There is also a smaller collection in Nottingham Record Office, QACP/5/1.

24 See for example Andrew Hassam, *Sailing to Australia: Shipboard Diaries by Nineteenth-Century British Emigrants* (Manchester, 1994).

25 For example, *Emigration: Letters from Sussex Emigrants* (London, 1835, 1837); 'Wiltshire emigrants to Canada', *Quarterly Review* 46 (1832), pp. 349–90; Poulett Scrope (ed.), *Extracts of Letters from Poor Persons who emigrated last year to Canada and the United States* (London, 1831); 'A bundle of emigrants' letters', *Household Words* 1 (1850), pp. 19–24.

26 See the useful discussion in Wendy Cameron *et al.*, *English Immigrant Voices: Labourers' Letters from Upper Canada in the 1830s* (Montreal, 2000), pp. xxxv–xxxix.

27 Cameron, *Assisting Emigration*.

28 Haines, *Emigration and the Labouring Poor*, p. 115.

29 Ibid., pp. 135–40, 253.

30 Ralph Goddard to Colonial Office, 24 Aug. 1819, repr. in G.M. Theal, *Records of the Cape Colony*, vol. 12 (Cape Town, 1902), p. 292.

31 John Scott to Colonial Office, 29 July 1819, PRO CO 48/45.

32 Cameron, *Assisting Emigration*, p. 100.

33 Haines, *Emigration and the Labouring Poor*, p. 6.

34 Gary Howells, ' "For I was tired of England, sir": English pauper emigrant strategies, 1834–60', *Social History* 23 (1998), pp. 181–94.

35 Anne Digby, *Pauper Palaces* (London, 1978), p. 101.

36 Geoffrey Best, *Mid-Victorian Britain, 1851–73* (London, 1979), p. 147.

37 For example, *Counsel for Emigrants, with Original Letters from Canada and the United States* (Aberdeen, 1834), p. 21.

38 Howells, ' "For I was tired of England" ', pp. 189–90.

39 For example, *Hints and Observations on the Disadvantages of Emigration to British America* (London, 1833); Susanna Moodie, *Roughing It in the Bush* (London, 1852).

40 Parkes, *Emigrant's Home Letters*, pp. 47, 98, 119.

41 Charles Hursthouse, *New Zealand or Zealandia, the Britain of the South* (London, 1857), p. 637.

42 Charlotte Erickson, *Invisible Immigrants: the Adaptation of English and Scottish Immigrants in Nineteenth-Century America* (London, 1972), p. 72.

43 George Russell, autobiography (1873), MS in Killie Campbell Library, Durban.

44 Frances Porter and Charlotte MacDonald (eds), *'My Hand Will Write What My Heart Dictates': the Unsettled Lives of Women in Nineteenth-Century New Zealand* (Auckland, 1996), p. 63.

45 Dudley Baines, *Emigration from Europe, 1815–1930* (Basingstoke, 1991), pp. 43–7.

46 Charlotte Erickson, 'Emigration from the British Isles to the USA in 1841: Part I', *Population Studies* 43 (1989), p. 362.

47 Raewyn Dalziel, 'Emigration and kinship: migrants to New Plymouth, 1840–43', *New Zealand Journal of History* 25 (1991), pp. 112–28.

48 Haines, *Emigration and the Labouring Poor*, p. 34.

49 Thomas Pringle, *Narrative of a Residence in South Africa* (Cape Town, 1966, first pub. 1835), pp. 12–13.

50 E.J. Wakefield (ed.), *The Founders of Canterbury* (Christchurch, 1868), p. 255.

51 Joy MacAskill, 'The Chartist Land Plan', in Asa Briggs (ed.), *Chartist Studies* (London, 1959), pp. 304–41.

52 James Methley, *The New Colony of Port Natal*, 3rd edn (London, 1850), p. 39.

53 J.S. Christopher, *Natal, Cape of Good Hope* (London, 1850), pp. 6–7.

54 John Moreland, shipboard diary, 14 July 1849, Killie Campbell Library, MSS A1273.

55 Coral Lansbury, *Arcady in Australia: the Evocation of Australia in Nineteenth-Century English Literature* (Melbourne, 1970), esp. pp. 52, 84; David Goodman, *Gold Seeking: Victoria and California in the 1850s* (Sydney, 1994), pp. 105–11.

56 See for example *Counsel for Emigrants . . . Concerning British America, the United States, and New South Wales* (Aberdeen, 1838), p. 38.

57 Quoted in Robin Haines and Ralph Shlomowitz, 'Emigration from Europe to colonial destinations: some nineteenth century Australian and South African perspectives', *Itinerario* 20 (1996), p. 142.

58 Scrope, *Extracts of Letters*, pp. 19–20.

59 *Quarterly Review* 54 (1835), p. 428.

60 George Menzies, letter from Chippawa, Upper Canada, in *Counsel for Emigrants* (1838), p. 38.

61 Quoted in Keith Pescod, *Good Food, Bright Fires and Civility: British Emigrant Depots of the Nineteenth Century* (Melbourne, 2001), p. xiv.

62 Keith McClelland, 'Masculinity and the "representative artisan" in Britain, 1850–80', in Michael Roper and John Tosh (eds), *Manful Assertions: Masculinities in Britain since 1800* (London, 1991), pp. 74–91.

63 L.M. Springall, *Labouring Life in Norfolk Villages* (London, 1936), p. 145.

64 Ibid., p. 143.

65 William Wingate (1855), quoted in Haines, *Emigration and the Labouring Poor*, p. 258.

66 Long, *Chronicle*, I, pp. 2–6.

67 William Pilkington to E.S. Godfrey, 24 Oct. 1819, Nottingham Record Office, QACP/5/1/4.

68 See Anna Clark, *The Struggle for the Breeches: Gender and the Making of the British Working Class* (London, 1995).

69 *Counsel for Emigrants* (1838), p. 22.

70 The phrase was actually Froude's, but credited to Carlyle. J.A. Froude, *Oceana* (London, 1886), pp. 132–3.

71 Quoted in Mark Baker, 'Some early Wiltshire emigrants to Australia', *The Hatcher Review* 2:17 (1984), p. 332.

72 Scrope, *Extracts of Letters*, pp. 14–15.

73 S.F. Surtees, *Emigrants' Letters from Settlers in Canada and South Australia Collected in the Parish of Banham, Norfolk* (London, 1852), pp. 8–9.

74 *Sidney's Emigrant's Journal*, 12 Oct. 1848, p. 13.

75 For example, John Ayliff, *The Journal of 'Henry Hastings', Albany Settler* (Grahamstown, 1963, first pub. 1847), p. 32.

76 Maxwell, *Reconsiderations*, p. 15; pers. comm., Steve Kotze, 26 August 2002.

77 See Baines, *Migration in a Mature Economy*.

78 Hassam, *Sailing to Australia*, p. 47.

79 For the place of emigration in melodrama and music hall, see J.S. Bratton *et al.*, *Acts of Supremacy: the British Empire and the Stage, 1790–1930* (Manchester, 1991), pp. 6–7.

CHAPTER 9

Manliness, masculinities and the New Imperialism, 1880–1900

I s there anything left to be said about the New Imperialism? So much has been written since the seminal analysis of J.A. Hobson in 1902 that the law of diminishing returns has surely begun to apply. In fact there is a striking imbalance in the scholarly literature. Most studies have concerned the politics and economics of colonial expansion. Yet the novelty of the New Imperialism lay not only in the feverish pace of overseas annexations, or in the tense atmosphere of international competition, but in the marked appetite of the British public for conquest, combat and heroism. That popular appetite was not only culturally significant in its own right; it was one of the conditions of a confident imperialist stance by Britain overseas. As Hobson argued, imperialism at this period served the interests of only a small powerful elite, which made it all the more crucial that there was what J.S. Bratton has called a 'psychological pay-off' for the nation at large.[1] Between the early 1880s and the conclusion of the South African War twenty years later, the empire occupied a more prominent place in the national psyche than before or since. This was the period when the death of Gordon evoked national mourning; when the relief of Mafeking was riotously celebrated in many cities; when military men like Roberts, Kitchener and Baden-Powell were household names; and when the advancing tide of pink on the map was a matter of widespread pride. Yet very little historical work has focused on what the empire really meant to the British people – on which social groups supported empire and why, and what impulses carried such large numbers of British people overseas. There has been an inconclusive and for the most part superficial debate about the impact of imperial propaganda on the lower classes,[2] and there is now a voluminous

Published here for the first time.

post-colonial literature on the place of empire in elite literary culture.[3] This is a scarcely adequate response to a major cultural theme with wide-ranging social implications.

In these debates gender has certainly not been ignored. A good deal is now known about the extent of women's commitment to – and revulsion from – the imperial project.[4] But surprisingly little attention has been paid to the terms in which the empire appealed to men.[5] More than most areas of national life, empire was seen as a projection of masculinity. As Joanna de Groot has put it, 'manliness and empire confirmed one another, guaranteed one another, enhanced one another, whether in the practical disciplines of commerce and government or in the escape zones of writing, travel and art'.[6] Kelly Boyd concurs with regard to one of those 'escape zones', boys' story papers.[7] There was a striking convergence between the language of empire and the language of manliness: both made much of struggle, duty, action, will and 'character'.[8] Given that masculinities in Britain were being placed under a variety of pressures in this period, it seems highly improbable that men's support for imperialism was unaffected. This proposition needs to be tested against the recorded experience of those who emigrated to the colonies or pursued their careers there. That task is still to be done. My purpose here is to suggest a framework of interpretation through a reappraisal of the secondary literature.

language of manliness & empire close

Empire was a man's business. By this I do not mean that men possessed an imperial monopoly, or that the empire aroused no interest in the other sex. Both missionary work and female emigration attracted a great deal of attention from women in late Victorian and Edwardian Britain.[9] Yet these concerns made comparatively few inroads on the construction of British imperialism, which, as Clare Midgley has pointed out, was 'an essentially masculine project'.[10] Empire was a man's business in two senses: its acquisition and control depended disproportionately on the energy and ruthlessness of men; and its place in the popular imagination was mediated through literary and visual images which consistently emphasized positive male attributes. Running through the history of the British Empire (as of other empires, no doubt) was the commonplace that overseas expansion depended on manpower, and on the supply of men of a certain type – practical, resourceful and self-reliant. Conversely, men who chose colonial careers or set off in search of adventure overseas were making a statement about their masculinity. Empire was, in a fundamental sense, a test of the nation's virility.

some female import

Two arguments can be made about gender and the New Imperialism. The first or 'weak' argument is that a heightened awareness of opportunities and threats overseas induced a harsher definition of masculinity at home;

if the empire was in danger, men must be produced who were tough, realistic, unsqueamish and stoical. A sense of crisis overseas prompted efforts to increase the appeal of imperial careers in the eyes of the young, especially by recasting the approved attributes of manliness.[11] The second or 'strong' argument reverses the relationship between imperialism and masculinity by locating the primary sense of crisis, not in the empire, but in the pattern of gender relations within Britain itself. According to this perspective, enthusiasm for the empire at the end of the century was a symptom of masculine insecurity within Britain. Anxieties which had their root at home could be displaced onto the empire as a site of unqualified masculinity, and both career choices and ideological loyalties were influenced as a result.[12] My suggestion here is that paradoxically both of these dynamics were working at once — that pessimistic appraisals of masculinity and of the empire played off each other in mutually reinforcing ways which powerfully conditioned the popular response to empire.

I

During the era of the New Imperialism the empire was widely perceived to be in danger. With the benefit of hindsight this may seem perverse. The empire had not yet reached its greatest extent; the first losses of territory did not occur until the 1920s; and the end of empire was scarcely in prospect before the 1940s. Contemporaries saw matters in a less sanguine light. The scale of colonial domination was now such that any failure to contain insurgency or attack called into question the imperial resolve of the British. Such failures came thick and fast between 1879 and 1885. The Zulu, the Boers, the Afghans and the Sudanese all inflicted humiliating reverses on the British, while Fenian violence reached new heights in Ireland.[13] General Gordon's death at Khartoum in 1885 was a catalyst for these anxieties. No imperial event at this time occasioned more alarm or soul-searching. The Sudan remained a running sore to British self-esteem until the 'reconquest' was accomplished thirteen years later. As one journal put it, 'There is the danger that not only in Africa, not only in Asia, but throughout the world, the idea should take root that England is too weak or too indifferent to hold her own.'[14] Fears for the security of the empire prompted a backward glance to the greatest crisis of the previous generation – the Indian revolt of 1857. From the mid-1880s there was a proliferation of novels set in the Indian Mutiny, as if there were still lessons to be drawn from that most catastrophic failure of control.[15]

On top of these anxieties, Britain's colonies faced the most threatening international scene for nearly a hundred years. The most novel feature of the New Imperialism was the number of nations who signed up to it, in the anxious realization that few areas of the globe now remained for colonial expansion: this was the last chance to secure boundaries, to 'protect' commercial interests, and to stake out spheres of future exploitation. As the *Pall Mall Gazette* complained, 'whereas, since Trafalgar, the Englishman has never found himself confronted by any other opponent but the savage with his spear, or the pirate in his prah, we now find every ocean highway furrowed by European ironclads, while over many a colonial frontier frowns the cannon of Continental rivals'.[16] British manhood must now prevail not only over the 'low' races, but over competitors whose inferiority could not be taken for granted. The complex threat posed by the situation in South Africa during the 1890s arose from a local population of European origin (the Transvaal Boers) potentially acting in concert with one of Britain's leading rivals (Germany).

The language of degeneration, which became so fashionable during the 1890s, brought home these fears, for it pointed the finger of blame at inadequacies on the part of the British themselves. Imperial reverses were a reflection on the virility of the British people. 'Degeneration' was a catch-all for pessimism about the birthrate, the nation's physical fitness, its mental and moral health, and its cultural vigour.[17] Social Darwinism was an important – though certainly not the only – strand of degeneration thought, and it produced a heightened sensitivity to any indication that the British race might be losing its place at the top of the hierarchy. Degeneration also had its puritanical wing: the British Empire was held to be vulnerable to the same danger which had allegedly brought the Roman Empire down – sexual depravity at its core – and this view was voiced not only by the cranks of the Social Purity movement but by mainstream educationalists and youth experts (including Baden-Powell).[18] The practical outcome of degeneration thought was an unprecedented scrutiny of the fitness of both sexes which had strongly imperial overtones: women as mothers of the race, men as the active, assertive element. As Lord Rosebery put it in 1900, 'An empire such as ours requires as its first condition an Imperial Race – a race vigorous and industrious and intrepid', exhibiting 'health of mind and body'.[19] The defence of the empire required more men and better men.

It might be thought that the principal anxiety here would be the fitness of working-class men for imperial service, above all for the military. Yet despite expressions of official concern, very little was done to address this issue.

Physical education in elementary schools was not a national requirement; it depended on the initiative of individual school boards, and it was intended to benefit school discipline as much as physical health.[20] The warning bells were only sounded during the South African War, when two out of five recruits were rejected as unfit. After the war this led to numerous initiatives to improve the physique of working-class boys,[21] and it also prompted the most ambitious youth movement in modern Britain. But even the Boy Scouts would have far less success with the working class than with the lower-middle class, and Baden-Powell continued to fulminate against the urban blight of enfeebled manhood.[22] In the period before the South African War, the most successful youth organization – and the model for all that followed – was the Boys' Brigade, founded in 1883. This is sometimes grouped with the Boy Scouts as a broadly 'imperial' organization, but the prime purpose of the Brigade was to continue with boys where Sunday school had left off: in the early years especially, the Brigade was far more concerned with promoting Christian manliness than imperial sentiment.[23]

The most material contribution made to the empire by the working class in this period was as emigrants. Nearly a million working-class people left for the colonies during the 1880s and 1890s.[24] The era of large-scale assisted emigration was over, so most emigrants made their own way as paying steerage passengers. Guaranteed employment was rare, and usually confined to the highly skilled. In contrast to the earlier part of the century, emigrants were drawn not to life in the bush or on the prairies, but to waged work in the growing cities of Canada and the Antipodes. Despite the lack of historical work on the social dynamics of emigration during this period,[25] it is likely that the motives of emigrants to the colonies were not greatly different from those who emigrated to the United States. The decisive consideration was the state of the labour market in Britain, and this was a particular concern during the mid–1880s when the Great Depression was at its most severe.[26] The government proved largely immune to the arguments of emigration pressure groups for state-assisted emigration, and their case anyway rested on the relief of poverty at home rather than the cementing of links with the colonies.[27] In this period what is remarkable about the working class is how little serious effort was made to mould them to the imperial project.

The main target for empire propaganda was not the working class but the 'service class' – the upper levels of society from whom colonial administrators and officers in the army and navy had traditionally been drawn. By the 1880s this grouping was nearly coterminous with the graduates of the public schools. During the period of reform and expansion of the public schools between the 1830s and 1860s, training boys for the empire had been incidental to the main purpose of the schools. Neither the curriculum nor the institutional ethos was consciously imperial. By the 1880s a major change had taken place. The schools vigorously recruited boys for colonial careers, and they laid claim to the role of educator for empire *par excellence*. Their contribution was not, by and large, educational in the narrow sense. The curriculum certainly reflected an imperial agenda – in history, geography, English literature and classics. But the public schools did not base their claim to service the empire on academic grounds. What they specialized in was manliness, or making men out of boys, and the agents in this process were not so much the school authorities as the boys themselves. Manliness was acquired through a process of physical hardening imposed by the often harsh living conditions at school. It was about renouncing the ministrations of women. And it was about learning to stand up for oneself in the company of men, both in the physical sense of showing courage, and in the social sense of finding one's place in a deeply hierarchical society.[28] These qualities had an obvious relevance to life on the imperial frontier, where conditions were Spartan, respectable female company scarce, and survival often depended on an overstretched chain of command.

Superimposed on this bedrock of schoolboy culture was a more sophisticated understanding of manly character, articulated by teachers and educational experts. This rested on the notion that the individual was, if not master of his fate in the eternal sense, at least fully responsible for the mark he made on the world. A high value was set on energy, as displayed in resolute action, and on self-control, particularly in suppressing the appetites and emotions which might sap the will. Whether in business or the professions or public life, the 'man of character' was someone who set the claims of duty above personal gratification, and who could draw on his moral resources to prevail over adversity.[29] These ideals still held true in the late Victorian era, but with one significant change. Compared with the age of Thomas Arnold, the character-talk of late Victorian Britain was much less individualistic. It redefined 'duty' as commitment to an overriding imperial loyalty and an identification with a set of collective imperial values. Teamwork subordinated the individual to the production of a 'type'.[30]

Two innovations of the late Victorian period confirmed the trend: the officer cadet corps and team sports. The origin of the cadet corps lay in the volunteer movement of the 1860s, but it was not until the 1880s that it became central to the school ethos, and not until the 1890s that membership became virtually *de rigueur*.[31] The cadet experience prepared boys for the idea – if not the actuality – of war within a colonial frame; it emphas-ized not just marksmanship, but physical and mental discipline. Team sports also dated back to the 1860s, when they had been promoted as a means of improving school discipline and as a channel for the academically less gifted pupil. By the 1880s they increasingly dominated school life, and their rationale had shifted. Team sports trained boys to obey (and later to give) orders; they subordinated the individual to the team effort; and they instilled stoicism in the face of pain and discomfort (hence the marginal-ization of undemanding sports like tennis and golf).[32]

By the 1890s the public schools were well focused on their imperial rationale. To the traditional training in survival skills had been added an explicit attention to physical fitness, military skills and team dynamics. The academic curriculum continued to be important, especially for boys seek-ing admission to the professions or the more technical departments of the army, but it was of declining importance in setting the tone of the school, and headmasters were more likely to worry about the dangers of swotting than about academic underperformance. As H.H. Almond (headmaster of Loretto) put it, in a future Indian Mutiny the scholar would be little use; it was 'the man of nerve, high courage, and animal spirits' who would make the difference.[33] By the end of the century such men were produced by the public schools in large numbers. In the 1870s and early 1880s anxiety had been expressed in the highest circles about the physical robustness of British officials in India: too much cramming for the entrance exam was believed to undermine the constitution, leading to early retirement and even insanity.[34] In 1894 Dr William Ord sought to put these fears to rest. The candidates he had examined, he said, 'have commended themselves as excellent specimens of the English youth of today: for the most part well set-up, clean-skinned, clean-limbed, and in all ways wholesome'.[35] The promotion of empire appears to have hit home, for a significant propor-tion of school-leavers went overseas – as high as one third in some cases.[36] The public schools, in short, had become adept at producing men for imperial service.

II

Too often analysis of the link between the public schools and the empire stops at this point, as if the attraction of empire were self-evident.[37] Yet it is not enough to identify and describe a propaganda drive. What needs to be explained is why this attempt to promote the empire with young men of the upper and middle classes was so successful. Why was the frontier image so appealing? Why did it seem plausible to so many that empire might be the making of them *as men*? Once imperial sentiment is placed in a gendered framework, it becomes evident that the empire in turn answered to profoundly felt masculine needs. The empire needed men; but men also needed the empire, as a resource, as a refuge and as an object of desire.[38]

In popular imagining empire was synonymous with adventure. The colonial world symbolized the freedom which was in theory available to men (unlike women) of cutting a lone path, of deviating from the norm, of fashioning their own destiny. For the black sheep, the misfit and the tearaway, life overseas held out the possibility of great personal riches, an exotic lifestyle, military escapades or the excitement of operating effectively beyond the law. The identification between empire and adventure might break down on the ground: where was the excitement in back-breaking farm work in Canada or an office job in a Bengal trading company? But in the metropolitan imagination the association of empire and adventure was well established. Martin Green has identified a tradition of imperial adventure in popular fiction dating back to Defoe's *Robinson Crusoe*.[39] From the mid-nineteenth century the volume of work in this mould increased dramatically, first as a rival to the moral fable for children, and then by the 1880s as the preferred reading-matter for adolescent boys, and for many adults too. Adventure fiction presented its readers with a romanticized picture of the overseas world, in which pluck and guts always won through.[40] Patrick Brantlinger maintains that in reality opportunities for overseas adventure were waning in the late nineteenth century, as the big problems of geography were solved.[41] This is to confuse personal with public objectives. There were fewer prizes for the headline-seeking explorer, but on an individual level the challenges were many and various. What produced the biggest surge of adrenalin was big-game hunting. As John MacKenzie has shown, this was a new preoccupation in the nineteenth century.[42] It fed on what purported to be reliable travel literature about the penetration of Africa, and on its embellishment in the hunting yarns of Mayne Reid and W.H.G. Kingston (also a propagandist for colonial emigration).[43]

This romanticization of the frontier had important implications for the popular image of the military. In late Victorian Britain firsthand knowledge of war was confined to a small proportion of the male population. But its pleasure and excitement could be vicariously enjoyed in a romanticized form. Soldiering was associated primarily with small-scale, fast-moving operations which allowed maximum initiative to young officers. Well before *Scouting for Boys* a frontier myth was in the making. Baden-Powell himself first gained public notice as the author of books about irregular warfare during the 1890s.[44] When public-school headmasters (and chaplains) spoke of the games field as a preparation for the battlefield, it was this kind of warfare they had in mind. School magazines in the 1890s regularly itemized the military achievements of men who had once excelled on the playing field; no greater honour could be brought on the school than death in action – the epitome of imperial 'sacrifice'.[45] A heroic, sanitized death was both the ultimate duty and the final chapter in a life of adventure.[46]

But 'adventure' is not an adequate framework for interpreting popular attitudes towards the empire. Taken at face value, it obscures both the strength of the 'push' factors involved, and the harsher and less romantic 'pull' factors. In the first place, adventure only made sense when set against the conditions at home from which it represented an escape. The appeal of adventure rested not just on the allure of the exotic and the dangerous, but on renunciation of the mundane. It promised escape from custom and convention, from the chains of matrimony and from respectable pieties about sex. Overseas adventure was, in Green's phrase, 'a breaking of the social contract', an appeal against moral reason.[47] Colonial postings had attracted men on these grounds for generations, but in the nineteenth century the gap between metropolitan respectability and colonial licence grew wider than ever. For any man who fretted against 'Victorian' conventions of domesticity and sexual continence, the colonies offered the promise of release, and the chance to explore alternatives ranging from concubinage to pederasty.[48] Since 'respectable' white women were still very thin on the ground in many colonies, there was less countervailing censure, and less chance of deviant behaviour being reported back home. In gender terms the other side of the coin was the homosocial culture of the colonies, appealing especially to young men. For the soldier, the administrator, the trader and the frontiersman, the empire was a site where comradeship was valued, domesticity disparaged and sexual escapades overlooked or approved. These traits were particularly appealing to graduates of the public schools, who embraced the opportunity to continue living in the homosocial culture they knew so well.[49] Empire represented an intensified version of the bachelor world which most young men inhabited between their late teens and marriage in their late twenties or early thirties.

In the second place, the attractions of the overseas world were about more than high spirits and heroism. The prospect of personal authority was fundamental. One of the measures of manliness in common understanding was the degree of mastery exercised over others within or outside the home. This was most true of the upper class, for whom the exercise of paternalist, face-to-face authority was a defining masculine attribute. Younger sons had traditionally been packed off to the colonies where they could fulfil the role which their cadet status denied them in Britain. The gentry provided the majority of officers in both the British army and the Indian army, and they had the edge in appointments to sought-after civilian posts. Real responsibility was given to individual officials, often with minimal supervision: decisions were made and enforced on the spot, supported by the consciousness of being part of a ruling caste not unlike the traditional sense of rank among the English gentry.[50]

The adventure genre tended to gloss over the extent to which that personal authority was underpinned by violence. The empire could not be run with kid gloves. It had been acquired by the use of force, and force would continue to be needed to extend the frontiers and to deal with troublemakers. With its skeletal or non-existent administration the frontier was a by-word for lawlessness, often met with summary justice. Since the moral and social complexities of the local situation were usually unknown, opinion in Britain could applaud the smack of firm government and the 'resolution' of the man on the spot. Fantasies of violent reprisal which were completely inadmissible in England could be freely indulged in a colonial setting – as in 1857 and again in 1865 during the Jamaican rebellion.[51] In the atmosphere of crisis which prevailed in the 1880s and 1890s there were renewed calls for a stiffening of masculine resolve, an unflinching readiness to take whatever steps were necessary – to behave in short as an 'imperial race'. When the chief secretary of Ireland was assassinated in Phoenix Park, Dublin, in 1882, Sir Alfred Lyall reflected on the appalling message this sent to Indian nationalists. What was needed, he remarked, was 'a little more fierceness and honest brutality in the national temperament'.[52] The journalist George Steevens was no less blunt: 'we became an Imperial race by dealing necessary pain to other men, just as we became powerful men by dealing necessary pain to other animals'.[53] Popular literature for boys echoed the same concern. Since the 1850s 'penny dreadfuls' had featured bloodthirsty yarns for boys and had been much criticized for it. Towards the end of the century, however, these magazines began to be seen in a much more positive light, and to influence writers like Rider Haggard and G.A. Henty.[54] As Richard Phillips observes, 'never before, in respectable Victorian literature, was violence so graphic, gratuitous and light-hearted, so calculated to entertain'.[55] Readers were reminded that 'honest brutality' was indeed expected of men.

This validation of violence was not, of course, the only moral tradition of British imperialism. Against it were pitched the humane methods which had been championed by the anti-slavery movement, and which were symbolized above all by the memory of David Livingstone and his appeal for Christianity and commerce. For imperialists cast in the missionary mould the appropriate model of manliness was one of patient endurance rather than bravery in battle. The antagonism of these two positions was made very clear in a number of public controversies, notably the sharply divided reactions to H.M. Stanley's blunt methods of African exploration.[56] But the great days of anti-slavery were long over. The Governor Eyre controversy on the eve of the Second Reform Act (1867) had signalled the turn of the tide. As Catherine Hall has put it, the 'manly citizen' now thought less of the plight of the oppressed and more of the need for authoritative rule in the empire.[57] Hobson's interpretation of popular jingoism has not enjoyed a very good press in recent years, but it is hard to dissent from his complaint that current events were 'falsified in coarse glaring colours, for the direct stimulation of the combative instincts'.[58] After all, this was a society which could take in its stride the 11,000 Sudanese slaughtered at the battle of Omdurman (as against a mere 48 killed in Kitchener's army).[59]

The association of the empire with personal wealth, unchecked indulgence of the appetites, personal authority and boisterous homosociality assured its appeal to middle- and upper-class men. To what extent did these attractions register with the working class? The extent of popular imperialist sentiment is particularly difficult to gauge. The scope and variety of empire propaganda directed at the working class is well documented. It embraced the daily press, music hall, advertising, leisure reading, youth organizations and the curriculum of state elementary schools.[60] Broadly speaking the jingo tone became more pronounced as the century drew to a close.[61] But all this begs the question of reception. Current scholarship amounts to little more than conflicting statements largely unsupported by research. Positive evidence of working-class imperial sentiment is surprisingly slim.

As the earlier discussion suggested, emigration was viewed primarily in an economic frame, ranging from the skilled engineer attracted to railway development overseas to the unskilled man trying his luck on the goldfields. The excitement of emigrating could hardly be denied, but the need for a secure livelihood was the first priority: 'adventure' usually required time and means. Music-hall song suggests that in popular culture emigration was associated as much with the human pathos of leaving home and family as with any active sense of colonization.[62] The association between empire and masculine authority may have been rather more telling. Racially stratified dependencies promised the satisfactions of personal authority to men whose authority in the normal run of things would have extended no further than a wife or an apprentice. John MacKenzie has sur-mised that service in the Indian army was attractive because soldiers from the poorest background in Britain were no longer at the bottom of the pile once they reached their postings.[63] The cheap black labour anticipated by prospective emigrants to South Africa promised not only prosperity but a real gain in personal status.[64] The privilege of race was available to all whites, no matter how lowly their social origins at home.

There was probably also some popular understanding of the military dimension of empire. By 1898 more than 22 per cent of the entire male population between the ages of seventeen and forty had previous military experience (though only a minority had actually served overseas).[65] It is reasonable to infer a considerable identification with martial values, as rep-resented both by the big names and by the common soldier who in the late Victorian era was much more respectfully treated than ever before.[66] But that favourable view of army life did not translate into buoyant recruitment. Not even during the South African War was there a rush to the colours. Richard Price has shown that the pace of enlistment was determined more by the ebb and flow of unemployment than by patriotic fervour. The war fever whipped up by the press had least impact on the working class, who took little part in pro-war demonstrations or in attacks on anti-war meet-ings. Not even 'Mafeking Night' – the most enthusiastic public affirmation of empire during this period – can be seen as proof of working-class jingo-ism. Price shows that the crowds on the streets were composed predom-inantly of middle-class youth: students, lawyers and clerks.[67] 'The truly jingo crowd', he writes, 'was not a working-class phenomenon.'[68]

III

The argument so far has turned on the varied appeal of empire as a marker of manhood, through its association with adventure, sexual licence, per-sonal authority and violence. These activities were pursued in the company of other men, or were intended to earn respect in their eyes; they were the currency in which masculinity was conferred or withheld by one's peers. But masculine status also depended on maintaining a dominant position with the opposite sex, through privileged access to the public sphere, domestic authority and the double standard of sexual conduct. The con-nection of these aspects of gender relations with empire is less obvious. But indirectly their implications for imperial commitment were important, particularly when relations between the sexes were perceived to be in flux.

If men's power was called into question, the attraction of empire as an unequivocal indicator of masculinity was likely to be intensified. That several categories of men were thrown onto the defensive in their relations with women during the 1880s and 1890s is highly relevant to understanding the popular appeal of an assertive imperialism.

In the 1880s and 1890s few men could recall a time when women had been so free or so subversive. The label 'first wave feminism' is mistaken if it suggests there had been no feminism at an earlier date; but it is apt in implying an unprecedented level of consciousness on questions of gender. 'The woman question' was all the more disturbing because it was not confined to a single issue but touched on a number of sensitive areas. The most material of these was employment. Office work was a traditional route into the middle class for the upwardly mobile working-class man. But in the late nineteenth century large corporations and some sections of the Civil Service began to recruit female typists and telegraphists as a cheaper and more 'docile' workforce. By 1901 women comprised 11 per cent of clerks, and in some cities like Birmingham the proportion was as high as 20 per cent by 1891. Male clerks opposed this trend not only because they feared redundancy or wage reduction, but because the gender status of their occupation was at stake. Office work had long had overtones of effeminacy: 'born a man, died a clerk' went the old saying. The point seemed proven by the entry of women into office work. Gregory Anderson's work on Manchester provides suggestive evidence of how male clerks reacted to this feared slur on their manhood. One correspondent in the *Manchester Guardian* in 1886 complained of the spectre of a world turned upside down: of girls 'unsexing themselves by taking men's place at the desk', of men driven to 'seek employment in drapers' and milliners' shops and restaurants'.[69]

These tensions in the lower middle class had imperial implications in at least two ways. In the first place, emigration became a much more attractive option. The YMCA administered a scheme in which they provided unemployed clerks with letters of introduction to farmers in Manitoba. The fact that 13,000 clerks applied from Manchester alone certainly testifies to the impact of clerical unemployment; but given the complete lack of agricultural experience that these men must have had, it also suggests a determination to embrace an unequivocally 'masculine' life.[70] In the second place, the social character of popular jingoism points to a masculine overcompensation on the part of lower-middle-class men. As we have seen, the working-class element in popular jingoism was much less than earlier studies supposed. The key constituency was lower-middle-class men, with clerks well to the fore, particularly during the Mafeking celebrations. This same group

[handwritten margin note: women beginning to work in trad. male roles (gender status of occupation under threat)]

was strongly represented in the City Imperial Volunteers and the Imperial Yeomanry who fought in the South African War.[71] Volunteering was in part a means of demonstrating the patriotism of those on the borderline of respectability, but it was also a specifically masculine assertion. The clerk who cheered on the army, or better still enlisted, was less vulnerable to the charge of having soft and useless hands. Noisy enthusiasm for the empire allowed him to rise above the demeaning feminine associations of his occupation.

The gender turbulence of the *fin de siècle* was not only about employment; it also affected sexuality and marriage. It was these areas which occasioned the greatest amount of feminist polemic – and the greatest degree of anxiety on the part of men. Partly because of the expansion in female employment, unmarried young women had greater freedoms than before. Smoking and cycling – symbols of the New Woman – stood for more fundamental challenges to patriarchal convention: women who lived alone or in all-women households, and who chose their own male company, and in some cases dispensed with it entirely. In the cities spinsterhood ceased to be automatically associated with personal failure; it was now recognized to be for some a preference. At the same time, the terms of marriage were visibly changing in women's favour. The Married Women's Property Act of 1882 gave wives control over the funds they brought into the marriage, while the courts were gradually liberalizing the terms on which wives could secure a marital separation or sole custody of their children.[72] These changes were reflected in a spate of outspoken feminist polemic by journalists and novelists, who attacked the institution of marriage and castigated the sexual practices of men. As portrayed in the press, the New Woman was engaged in not merely self-improvement but also sex warfare. One did not have to accept the New Woman at face value to see a failure of masculine authority in the most intimate areas of life.

Of course the response of many men was to engage in an unyielding defence of patriarchal marriage. They were supported by fashionable writers on science who tried to shore up traditional wisdom about sexual difference by adapting the theory of evolution to their ends.[73] But in the context of empire the most telling male reaction was to vacate the disputed ground altogether by disparaging domesticity. Middle-class culture of the period was moulded by the experience of two – and sometimes three – generations of masculine domesticity. What had appealed to the early Victorians as a necessary retreat from the often alienating world of work now tended to appear routine-bound and stifling. This reflected the tastes of a younger generation for whom the allure of the city outweighed its more negative

[margin handwritten note:] New Woman challenge to patriarchal conventions

features. It also reflected the way in which the conventions of domesticity had become more formulaic and more constraining, policed by etiquette manuals of increasing complexity. Men's boredom was tinged by sometimes overt sexual antagonism, the wife carrying the blame for this more intrusive routine. It was she who demanded punctuality and at least outward deference. On this view domesticity for men meant submitting to a feminized ambience. Many writers commented on how such a life made men dull and spiritless.[74] As Robert Louis Stevenson put it, 'the air of the fireside withers out all the fine wildings of the husband's heart'.[75]

It is important not to exaggerate the extent of the 'flight from domesticity'.[76] The turn away from marriage was class-specific. It did not affect the working class, nor the lower middle class, for whom the close of the century was the acme of domesticity.[77] But among the business and professional classes the trend was clear. An increasing proportion of young men postponed marriage until they were on the threshold of middle age; others remained bachelors all their lives, in some cases placing the survival of the family name in doubt.[78] Professions like the army or public-school teaching which either precluded marriage or presumed the attraction of an alternative all-male society acquired a higher profile. Gentlemen's clubs and passionate (or 'Uranian') male friendship flourished as emotional alternatives to marriage.[79] The personal histories of empire-builders include many references to the trammels of domesticity: the most prominent were either single for life (Gordon, Rhodes, Kitchener), or else married well after their empire-building days were over (Milner, Baden-Powell, Lugard).[80] The equivocal standing of domesticity was perhaps best symbolized by Kitchener's refusal to accept married officers under his command in the Sudan campaign of 1897–8 – the most coveted military posting of the day.[81]

In this context the traditional image of the colonies as pre-eminently a man's world was greatly reinforced. Of course the reality of empire included the settler wife and the missionary couple, but they did not figure prominently in popular representations of the empire, which was equated with the complete antithesis of feminine domesticity. This message came over loud and clear in the work of Stevenson and Rider Haggard, which spanned the gap between high-bow and low-brow, and in the hugely successful novels of G.A. Henty, read primarily by adolescent boys. Their stories were exciting, full of action, bracingly masculine, and staged in a real or invented colonial setting. Their heroes hunted, plundered or conquered, shored up by the silent bonds of men's friendship; and they were unencumbered by the presence of females: 'there is not a petticoat in the whole history', Allan Quatermain reassures his audience in King Solomon's Mines.[82]

The message of male panic is particularly clear in Kipling's early novel, *The Light That Failed* (1891), in which death in a desert battle is presented as a wholesome escape from a degenerate London and a rejecting New Woman sweetheart.[83] A generation of boys and young men (not to mention many of their sisters) was brought up on an image of masculinity which was self-reliant, extrovert, achieving and entirely detached from women.

It is worth considering what bearing this analysis has on emigration. The majority of emigrants from Britain in the late nineteenth century were indeed young single men, travelling without family ties.[84] But this does not mean that they were in flight from domesticity. Most working-class bachelors seem to have regarded emigration as a step towards independence of the traditional kind. They expected either to marry and settle in the new country, or to make enough money to sail back to England and set up home there (in the era of cheap steamship travel, this was an increasingly realistic prospect). That continuing link between emigration and marriage prospects accords with working-class notions of manliness, and it is also reflected in the changing character of the colonies themselves. In Australia especially, the folk emphasis on the gold rushes has tended to obscure the fact that it was the same period which saw the rapid growth of settled urban society in the colonies, and this was the ultimate destination of most emigrants from Britain.[85]

But there was another kind of emigrant – the man who was positively attracted to the homosocial life of the frontier – whether it be a mining town in British Columbia, a ranch in the Canadian West, a sheep station in New Zealand, or a paramilitary force in southern Africa. In these regions the demographic preponderance of men in the colonies was even more pronounced, and there were few white women of any description. For such emigrants all-male society was not so much a privation to be endured as a glamorous attraction. The bachelor emigrant bound for the frontier interpreted 'independence' differently from the married man. For him it meant independence *from women* – living outside the family nexus, being free to 'up sticks' and move on. As one New Zealand itinerant explained in 1890, 'we do not marry because we prefer to spend our money in other ways, because an establishment is a nuisance; because a wife is not so necessary to our happiness as other luxuries; because there is no good like independence'.[86] Significantly, this aspect of colonial life was over-represented in Britain itself, where the colonist tended to be identified with the bushman ideal: rough, self-reliant, independent, rejecting domesticity and instead prizing the values of 'mateship'.[87] The bushman and his equivalent in other colonies included many men of proletarian origins in Britain, but the strongest evidence we have of the appeal of a men-only life overseas relates to the upper and middle classes. These classes were disproportionately represented among emigrants to colonial destinations. In the 1890s the middle class accounted for 26 per cent of all emigrants, and 38 per cent of those going to Australia.[88]

For middle-class men a large part of the attraction of the colonial world was its distinctive gender regime. A spell in the colonies promised a homosocial paradise, governed by clear-cut masculine values. Life there was not subject to constant negotiation with the opposite sex. The New Woman would not be encountered overseas (how many Olive Schreiners were there in South Africa?). For those who were bored by feminine domesticity, or frightened of being drawn into marriage, the wide-open spaces of prairie and bush and the rough democracy of the frontier stood for a world which was free of the constraints of respectability. Instead there was the prospect of a much more relaxed sexual regime. In major all-male concentrations like the goldfields there was unregulated prostitution, while in racially stratified colonies like Natal domestic servants were much more vulnerable to sexual liberties from their masters than servants in Britain. In both cases there was far less risk of social exposure than at home.[89] Marriage was not necessarily renounced, but it was projected into the distant future, after life had been lived to the full and a fortune had (hopefully) been made. In the meantime the colonies provided a space in which sexual difference appeared to be clear-cut and unchallenged, and masculinity could be lived out without compromise.

IV

The New Imperialism, it is now widely recognized, was not so much an assertion of strength as a symptom of weakness. The excesses of imperial fervour may have looked like the high point of national self-confidence, but they were in reality an overwrought reaction to an increasingly perilous international situation. Except between 1899 and 1902 Britain did not consider itself at war, yet the need to 'defend' the empire and to be vigilant against foreign rivals was repeatedly articulated during the 1880s and 1890s. Psychologically this situation called for a heightened awareness of empire within Britain; materially it demanded an increase in the quantity and quality of manpower available for imperial service. The failure to vigorously promote this programme with the working class became a cause of serious alarm after the South African War. In the middle and upper classes, on the other hand, a determined effort was made to remoralize manhood for imperial service, and with considerable success. By 1900 empire had become central to the identity of an expanded service class, and imperial attributes underpinned the prevailing myth of British national character.

That class distinction applied also to the 'gender panic' in *fin-de-siècle* Britain. Among the working class the gender balance in employment was less disturbed than in the lower middle class, and there is no reason to suppose that marriage was any less central to masculine self-realization than it had been in the past, or that domesticity was more burdensome to men. But considerations of this kind had considerable weight at other levels of society. Changes in employment, marriage and the lifestyle of young women demonstrably caused anxiety among men of the lower middle and middle classes, and some of this anxiety was displaced onto the empire, partly as an unequivocally masculine loyalty, and partly as an actual destination where men might lead manly lives. Thus on the one hand men in Britain were being recast to fit them for an imperial role; on the other hand the empire itself had become a widely recognized means of 'making men'. It is a measure of the complex interpenetration of the imperial and the masculine that both these functions were pursued at the same time. Together they account for much of the metropolitan character of the New Imperialism.

Notes and references

1 J.S. Bratton *et al.*, *Acts of Supremacy: the British Empire and the Stage, 1790–1930* (Manchester, 1991), p. 18.

2 The debate began with Gareth Stedman Jones, 'Working-class culture and working-class politics in London, 1870–1900: notes on the remaking of a working class', *Journal of Social History* 7 (1974), repr. in his *Languages of Class: Studies in English Working Class History, 1832–1982* (Cambridge, 1983). The most recent contribution is Jonathan Rose, *The Intellectual Life of the British Working Class* (London, 2001), ch. 10.

3 The seminal works are Patrick Brantlinger, *Rule of Darkness: British Literature and Imperialism, 1830–1914* (Ithaca, 1988), and Edward Said, *Culture and Imperialism* (London, 1993). Critical work on Kipling has, perhaps not surprisingly, come closest to an understanding of the popular springs of imperialism. See esp. Robert H. MacDonald, 'The Laureate of Empire – and his chorus', in his *The Language of Empire: Myths and Metaphors of Popular Imperialism, 1880–1918* (Manchester, 1994).

4 See esp. Antoinette Burton, *Burdens of History: British Feminists, Indian Women, and Imperial Culture, 1865–1915* (Chapel Hill, 1994).

5 The most recent survey of imperial culture in this period does not deal with masculinity at all. John M. MacKenzie, 'Empire and metropolitan cultures', in Andrew Porter (ed.), *The Oxford History of the British Empire*, vol. III (Oxford, 1999), pp. 270–93.

6 Joanna de Groot, '"Sex" and "race": the construction of language and image in the nineteenth century', in Susan Mendus and Jane Rendall (eds), *Sexuality and Subordination* (London, 1989), p. 122.

7 Kelly Boyd, *Manliness and the Boys' Story Paper in Britain: a Cultural History, 1855–1940* (Basingstoke, 2003), p. 125.

8 H. John Field, *Toward a Programme of Imperial Life: the British Empire at the Turn of the Century* (Oxford, 1982) provides a sensitive commentary on these terms, but does not place them in a gendered context.

9 Julia Bush, '"The right sort of women": female emigrators and emigration to the British Empire, 1890–1910', *Women's History Review* 3 (1994), pp. 385–410; Lisa Chilton, '"A new class of women from the colonies": *The Imperial Colonist* and the construction of empire', *Journal of Imperial and Commonwealth History* 31 (2003), pp. 36–56; Judith Rowbotham, '"Soldiers of Christ?" Images of female missionaries in late nineteenth-century Britain', *Gender & History* 12 (2000), pp. 82–106.

10 Clare Midgley (ed.), *Gender and Imperialism* (Manchester, 1998), p. 14.

11 This argument runs through the recent secondary literature on manliness, but is most clearly stated in Field, *Toward a Programme of Imperial Life*.

12 An interpretation along these lines is sketched in Leonore Davidoff, 'The family', in F.M.L. Thompson (ed.), *The Cambridge Social History of Modern Britain*, vol. 2 (1990), p. 105, and in Elaine Showalter, *Sexual Anarchy: Gender and Culture at the Fin de Siècle* (1991), pp. 4–6, 78–95.

13 For the impact of these reverses, see Ronald Robinson and John Gallagher, *Africa and the Victorians: the Official Mind of Imperialism* (London, 1965), chs 3–5, and Peter Marshall, 'The imperial factor in the Liberal decline, 1880–1885', in J. Flint and G. Williams (eds), *Perspectives on Empire* (Harlow, 1973), pp. 134–5.

14 *The Statist*, Feb. 1885, quoted in Bernard Porter, *The Lion's Share* (London, 1975), p. 116.

15 Mary A. Procida, *Married to the Empire: Gender, Politics and Imperialism in India, 1883–1947* (Manchester, 2002), p. 120.

16 *Pall Mall Gazette*, 4 Feb. 1885, quoted in Porter, *Lion's Share*, p. 118.

17 Daniel Pick, *Faces of Degeneration: a European Disorder, c. 1848–c. 1918* (Cambridge, 1989).

18 See for example J. Ellice Hopkins, *The Power of Womanhood: or Mothers and Sons* (London, 1899), pp. 161–6.

19 Lord Rosebery, *Questions of Empire* (London, 1900), pp. 23–4.

20 Peter C. McIntosh, *Physical Education in England since 1800*, rev. edn (London, 1968).

21 Anna Davin, 'Imperialism and motherhood', *History Workshop Journal* 5 (1978), pp. 9–65.

22 Michael Rosenthal, *The Character Factory: Baden-Powell and the Origins of the Boy Scout Movement* (New York, 1986); Robert H. MacDonald, *Sons of the Empire: the Frontier and the Boy Scout Movement, 1890–1918* (Toronto, 1993); Allen Warren, 'Sir Robert Baden-Powell, the Scout movement and citizen training in Great Britain, 1900–1920', *English Historical Review* 101 (1986), pp. 376–98.

23 John O. Springhall (ed.), *Sure and Steadfast: a History of the Boys' Brigade, 1883–1893* (London, 1983).

24 The figures for emigration cannot be broken down in class terms, but the overall figures give some indication of the scale of increase. Total emigrants from England, Wales and Scotland to British North America, Australasia and South Africa were 650,800 during the 1880s and 452,600 during the 1890s. P.J. Cain, 'Economics and empire: the metropolitan context', in Porter, *Oxford History*, p. 47.

25 For an impressive exception, see Rollo Arnold, *The Farthest Promised Land: English Villagers, New Zealand Immigrants of the 1870s* (Wellington, 1981).

26 N.H. Carrier and J.R. Jeffery, *External Migration: a Study of the Available Statistics, 1815–1950* (London, 1953), pp. 95–6.

27 H.L. Malchow, *Population Pressures: Emigration and Government in Late Nineteenth-Century Britain* (Palo Alto, 1979).

28 J.R. de S. Honey, *Tom Brown's Universe: the Development of the Victorian Public School* (London, 1977), pp. 209–17.

29 Stefan Collini, 'The idea of "character" in Victorian political thought', *Transactions of the Royal Historical Society*, 5th series, 35 (1985), pp. 29–50.

30 Field, *Toward a Programme of Imperial Life*.

31 Hugh Cunningham, *The Volunteer Force* (London, 1975).

32 J.A. Mangan, *Athleticism in the Victorian and Edwardian Public School: the Emergence and Consolidation of an Educational Ideology* (Cambridge, 1981).

33 H.H. Almond (1897), quoted in J.A. Mangan, *The Games Ethic and Imperialism: Aspects of the Diffusion of an Ideal* (London, 1986), p. 28.

34 Mrinalini Sinha, *Colonial Masculinity: the 'Manly Englishman' and the 'Effeminate Bengali' in the Late Nineteenth Century* (Manchester, 1995), pp. 107–8.

35 Dr W. Ord (1894), quoted in W.J. Reader, *Professional Men* (London, 1966), pp. 89–90.

36 This proportion also includes a significant number of public schoolboys who emigrated to the colonies to sample a frontier life under their own steam. F. Musgrove, *The Migratory Elite* (London, 1963), pp. 19–21; Patrick Dunae, *Gentlemen Emigrants: from the British Public Schools to the Canadian Frontier* (Vancouver, 1981), p. 60.

37 For example, Mangan, *Games Ethic.*

38 Thus for Kipling, empire-building was valued less for the sake of the empire than for the qualities which it nurtured in the empire-builder. Andrew Rutherford (ed.), *Kipling's Mind and Art* (Edinburgh, 1964), p. 185.

39 Martin Green, *Dreams of Adventure, Deeds of Empire* (London, 1980).

40 Jeffrey Richards (ed.), *Imperialism and Juvenile Literature* (Manchester, 1989).

41 Brantlinger, *Rule of Darkness*, pp. 37–45.

42 John M. MacKenzie, *The Empire of Nature: Hunting, Conservation and British Imperialism* (Manchester, 1988).

43 J.S. Bratton, *The Impact of Victorian Children's Fiction* (London, 1981), pp. 115–33.

44 MacDonald, *Sons of the Empire*, pp. 62–3, 68–70, 82–7.

45 Mangan, *Games Ethic*, pp. 58–70.

46 See for example the instant mythologization of Allan Wilson's stand against the Ndebele in 1893: MacDonald, *Language of Empire*, pp. 131–5.

47 Martin Green, *The Adventurous Male* (University Park, PA, 1993), p. 71.

48 Ronald Hyam, *Empire and Sexuality: the British Experience* (Manchester, 1990).

49 Dunae, *Gentlemen Emigrants.*

50 On the personal way in which authority was exercised in the colonies, see Kathryn Tidrick, *Empire and the English Character* (London, 1980).

51 Catherine Hall, *Civilising Subjects: Metropole and Colony in the English Imagination, 1830–1867* (Cambridge, 2002), pp. 243–64, 406–24.

52 H.M. Durand, *Life of Lyall* (London, 1913), p. 264.

53 George W. Steevens, 'The new humanitarianism', *Blackwood's Magazine* 163 (1898), p. 104.

54 Patrick Dunae, 'Boys' literature', *Victorian Studies* 24 (1980), pp. 105–21; Boyd, *Manliness and the Boys' Story Paper*, p. 124.

55 Richard Phillips, *Mapping Men and Empire* (London, 1997), pp. 69–70. Note however that Louis James has identified the 1870s as the high point of violence in adventure writing for boys. Louis James, 'Tom Brown's imperialist sons', *Victorian Studies* 17 (1973), p. 99.

56 See Iain R. Smith, *The Emin Pasha Relief Expedition* (Oxford, 1972).

57   Catherine Hall, 'A response to the commentators', *Journal of British Studies* 42 (2003), p. 538.

58   Hobson, *Imperialism*, p. 234.

59   P.M. Holt, *The Mahdist State in the Sudan*, 2nd edn (Oxford, 1977), p. 240.

60   See in particular John M. MacKenzie (ed.), *Propaganda and Empire* (Manchester, 1986); John O. Springhall, *Youth, Empire and Society: British Youth Movements, 1883–1940*; Paula M. Krebs, *Gender, Race and the Writing of Empire: Public Discourse and the Boer War* (Cambridge, 1999); Valerie Chancellor, *History for their Masters* (Bath, 1970); Kathryn Castle, *Britannia's Children: Reading Colonialism through Children's Books and Magazines* (Manchester, 1996); Boyd, *Manliness and the Boys' Story Paper*, ch. 7.

61   Chancellor, *History for their Masters*, pp. 124–30, 137–8; Krebs, *Gender, Race and the Writing of Empire*, pp. 4–22.

62   Penny Summerfield, 'Patriotism and empire: music-hall entertainment, 1870–1914', in MacKenzie, *Propaganda and Empire*, pp. 17–48.

63   John M. MacKenzie (ed.), *Popular Imperialism and the Military, 1850–1950* (Manchester, 1992), pp. 111–12.

64   Simon Dagut, 'The migrant voyage as initiation school: sailing from Britain to South Africa, 1850's–1890s' (unpubl. conference paper, University of Western Australia, 1999), p. 12.

65   Michael Blanch, 'British society and the war', in Peter Warwick (ed.), *The South African War* (Harlow, 1980), p. 215.

66   MacKenzie, *Popular Imperialism and the Military*.

67   Richard Price, *An Imperial War and the British Working Class* (London, 1972).

68   Ibid., p. 176; Blanch concurs: 'British society and the war', p. 235.

69   Gregory Anderson, *Victorian Clerks* (Manchester, 1976), pp. 56–60.

70   G.L. Anderson, 'The social economy of late Victorian clerks', in Geoffrey Crossick (ed.), *The Lower Middle Class in Britain* (London, 1977), p. 122.

71   Richard N. Price, 'Society, status and jingoism: the social roots of lower middle-class patriotism, 1870–1900', in Crossick, *Lower Middle Class in Britain*, pp. 89–112. See also Blanch, 'British society and the war'.

72   A. James Hammerton, *Cruelty and Companionship: Conflict in Nineteenth-Century Married Life* (London, 1992).

73   Cynthia Eagle Russett, *Sexual Science: the Victorian Construction of Womanhood* (Cambridge, 1989).

74   John Tosh, *A Man's Place: Masculinity and the Middle-Class Home in Victorian England* (London, 1999), pp. 172–82.

75   Robert Louis Stevenson, *Virginibus Puerisque* (London, 1918), p. 5.

76 My view has been criticized for generalizing from too few examples: A. James Hammerton, review of *A Man's Place* in *Journal of Family History* 25 (2000), pp. 552–4, and Robert Morrell, 'The family man and empire: Sir Albert Hine of Natal, 1875–1903', *Journal of Natal and Zululand History* 18 (1998), pp. 20–44.

77 A. James Hammerton, 'Pooterism or partnership? Marriage and masculine identity in the lower middle class, 1870–1920', *Journal of British Studies* 38 (1999), pp. 291–321.

78 The families of W.E. Gladstone, Edward Benson and Francis Rhodes (father of Cecil Rhodes) are cases in point.

79 Hammerton, *Cruelty and Companionship*, ch. 5; Tosh, *A Man's Place*, pp. 178–82.

80 Margery Perham, *Lugard: the Years of Adventure* (London, 1962), pp. 61–73; Tim Jeal, *Baden-Powell* (London, 1989), pp. 26, 345, 411, 569; Janet Adam Smith, *John Buchan* (London, 1965), pp. 45, 68–9, 165.

81 G.W. Steevens, *With Kitchener to Khartum* (Edinburgh, 1898), p. 50.

82 H. Rider Haggard, *King Solomon's Mines* (London, 1885), p. 9.

83 Rudyard Kipling, *The Light That Failed* (London, 1891). For perceptive commentary, see Preben Kaarsholm, 'Kipling and masculinity', in Raphael Samuel (ed.), *Patriotism* (London, 1989), vol. III, pp. 215–26; and Joanna de Groot, ' "What should they know of England who only England know?" Kipling on the boundaries of gender, art and empire', in Geoffrey Cubitt (ed.), *Imagining Nations* (Manchester, 1998), pp. 173–89.

84 Dudley Baines, *Migration in a Mature Economy: Emigration and Internal Migration in England and Wales, 1861–1900* (Cambridge, 1985), pp. 84–5, 130–6.

85 Geoffrey Sherington, *Australia's Immigrants, 1788–1978* (Sydney, 1980); Arnold, *Furthest Promised Land*.

86 Quoted in Jock Phillips, *A Man's Country? The Image of the Pakeha Male – A History*, 2nd edn (Auckland, 1996), pp. 37–8.

87 Marilyn Lake, 'The politics of respectability: identifying the masculinist context', *Historical Studies* 22 (1986), pp. 116–31.

88 Musgrove, *The Migratory Elite*, pp. 19–21.

89 Hyam, *Empire and Sexuality*, pp. 106–10; Norman Etherington, 'Natal's black rape scare of the 1870s', *Journal of Southern African Studies* 15 (1988), pp. 42–3.

Index